Wordsworth's Poetic Theory

Wordsworth's Poetic Theory

Knowledge, Language, Experience

Edited by

Alexander Regier

and

Stefan H. Uhlig

First published 2010 by
PALGRAVE MACMILLAN

Palgrave Macmillan in the UK is an imprint of Macmillan Publishers Limited, registered in England, company number 785998, of Houndmills, Basingstoke, Hampshire RG21 6XS.

Palgrave Macmillan in the US is a division of St Martin's Press LLC, 175 Fifth Avenue, New York, NY 10010.

Palgrave Macmillan is the global academic imprint of the above companies and has companies and representatives throughout the world.

Palgrave® and Macmillan® are registered trademarks in the United States, the United Kingdom, Europe and other countries.

ISBN-13: 978-0-230-52544-3   hardback

This book is printed on paper suitable for recycling and made from fully managed and sustained forest sources. Logging, pulping and manufacturing processes are expected to conform to the environmental regulations of the country of origin.

A catalogue record for this book is available from the British Library.

A catalog record for this book is available from the Library of Congress.

10   9   8   7   6   5   4   3   2   1
19 18 17 16 15 14 13 12 11 10

Printed and bound in Great Britain by
CPI Antony Rowe, Chippenham and Eastbourne

Contents

Notes on Contributors

Andrew Bennett is Professor of English at the University of Bristol. He has published widely on Romanticism, poetics, and literary theory: his books include *Keats, Narrative and Audience: The Posthumous Life of Writing* (1994), *Romantic Poets and the Culture of Posterity* (1999), *Wordsworth Writing* (2007), and *Ignorance: Literature and Agnoiology* (2009).

Peter de Bolla is Professor of Cultural History and Aesthetics at the University of Cambridge. His books include *The Discourse of the Sublime: Readings in History, Aesthetics and the Subject* (1989), *Art Matters* (2001), *The Education of the Eye: Painting, Landscape and Architecture in Eighteenth-Century Britain* (2003), and *The Fourth of July and the Founding of America* (2007).

Claudia Brodsky teaches comparative literature at Princeton University. She is co-editor, with Toni Morrison, of *Birth of a Nation'hood* (1997), and the author of *The Imposition of Form: Studies in Narrative Representation and Knowledge* (1987), *Lines of Thought: Discourse, Architectonics and the Origin of Modern Philosophy* (1996), and *In the Place of Language: Literature and the Architecture of the Referent* (2009).

Soelve Curdts received her Ph.D. from Princeton University, where her doctoral thesis won the biennial award for the best dissertation in comparative literature. Curdts's research focuses on literature and philosophy in English, German, Russian, and French. Her publications include articles on Turgenev, Baudelaire, Hegel, Flaubert, and Dostoevsky. She is currently at work on a book entitled *The Graveyard of Europe*.

Frances Ferguson is Mary Elizabeth Garrett Chair in Arts and Sciences at Johns Hopkins University. She has written three books, *Wordsworth: Language as Counter-Spirit* (1977), *Solitude and the Sublime* (1992), and *Pornography, the Theory* (2005), and essays on literary theory and a variety of eighteenth- and nineteenth-century topics.

Paul Hamilton is Professor of English at Queen Mary, University of London. He has written books on Romanticism and on historicism, and his most recent monograph is *Coleridge and German Philosophy* (2007). He is currently writing a comparative study of Romantic writing and theory.

Geoffrey Hartman is Sterling Professor of English and Comparative Literature (Emeritus) and Senior Research Scholar at Yale. His latest book is *A Scholar's Tale: Intellectual Itinerary of a Displaced Child of Europe* (2007). He is a co-founder of the Fortunoff Video Archive for Holocaust Testimonies and continues as its Project Director.

Mary Jacobus is Grace 2 Professor of English, and the Director of the Centre for Research in the Arts, Social Sciences, and Humanities (CRASSH) at the University of Cambridge. She has published many books and essays on Wordsworth, Romanticism, psychoanalysis, feminism, and visual art. She is currently working on a book entitled *Romantic Things: A Tree, A Rock, A Cloud.*

Simon Jarvis is Gorley Putt Professor of Poetry and Poetics at the University of Cambridge. Among his books are *Adorno* (1998) and *Wordsworth's Philosophic Song* (2007).

Alexander Regier is Assistant Professor of English at Rice University. His study *Fracture and Fragmentation in British Romanticism* (2010) addresses imaginative and philosophical writing. He has published on Wordsworth, rhetoric, utopianism, and the aesthetics of sport. He is currently preparing a comparative study of theories of language with attention to Hamann, Blake, Wordsworth, and Benjamin.

Stefan H. Uhlig is Lecturer in English Literature at the University of Cambridge. He has published on the idea of world literature, eighteenth-century conversation, and the value of ordinary life in Gray and Wordsworth. He is writing a study of the conceptual resources of literary studies, and is co-editor of *Aesthetics and the Work of Art: Adorno, Kafka, Richter* (2009).

Introduction

Alexander Regier and Stefan H. Uhlig

What is the place of theory in Wordsworth's poetry and poetics? This question motivates the present volume of essays. By seeking answers to it across Wordsworth's prose and verse, our contributors confront a lasting challenge in Romantic writing. They explore Wordsworth's reflective views of his own work and, by extension, the compelling implications of his theorizing for the shape of poetry, and its significance as art, since the Romantic period. Wordsworth's decisive reassessment of what makes for poetry, and what its forms and affects might achieve, conjoins persistent questions about style, morality, aesthetics, kinds of knowing, and the theory of language. Moreover, Wordsworth makes his contribution to our modern ways of thinking about poetry both inside his poetic writing and alongside it, stepping back. His sharply theoretical critique of poetry's traditional routines therefore involves a no less knowingly poetic mode of theory. Wordsworth's efforts to straddle the attendant tensions and dichotomies has not always found favour with his various readerships. Yet his poetic theory forms a decisive part of his work's claim on us.

One consequence of his intrinsically reflective stance towards his work is that the legacy of Wordsworth's writings is at once less definite and more capacious than what we might think of simply as a series of compelling works. It is not just that much of his most consequential verse exists in variously unfinished drafts. More taxingly for us as readers, Wordsworth's effort to rewrite the potential as much as the grounds of poetry involves a deeply thoughtful set of working practices. Even by the standards we associate with the Romantic period, his poems carry an effective charge of knowingness and circumspection that is as hard on his verse as a poetic enterprise as it is demanding on his readers. Furthermore, Wordsworth supplemented his poetic writing with

1

a framework of extensive critical essays. And these are both tremendously ambitious prose and tightly bound up with the works which they most often introduce, or else astutely trail in various ways. The contributions gathered here explore the interactions between theory and practice which arise from these purposely mixed or polyphonic forms.

Wordsworth's first readers had no doubt that they were grappling with a poet who was drawn to theory. Most took his thought-out stance against what he described as a derivative and self-regarding art of poetry to count against his longer-term appeal. Others, in contrast, read precisely Wordsworth's zeal to amplify his voice through more reflective registers (or by supplying his own critical preambles and reports) as evidence that this poet was marking the beginning of an epoch. It seemed on all sides undeniable (though it was also constantly remarked upon) that the compulsive idiosyncrasies of these new writings with their plain, yet also fundamentally disruptive, style had to be viewed in light of Wordsworth's programmatic impetus. From poems like 'The Idiot Boy', offered in *Lyrical Ballads*, to *Peter Bell* or *The Excursion* in 1814, his publications generated critical responses which took his prominence as a committed theorist to be integral to his aspirations as a writer. Wordsworth's poems were routinely read as championing more than their own, perhaps already sly or disingenuous, versions of ordinariness. That is to say they looked not least to be colluding with an effort in which this unusually knowing poet seemed determined to upend the art of poetry itself. Of course, Wordsworth himself did much to prompt such expectations and anxieties. The notices, notes, prefaces, and afterwords with which he packaged most of his poetic output present an exceptionally – in their sheer volume as much as their intellectual energy – substantial contribution in the history of anglophone poetics. Yet it is striking how acutely and consistently Wordsworth's poetic forms were at the outset read as themselves features of a quest to recast poetry itself: its diction no less than its aspirations and its consequence.

To start with, few reviewers of *Lyrical Ballads* even broach the volumes' poems and their noted 'strangeness' without redeploying the 1798 Advertisement's first principles for their own purposes.[1] These early critics cite especially the axiom that, in their divergence from canonically poetic idioms, the poems of *Lyrical Ballads* must be treated 'as experiments',[2] and thereby also signal that the poems' conversational, plain style is best reviewed as an 'experimental' one.[3] In 1800, Wordsworth's Preface openly acknowledges a 'theory' on which these unconventional efforts, he reports, 'were written'. The poet even contemplates a 'systematic defence' of this professed theory in terms that would require him, or any other critical apologist, to shoulder vast historiographical as well as analytic tasks.[4] As if to give this gesture its commensurate (or, for detractors, its incriminating) due, the presence of a palpably 'new system' comes to headline the majority of otherwise quite disparate reactions to the poet's works as they successively appear.[5] In arguments like Francis Jeffrey's earliest response to *Lyrical Ballads*, Wordsworth's divergence from 'established systems' in both 'poetry and criticism' looks principally like a counter-theory.[6] The poet's 'flagrant' contribution to the Lake school's 'positive and *bona fide*' disavowal of 'art altogether' – in the sense of a determinable craft – mainly derives from having promulgated 'a kind of manifesto' in the Preface.[7] But as Jeffrey's fear not just for criticism but for poetry itself confirms, the poet's readers widely sense that his reflective drive is just as integral to his emphatically creative works as it is to his prefatory notes. John Wilson is by no means alone in speculating that much of the poems' cognitive 'advantage to the world' will stem from their 'containing in them a system of philosophy', a structure whose 'subjects of investigation' are said to join moral with anthropological concerns.[8]

Wordsworth's subsequent volumes of poetry were likewise standardly received as if they not just featured individual works, but also manifested the connected 'principles', or 'plan of writing', which publicly continued to typify his enterprise. This imbrication of the primary and secondary – of what has clearly been reflected on and yet claims to be underived in Wordsworth's work – strikes readers whether with or without prompting from his critical essays. Of all his numerous collections, the two-volume *Poems* of 1807 is the only one to offer no explicit prose aside from notes. Yet Jeffrey finds the volumes' gleanings from the 'compositions' of the intervening and presumably 'maturer years' defined, if anything more strongly than their earlier counterparts, by joint 'peculiarities'. Such an apparent pattern is, in this perplexing author's case, clearly enough to let Jeffrey infer that these new poems were again 'avowedly' designed 'for the purpose of exalting a system' – one which had 'already excited', and looked further set to generate, 'a good deal of attention' in the past and future stages of this literary trial.[9]

Thus both sceptics and defenders found it easy to agree, if on nothing else, that what Leigh Hunt dubbed 'the theory of Mr. Wordsworth' was an unmistakable and, for the poet's readership, an ineluctable component of this wilfully plain poetry.[10] Even the slightest poem seemed to confront the reader not just with itself, but with implicit claims made for a whole 'new species'.[11] As Charles Burney helped to clarify, this interplay between the poem and its critically tendentious type would, if successful, redefine the *'genus'* poetry through its most lowly *'species'*.[12] In terms of traditional poetics, the least distinguished features of the token thus looked ready to demote the type itself. In their concerted challenge to 'a higher species of versification', Wordsworth's poetry and criticism clearly challenged not just classical poetic theory, but any simple view of theory's relationship with art.[13] It is then not surprising that the poet's more enthusiastic readers frequently exchanged the two in acts of playful speculation. For Henry Crabb Robinson, the verse prologue to *Peter Bell* was so replete with 'Wordsworth's theory', that is to say 'a vindication of his practice', that Crabb Robinson's interpretive response is to provide 'an abstract' of the prologue's allegorical significance.[14] As early as 1802, Coleridge contrasted 'the extreme elaboration & almost constrainedness of the Diction' in Wordsworth's Preface with his poems' 'general style'. And in agreement Sara Hutchinson was said to have, 'with some acuteness', wished parts 'of the Preface to have been in Blank Verse – & vice versa &c'.[15] According to Crabb Robinson, Wordsworth's enduring impact as a theorist might even rest on his ability to 'incorporate all his critical ideas into a work of taste', whether in 'the dialogue or novel form'.[16] Like several others, Robinson reacted not least to an effective reconception of the place of theory, at once within and in relation to the poet's work.

It is, of course, one of the signal paradoxes of Wordsworth's recasting of poetic theory that it has made him look like, at the same time, the most and the least conceptually involved of perhaps any major poet. Right from the start, this author of a ceaselessly self-implicating theory was just as commonly described as a distinctly anti- or at least atheoretical poetic figure in what could be called the true sense of his work – at least as that sense has been urged by those who have viewed him in this way. Coleridge's censure of the Preface in the *Biographia Literaria* was fuelled not least by 'delight, how little a mere theory, though of his own workmanship', in real terms 'interferes' – by dint of Wordsworth's higher creativity – 'with the processes of genuine imagination'.[17] Many have since agreed with William Whewell's judgement of not only this but, by the force of his example, any poet's sustained theorizing when he wrote that if and where Wordsworth 'has got wrong', 'it pleases me to find that it is in consequence of his theory'. 'What', after all, 'has a poet to do with a theory?' – a practitioner who should appropriately 'mind' rather than think about 'his business'.[18] Along the same lines, Matthew Arnold's well-known introductory essay to his selection of the poet's works (minus the criticism) defended, in 1879, the 'body' formed by 'Wordsworth's best work', and its connections 'with *life*, as a whole', against 'Wordsworthians' who lay 'far too much stress upon what they call' – in the sense of a coherent set of insights – 'his philosophy'.[19] Arnold considered Wordsworth's reflective poetics only in the guise of his 'ingenious', yet 'farfetched' and divisive, classification of the poems in 1815. Again, the antidote to pointless innovation on the systematic plane was simply to allow poetry to 'speak for itself' and, unreflectively, as poetry.[20] Arnold's recourse to classical 'conditions', thought of as 'immutably fixed' by the Greek poetic 'laws' of truth and beauty, sought straightforwardly to void the poet's challenge to the critical tradition. In contrast, early in the century that conspicuous intervention had been reckoned the 'commencement' of a revolution,[21] or the 'open violation' of 'all existing authority' over how we may conceive of, and accordingly read, poetry.[22]

Such celebrations of Wordsworth as the most uncomplicatedly creative and, by extension, the least theoretical of all Romantic writers have had influential afterlives. Yet what is most revealing for our present purposes is how the alternative, split recognition of Wordsworth as either system-poet or instinctive genius points to a vital tension in his own, intentionally poetic modes of theorizing. In fact, Wordsworth's most openly reflective writings are themselves routinely troubled by their implication that they may endorse, or even share, an independent theoretical account of poetry. The poet's effort to construct a general, indeed a systematic case for his achievement is throughout as warily defensive as it is ambitious and sustained. Right from the start in the Advertisement, Wordsworth instructs us categorically that 'evidence' for poetry's supreme distinction as a cultural form 'is to be sought, not in the writings of Critics, but in those of Poets themselves'. And in this motion to deregulate the poet's work, our 'pre-established' and thus generalizing 'codes of decision' are arraigned as 'that most dreadful enemy' to the specific pleasures we would otherwise be free to take in works that may be singularly great (*PW*, 1:116). Yet at the same time as they sound these urgent cautionary notes, the arguments of Wordsworth's criticism also raise the expectation that a body of poetic writing might reward ambitious theoretical analysis. And sometimes Wordsworth even leads us to believe that his own work has all along derived part of its force from organized assumptions and criteria.

In the passage we noted above, Wordsworth maintains in the 1800 Preface that he has been asked to raise his chances of success by framing his collection with 'a systematic defence of the theory, upon which the

poems were written'. His response does nothing to reject the implication that this theory exists, and that it could in fact be rigorously
defended. If anything, the poet seems to magnify the function of concerted thought when he insists that such a vindication must exceed the
reach of a mere preface to a book of poetry. 'I was unwilling to under-
take the task', Wordsworth reports, not least because to justify these
poems even their own author would need to resort to specialized and
rather comprehensive modes of retrospection and analysis:

> For to treat the subject with the clearness and coherence, of which
> I believe it susceptible, it would be necessary to give a full account of
> the present state of the public taste in this country, and to determine
> how far this taste is healthy or depraved: which again could not be
> determined, without pointing out, in what manner language and the
> human mind act and re-act on each other, and without retracing the
> revolutions not of literature alone but likewise of society itself.
>
> (*PW*, 1:120)

These dizzying ambitions for a theory of poetry were never likely to be
realized in Wordsworth's texts alone. Indeed his own engagements with
a theoretical perspective are by no means clearly captured by these intimations, in the Preface, of an organized critique of taste, a philosophy
of language, or an evolutionary account of literary and social forms.
But when his 1802 Appendix to *Lyrical Ballads* recalls what has already
been 'explained', although 'imperfectly', Wordsworth's commitment to
at least the promise of a theoretical account is amply reconfirmed. The
Preface may have done no more than outline certain 'detached parts',
yet there is every expectation that a full-fledged 'system' of poetic writing may in time be formed (*PW*, 1:164 n.). In various ways, the following essays pursue this thought across a range of Wordsworth's poetry
and prose.

Not least because of Wordsworth's own ambivalence about a separate
role for thought alongside poetry's distinctive voice, his readers have
long doubted the significance of his irregular and sometimes intricate
recourse to theory. Indeed, despite extensive contributions to poetic
criticism, Wordsworth himself would later in his life insist that he had
never truly 'felt inclined to write criticism, tho' I have *talked*, and am
daily talking, a great deal'.[23] And when an unsuspecting memoirist of
his career lent too much weight to 'this word *theory*', he rather stridently
protested that, far from having worked hard to recruit it for the future
work of poets, he 'never cared', in fact, 'a straw about the theory'.[24] For

all that, few other poets or critics have worked as stringently through the complexities, the risks, and the promise of coherent thinking about poetry, whether within or at a distance from its primary forms. By focusing on his unique construction of the pathways between creativity and thought, this volume seeks to amplify our understanding of Wordsworth's enduring presence as a poet who is able to transform our access to writing as art.

Our first four essays all take as their main concern the cluster of texts surrounding *Lyrical Ballads*. Andrew Bennett opens the volume by considering how Wordsworth's poetic theory articulates the relation of poetry, knowledge, and ignorance in the 1802 Preface. Wordsworth, as we know, insists in a rather categorical fashion that poetry has an epistemic element. Bennett observes that, while Wordsworth makes a number of apodictic claims linking poetry and knowledge, he does not simply equate the two. Bennett suggests that the poet's essay, by self-consciously pointing towards the limitations of its absolute claims, in fact invokes the counterpart of knowledge, namely ignorance. In the interplay between these epistemic and poetical spheres, poetry turns out to be the medium which allows us to reconsider our parameters of knowledge. Bennett's discussion of 'poetic ignorance' thus engages with a redefinition of the relation between knowledge and poetry. Implicitly, Wordsworth frames poetry as resistant to knowledge as conventionally understood. Instead of equating it with epistemological insight, knowledge is here associated and identified with pleasure. In fact, Bennett shows that by redefining knowledge as pleasure, Wordsworth largely manages to eliminate the former from poetry. Despite his bullish claims about the epistemic power of poetry, it turns out that his poems often resist these claims. In fact, they tend to situate themselves outside the sphere of ordinary knowledge. Many explore what they, poetically, cannot know rather than display their insights. This new calibration allows Bennett to explain how the poems of *Lyrical Ballads* in fact do not bear out the kinds of knowledge claim we might have taken them to make. Instead, they act on a poetics of ignorance which is formulated in the Preface, although, in its discursive form, the latter can hardly itself lay claim to that ignorance.

Stefan Uhlig begins his discussion with another text associated with *Lyrical Ballads*, namely the Advertisement. He extrapolates what one might call a 'structural claim' about Wordsworth's poetic theory, namely that its opening moves involve an argument about poetic objecthood. Uhlig's analysis of the kind of novelty sought by *Lyrical Ballads* focuses on their status as poems, and what a reader might understand or expect to fit that category. He begins by reading Wordsworth's brief commentary as a cautious contextualization for potential readers at the point of publication. For Uhlig, the Advertisement implicitly claims to advance a new way of conceptualizing poetry. Wordsworth's text centres on the poem as defined through its affective engagement with the reader or the poet. It does not comply with patterns set by other well-made objects, namely with their typification via properties or their attributes, be they circumscribed historically or analytically. Instead, a poem is defined through its affective potentialities. And poems therefore have a special status in relation to how they may be recognized, specified, and evaluated as such. The main part of the essay clarifies this status of what Uhlig terms 'poetic objecthood'. Uhlig's claim about the Advertisement here is twofold. He suggests first that, for Wordsworth, poems do not need to adhere to parameters which had become prevalent in the identification of poems, say through neo-classical standards of taste. Secondly, he takes Wordsworth to argue that poems display neither a specific range of properties that could serve as necessary or sufficient conditions nor a list of features that would help to mark them out as poetry. Wordsworth's poetic theory looks in part so innovative because it calls on readers for a judgement that cannot simply rely on identification. This judgement will be unpredictable, and in a crucial sense it needs to be. Uhlig explains why this account of poetry goes far beyond a mere Wordsworthian idiosyncrasy. The special status of poetic objecthood as urged in the Advertisement is, for him, analogous to Kant's understanding of the objects of aesthetic judgement as proposed in the *Critique of Judgement*. Uhlig shows how instructive this analogy between Wordsworth's concise Advertisement and a foundational text in aesthetics may prove. Apart from his discussion of Wordsworth and Kant, the structure of Uhlig's argument is also noteworthy here. Its illumination of, and by, analogy does not make any claim for historical influence. It rather allows us to consider Wordsworth's poetic theory from within the Romantic corpus. And it reminds us that, for all the discursive clarity which the Advertisement, the *Critique*, or other critical arguments might provide, we enjoy and recognize poems on account of their affective power, not because we have – as Wordsworth feared – been reasoned into it.

Peter de Bolla's essay begins by suggesting that the seemingly simple question, 'What is a lyrical ballad?', opens up a set of issues that are crucial to the wider Wordsworthian project. Any attempt to answer such a question will again bear on the formulation of the category of knowledge in Wordsworth's poetics. And once more we find that his poetic theory is not bound to the epistemological or poetical frame-work we are accustomed to employing. In a discussion of the possible alternative models of knowledge, de Bolla invokes what he calls the 'thingliness' of Wordsworth's poetry, a term which ultimately refers to the materiality of the word itself. According to de Bolla, the thingli-ness of poetry is what enables it to offer an experience that intimates a different model of knowledge, or epistemology. This would include, as his discussion shows, a powerful reconsideration of the claim that the poems collected in *Lyrical Ballads* are 'experiments'. These poems are not merely unconventional. More than that, Wordsworth's experi-ments demand a serious engagement with the possibility of shifting the parameters of our conventional standards of epistemology, with all the risks which such a shift may imply. These include precisely the idea that knowledge may prove to be a form of experience, mediated through the thingliness of language. Wordsworth's experiments would thus be more than part of a genealogy of poetic innovations and changes. They would invite us to meditate on the deeper risks of reconsidering the parameters that make poetry, and the special form of knowledge it produces, possible in the first place. According to de Bolla, they hereby also urge us to consider the existential choices involved in being a poet. He offers two examples from *Lyrical Ballads* of how thingliness invades Wordsworth's poetry, and our interpretations. 'Anecdote for Fathers' is seen to meditate on a positive status for lying in a setting that might be expected to yield knowledge. In the Lucy poems, more explicitly, de Bolla finds the materiality of a single letter, its thingliness, to constitute a stumbling block for our reading and understanding of the poem's larger claims. Both readings show that the notion of thingliness is not only attached to objects we would situate in the domain of knowledge. It turns out that thingliness and knowledge can ultimately also function in reverse. That is, the things or words we know to be around us might themselves hold knowledge which we can, in turn, access only through a new understanding of poetry. The thingliness of words may alert us to the possibility that they are carriers of knowledge of a different sort, a knowledge that can make us reconsider both the status of language and the criteria we use to judge its claims. De Bolla's closing paragraphs urge us not to limit our attention to the poetological aspect of what he calls 'Wordsworth's experimental epistemologies'. He suggests that once we consider the avenues that the poet's experiments and their language can open up for us – once we realize how they might carry knowledge of a different kind, and its experience – we become ethically enjoined by his poetic theory.

In his 'Words Worth Repeating', Alexander Regier conjoins two aspects of Wordsworth's poetic theory. First, he offers a reading of the Note to 'The Thorn' that uncovers the poet's seemingly contradictory account of repetition as a source of both a pleasurable celebration of the richness of language and a painful reminder of its necessary limitations. It emerges that the Note is a condensed example of how Wordsworth negotiates the complex relation between ideas, words, and objects that lies at the heart of his poetics. Regier argues that, via a discussion of repetition, Wordsworth advances an account of language as located in a realm between the material and immaterial. The rhetorical moves of repetition and tautology illustrate and enact this double nature of the linguistic. Language, at the very moment it is supposedly defined, becomes the site of an ambiguous and inextricable relation between the material and the immaterial. Regier suggests that this understanding of language points directly to the *Essays upon Epitaphs* and their related views. Here words come similarly to locate themselves between the material and the immaterial, the spiritual and the earthly. But rather than diagnosing this position as a stultifying tension, Regier proposes that Wordsworth allows the reader to renegotiate one of the governing principles of language and analysis. In fact, Wordsworth's account of language points towards a poetic principle of non-resolution that lies at the heart of his poetic theory. The poet here presents us with an approach that discards a progressive dialectics in favour of a distinction 'finer than that of contrast'. The essay closes by delineating how the wider purchase of such a reading may reconfigure the oppositions through which Wordsworth is often understood.

In her contribution, Claudia Brodsky returns to several decisive moments in the Preface to *Lyrical Ballads*. Her discussion shows how Wordsworth's definition of the poet includes a particular receptivity to the complexity of experience. In her account, the poet's self-definition is rooted in the type of relation he needs to negotiate between interior and exterior experience, not only as an individual but also in his poetry. One of the signal instances of this negotiation is the effort to relate the activity of reading to our immediate empirical experiences. For Wordsworth, these two engagements are especially proximate because each poem goes beyond simply re-enacting experience, inviting us to add to it. Thus his poetic theory situates the relevance of reading poetry close to the immediate empirical experience which constitutes our common life. While the two are not identical, any satisfactory description of one will necessarily include the other. There is then, in Brodsky's view, a tight link between Wordsworth's investment in poetry and what we think of as conditions framing our experience, including the conceptual limits we retain in order to account for that experience. Exploring the boundaries of these constructions, Wordsworth sees in poetry's ability to represent memory a power to transcend the limits which human consciousness commonly draws for itself. With Wordsworth, but also invoking Kant, Brodsky identifies this capacity as the sublime. She points out that, considering the complexity and ambition of the poet's aims, it must be crucial that he insists on the simplicity of the language of poetry, its medium. While poetry is complex in its subject matter, there are no predetermined codes through which such complexity is to be explored. Hence the question becomes how a (seemingly) non-complex language may circumscribe and represent experience and a realm of consciousness that in fact reach beyond consciousness. Brodsky seeks to resolve this puzzle by paying close attention to one of the most central moments in Wordsworth's poetics, namely his definition of poetry as 'the spontaneous overflow of powerful feelings', composed by a poet who 'had also thought long and deeply'. Brodsky argues that critics have wrongly thought themselves familiar with the meaning of this passage by focusing on the question of feeling and emotion rather than considering the equally important reference to the centrality of reflection in poetic composition. When read in its entirety, the passage illustrates that Wordsworth's description of poetry as complex action (or indeed as an event) avoids the reductionism entailed by concentrating on any single aspect of a creative process. However, the resulting difficulty of this poetic theory is similarly twofold. Brodsky reminds us that the purpose of poetry is, for Wordsworth, the production of knowledge. It follows, however, that the purpose of poetry is at odds with its language – a medium which produces a power whose effects are not captured by knowledge. Neither in its medium nor in its effects does the power of language match the point of poetry, a contradiction that weaves its way into all of Wordsworth's poetry. Brodsky closes with a brief, yet incisive reading of the Lucy poems as a lyric correlative to this deep strain in Wordsworth's theory.

In her piece on the *Essays upon Epitaphs*, Soelve Curdts explores how seriously the poet's enterprise takes both an ostensibly prosaic world and prose itself. On the one hand, her discussion draws, like Uhlig's, on Kant's critique of conventional hierarchical distinctions between aesthetic and ordinary objects. On the other, Curdts takes her cue from Hegel's striking claim that man will 'speak of external things', strictly conceived, 'only once prose, or thinking has penetrated all relations so that man everywhere conducts himself by thinking abstractly'.

Her study argues that if Wordsworth's poetry and poetics are prosaic in Hegel's sense, this precedence of thought over its external objects must preclude any direct transition from a consciousness of nature to self-consciousness. Instead the poet's engagement with the natural world will be already marked by man's commitment to all-comprehending thought. And where the world appears in these reflections, its poetic presence will be overlaid by consciousness itself, as present to the mind precisely in our most engaged attentions to external things. In pursuit of this dialectic of prose, Curdts shows how even at moments when the poet turns away from nature – say in book six of *The Prelude* – such disregard serves to realign his mind with the antithesis from which it turns all the more decisively. In the manner in which the *Essays* support a 'principle of immortality', this poetry of prose treats its own 'origin and tendency' as if they were 'notions inseparably co-relative'. At the same time, Wordsworth's case against 'poetic diction' seems to rival even Kant's insistence that the fine arts need neither rules nor precedents for their distinctive role. While Wordsworth's scope for poetry can thus extend across the most prosaic objects, circumstances, or events, Curdts finds this poetic theory to be boldly engaged with its own thinking, and to be offering us a poetics of the prosaic.

Frances Ferguson describes her essay, in Wordsworthian terms, as an experiment. She tries to move beyond the generalized significance of sets of poems in their historical context by focusing attention on a specific tension between writing and orality. Her essay clarifies its central relevance to, and within, Wordsworth's poetic theory. The notion of orality, as Ferguson points out, emerges in late opposition to print culture (which, in turn, is necessarily bound up with our modern conception of literature). It is telling, in this context, that the volumes of *Lyrical Ballads* invoke a range of versions and relations of orality and poetic form. Ferguson selects 'The Thorn' as an example of a poem that works through complex layers of orality. She concentrates on the pertinent, and surprisingly neglected, role of audience – at once imagined and real – in a reading that is not confined to the internal workings of the poem (or the collection of which it forms a part). How audience is projected in 'The Thorn' may clarify the specificity and prominence of reading situations, for both listeners and readers, around 1800. Ferguson reveals how literary anthologies, often edited by Dissenters, became an important factor in the development of the literary marketplace, and help us grasp how Wordsworth conceives of his audience.

Against this background, Ferguson provides a detailed reading of 'The Thorn' that re-establishes the centrality of the narrator and focuses particularly on questions of genre. She argues that the narrator's uncomfortable and shifting tone, noticed by many previous readers of the poem, is ultimately linked to his 'insensitivity' vis-à-vis his imagined auditors. The problem, and this is thematized quite deliberately by Wordsworth, is that the narrator talks at the audience, rather than to them. The significance of this dynamic becomes clear when Ferguson presents 'The Thorn' as part of a larger collection of poems which redefines itself, and its aesthetic mission, through its relation with the public. Her historical perspective illuminates how the public voice of Dissenters' anthologies becomes crucial in forming a new concept, experience, and praxis of orality for the written transmission of texts. Their role as popular sources of reading materials makes it imperative that their aesthetic standards be maintained. Joining historical and formal insights, Ferguson suggests that there is in the end an ethical component to Wordsworth's figurations of his listeners and readers.

Paul Hamilton's contribution adds a more urgently historical stance to this volume. His argument is that the late Wordsworthian text of *The Excursion* exceeds its own conservative restrictions and stipulations regarding the definition of the human species as a central aspect of poetics. The text is shown to do this with a radicality that is historically significant, both for our understanding of Romanticism and in reappraising its intellectual genealogy (including an early Marxism which Hamilton invokes). Throughout the essay, Hamilton trusts in the contemporaneity of Romantic texts, and in their power to contain self-criticism in a way that is at once productive and instructive. He focuses on *The Excursion*, a poem that is often vilified for its conservatism and doctrinal Christianity. Hamilton shows, by way of contrast, that one of its chief concerns is how to theorize the irreducible but impossibly difficult set of differences between nature, species, and cognizing individual. The human subject cannot escape a residue of anthropocentrism in his account of the natural world. However, this remainder might allow for an interconnection between species and surrounding world, rather than their division. Hamilton offers a detailed analysis in support of his case that there is a progressive function underwriting the main claims of *The Excursion*, while finding this dynamic to be neither simple nor linear. Hamilton's aim is to show that precisely the instances which might indicate a lack of progression, the moments that thematize the difference between natural world and human subject, often contain a concentrated version of Wordsworthian hope. This, then, is also the ethical core of Hamilton's own intervention. He does not deny his discomfort with Wordsworth's political embrace of religion or imperialism in *The Excursion*. But, he claims, the poem simultaneously seeks to define the human species in relation to the natural world in a manner that is best described as progressive. According to Hamilton, Wordsworth is caught between a religiously orthodox recovery of the individual and a set of radical assumptions about the indeterminacy of the human species which the poem, perhaps unwillingly, articulates. *The Excursion* turns out to accommodate the interdependence of species and individual by mediating this relationship through language. An openness to cross the boundary between the two, despite its troubled politics, lies at the heart of Wordsworth's poetic impulse. For Hamilton this reveals a deeply positive aspect to the poem, often sidelined by criticisms of its aesthetic and political programme. In his account, Wordsworth's writing forms part of a genealogy of efforts, both discursive and poetical, to understand the question of species in a humanist and philosophically progressive mode.

In his reflections on the poet's 'late melodics', Simon Jarvis joins some of our other contributors in exploring Wordsworth's typically constructive yet, by the same token, oddly self-effacing oppositions. More precisely, Jarvis works his way towards an ultimate – at once antagonistic and collaborative – conjunction between verse and thought via more local tensions between the compelling, if also disturbingly occult, appeal of musicality and its desired confluence with poetry's imaginative work. The basic questions are, first, what role Wordsworth envisages for music as accompanying verse (say, classically, as a component of the lyric) and, secondly, to what extent the charms of metre, and of rhythm generally, are best conceived as musical. Jarvis pursues the poet's deep ambivalence about the power of music as, by turns, entrancing idol and intrinsically poetic force across a range of criticism and remarks, chiefly from 1815 onwards, and in several late and highly, as Jarvis describes them, thoughtful lyric poems. Pope's troublingly seductive verse is a strong precedent for Wordsworth's sense of music as at once enchanting and potentially obstructive for original poets and their readership. Related links between a strictly natural song and superstition, or entrancing magic, surface in the sonnet 'On Approaching the Staub-Bach, Lauterbrunnen'. At the same time, Jarvis detects more complex attitudes to pagan idols and imaginative form in the 1815 Preface's tribute to Milton and Spenser as exemplary, yet also classically inspired, poets. His primary exhibits are, in this regard, the 'Ode to Lycoris' and its subsequent Fenwick note. In these materials, he shows the poet wanting to 'relax', or even be released from, some of the austerity of his original renunciations of the definite, anthropomorphic forms (as drawn from, say, ancient mythology and its personifying drive) which make up such a large part of the poet's heritage. Here, as in Jarvis's final analysis of 'On the Power of Sound', any straightforward contrast between music's dark and beneficial magic, its poetically enslaving and enabling powers, gives way to a firmly dialectical account of preservation within overcoming. One of the central lessons which this study draws from Wordsworth's deep ambivalence about prosodic music is its distance from a simple faith in pleasure or, as Jarvis terms it, the aesthetic view of musicality. Instead, Jarvis throughout invests in an account of music – and of Wordsworth's later verse by way of music – as at once bound up in rivalry with thought and as 'performatively' rational. Wordsworth's engagement with music as the counterpart of lyric thus looks to be sublated in a late style that is more than ever devoted to the modulated, even the 'irrational', rationality Jarvis describes with Wordsworth as the poet's 'philosophic song'.

In her essay, Mary Jacobus follows several avenues in thinking about the role of communication, signs, and sensual experience in Wordsworth's poetics. Her immediate point of entry is a meditation on how the condition of deafness, a recurrent figure in Wordsworth, may be key to furthering our understanding of the role of language in his work. Reconsidering the role of deafness (which Jacobus views less as a disability than a condition that can open up previously neglected ways of perceiving the world) proves a way of thinking about the role of natural and conventional sign systems far beyond the standard forms of speech or writing. Thematically, the texts surrounding Wordsworth's figure of the deaf Dalesman are the most forceful site of this concern in his oeuvre. Yet Jacobus also reminds us that this issue is, importantly, not just internal to Wordsworth's poetic work but also links his insights to their historical context. She pinpoints the late eighteenth century as a historically important moment in our cultural attitudes to the deaf. Theories of deafness and sign language at that time become part of the philosophically charged sphere of the theory of language, and this specific link is more than accidental. Jacobus draws on numerous sources which chart changing views of deafness in more than simply medical or ethical terms, and clarifies how this development is tied in with efforts to make the deaf 'speak', to reappraise sign language, for example, as more than a poor imitation of real speech. This broader dimension links the theme, and contemporary theorizations, of deafness to Wordsworth's work more intimately than mere context. The essay's argument suggests that his poetic writing entertains a deep conceptual link with these contemporary reflections on the deaf. For Wordsworth, the effort to rethink the linguistic as located not simply in speech that can be heard goes hand in hand with his reflections on the epitaphic nature of poetry. Through this interconnection, the figure of 'composing sound' becomes vital for an understanding of poetry per se. The mute inscription proves significant not just for the reflections of the *Essays upon Epitaphs*: the poetry itself provides an equally sustained test of its leverage in reinvestigating language beyond its received understanding.

The collection aptly closes with a contribution by Geoffrey Hartman, surely the most esteemed Wordsworthian of our day. It is telling that such a distinguished scholar should conclude our volume on an openly conjectural note by speculating about 'Wordsworth and Metapsychology'. Hartman muses on Wordsworth's strong sense of the material world, in its timelessness and universality, as a condition that underwrites all poetry. The subtly shaded way in which Wordsworth suspects that this material world is not altogether insensate is Hartman's cue to link the Romantic poet with Freud's conjectures on metapsychology. Poetry contains both the (for Freud, ultimately inexplicable) force that lies behind life's inception and its counterpart, the death drive. Crucially, however, Hartman shows how poetry intimates that this ostensibly destructive tendency is potentially remedial. Wordsworth's metapsychology, accordingly, involves not just a drive that wills the inanimate. Instead, the poetic mind fosters a further residue which, through recall, keeps present the very animating force that brought it into existence. Through the Lucy cycle Hartman illustrates how the poet's metapsychology knowingly accommodates this tension in poetic practice. Without leaving Wordsworth's work behind, Hartman allows us to see how this approach can be generalized beyond the poet's individual case, and how it may shape the evolution of our imagination no less than its relation to the natural world. Wordsworth's example is especially telling because he insists that, in articulating the relation between animate self and inanimate surroundings, the subject also insists on the importance of certain dimensions of the non-human. The disturbing aspects of this relation remain a part of the imagination's development (rather than being suppressed or denied). Hartman finds a deeply original way of showing how the link between poetic creation, destructive force, and memory is central to Wordsworth's poetic theory.

Conjointly and in their own characteristic terms, the studies in this volume chart the continuities in Wordsworth's theory as much as the divergences and contrasts which, if anything, intensify its critical effect. Whereas our opening essays focus firmly on the kinds of knowing, or indeed of judgement, that may be available through poetry, we are soon led to Wordsworth's deep critique of language in, and for the benefit of, his poetic work. At the same time the question of experience, and of distinctively poetic affects, proves decisive for a range of our contributors' concerns. The implications of oral or textual exchange, of musicality, or even of the absence of all sound derive in various ways from Wordsworth's reconfiguration of a poem's claim on us as an experiential one. The nature of this interaction between poet, poetry, and readers, we will see, comes to reflect on even our condition as the members of a species. Just as the present volume in this manner intersects no less than it traverses themes of knowledge, language, and experience, our contributions test any straightforward timeline for the poet's self-critique. We start with essays that attend to the initiatory notes and prefaces of *Lyrical Ballads*. Yet their concerns address, and are in turn engaged by, arguments in the full range of texts to which our further contributions turn. And from the outset Wordsworth's poetry, with its own perspicacity, inflects and amplifies our authors' lines of argument. No less than Wordsworth's intellectual stakes, this dialogue between his different modes of writing yields deeply intriguing, complex opportunities for thinking about poetry. We hope the present volume may serve to extend these resources.

Notes

1. Robert Southey, unsigned review of *Lyrical Ballads* (1798), *Analytical Review*, 28 (December 1798), p. 583; repr. *William Wordsworth: The Critical Heritage. Volume I, 1793–1820*, ed. Robert Woof (London: Routledge, 2001), p. 68 (hereafter cited as *CH*).
2. Southey, *Analytical Review*, 28 (1798), p. 583; *CH*, p. 68.
3. Robert Southey, unsigned review of *Lyrical Ballads* (1798), *Critical Review*, 24 (October, 1798), p. 198; *CH*, p. 66.
4. *The Prose Works*, ed. W. J. B. Owen and Jane Worthington Smyser, vol. 1 (Oxford: Clarendon Press, 1974), p. 120. This edition hereafter indicated as *PW* and cited by volume and page numbers in the text.
5. Francis Jeffrey, unsigned review of Robert Southey's *Thalaba*, *Edinburgh Review*, 1 (October, 1802), p. 66; *CII*, p. 156.
6. Jeffrey, *Edinburgh Review*, 1 (1802), p. 63; *CH*, p. 153.
7. Jeffrey, *Edinburgh Review*, 1 (1802), p. 65; *CH*, p. 156.
8. John Wilson ('Christopher North'), letter to Wordsworth (1802), quoted from *CH*, p. 111.
9. Francis Jeffrey, unsigned review of *Poems* (1807), *Edinburgh Review*, 11 (October 1807), p. 215–16; *CH*, p. 187.
10. Leigh Hunt, *The Feast of the Poets, with Notes* (London: James Cawthorn, 1814), p. 90; *CH*, p. 333.
11. Alexander Carlyle, letter to Miss Mitchelson (c. 1802), in *Autobiography*, ed. John Hill Burton (London: T. N. Foulis, 1910), p. 593; *CH*, p. 114. Cf. John

Stoddart on Wordsworth's 'necessary justification' of his 'species of poetry'. Unsigned review of *Lyrical Ballads* (1800), *British Critic*, 17 (February 1801), p. 125; *CH*, p. 139.

12. Charles Burney, unsigned review of *Lyrical Ballads* (1798), *Monthly Review*, 29 (June 1799), p. 203; *CH*, p. 75.

13. Burney, *Monthly Review*, 29 (1799), p. 202; *CH*, p. 74.

14. Diary, 4 June 1812, in *Books and Their Writers*, ed. Edith J. Morley, vol. 1 (London: J. M. Dent, 1938), p. 94; *CH*, p. 305.

15. To Robert Southey, 29 July 1802, *Collected Letters. Volume II, 1801–1806*, ed. Earl Leslie Griggs (Oxford: Clarendon Press, 1956), p. 830; *CH*, p. 118.

16. Diary, 16 April 1815, in *Books and Their Writers*, vol. 1, p. 165; *CH*, p. 819.

17. *Biographia Literaria*, ed. James Engell and W. J. Bate, vol. 2 (London: Routledge & Kegan Paul, 1983), pp. 59–60.

18. To Hugh James Rose, 30 August 1817, in *The Life and Selections from the Correspondence of William Whewell*, ed. Mrs. Stair Douglas (London: C. K. Paul, 1881), p. 31; *CH*, p. 985.

19. Matthew Arnold, 'Wordsworth', in *English Literature and Irish Politics*, ed. R. H. Super (Ann Arbor: University of Michigan Press, 1973), pp. 44, 48.

20. Arnold, 'Wordsworth', pp. 43–4.

21. Hunt, *Feast of the Poets*, p. 107; *CH*, p. 338.

22. Jeffrey, *Edinburgh Review*, 11 (1807), p. 214–31; *CH*, pp. 201, 199.

23. To Sir William Rowan Hamilton, 4 January 1838, in *The Letters of William and Dorothy Wordsworth: The Later Years. Part III, 1835–1839*, ed. Ernest de Selincourt, rev. Alan G. Hill (Oxford: Clarendon Press, 1982), pp. 508–9.

24. Geoffrey Little, ed., *Barron Field's Memoirs of Wordsworth* (Sydney: Sydney University Press, 1975), pp. 47, 62.

1
Wordsworth's Poetic Ignorance

Andrew Bennett

1

Wordsworth's uncompromising, exaggerated, essentially unfalsifiable claims for the knowledge production of poetry in the Preface to *Lyrical Ballads* are extraordinary, and possibly unique.[1] In a paragraph added in 1802 as part of a long disquisition on the language of poetry, the nature of the poet, and the relationship between poetry and knowledge, Wordsworth makes three substantive claims:

1. that poetry is 'the breath and finer spirit of all knowledge'
2. that the poet 'binds together by passion and knowledge the vast empire of human society'
3. that poetry is 'the first and last of all knowledge'.[2]

There are two observations to make about these claims. In the first place they are unequivocally totalizing. Poetry, Wordsworth says, encompasses or articulates or defines *all* knowledge; poetry 'binds together' *all* of human society, through knowledge. The second observation is that the reverse is the case: the assertions are profoundly equivocal. Wordsworth is not, not quite, claiming that poetry *is* knowledge, is a form of knowing or is knowledge-yielding. Instead, in claiming that poetry constitutes the 'breath and finer spirit' of knowledge, he is suggesting that it is something like the soul, in a dualistic epistemological model, to the 'body' of knowledge; in claiming that poetry is that which 'binds together' human society, he is suggesting that it does so 'by' knowledge, by using or exploiting it (rather than constituting it); in claiming that poetry is the 'first and last' of knowledge, he again suggests that it is not quite knowledge itself – poetry defines the limits of knowledge, tells us where knowing ends, without itself yielding knowledge as such outside of this meta-epistemic policing function. In effect, in fact, Wordsworth is attempting to redefine knowledge itself – to rethink knowledge as and in relation to both passion and poetry, and trying to rethink poetry both as, and as not, knowledge-yielding.

Wordsworth's essentially hyperbolic, even rather frantic, claims for the knowledge-based power and effect of poetry are generated no doubt by poetry's dwindling epistemic authority within the context of Enlightenment advances in philosophy and especially science. But even within his explicit formulation of these claims – or perhaps precisely because of their exaggeratedness, because of their impossibility – what also haunts Wordsworth's claims about poetic knowledge is the other of knowledge. And I want to suggest that one way to engage with Wordsworth's poetic epistemology is to think about what we might call 'poetic ignorance'. Because even in these formulations of the epistemological force of poetry, Wordsworth is in fact presenting poetry as, or as at, or even as finally beyond, the limits of what is or what might be conceived of as cognition. In order to justify his totalizing claims, in other words, Wordsworth has to redefine both poetry and knowledge and to rethink the relationship between the two.[3] As a result, what is called poetry comes at times to look like that which, by definition, knowledge resists, and that which resists knowledge.

Take, for example, the phrase 'breath and finer spirit of all knowledge'. In his subtle and philosophically informed examination of Romanticism's ambivalence with regard to epistemology and philosophical scepticism, *Knowledge and Indifference in English Romantic Prose* (2003), Tim Milnes has recently argued that in this phrase Wordsworth presents the 'collapsing of form and content and the rehabilitation of knowing through figuration'.[4] But an alternative reading of the phrase would suggest that what collapses here is precisely knowledge, precisely the possibility of poetic knowledge, that the figuration involved in the sentence is that which resists knowing. What would the 'breath' of knowledge be, and what would be its 'finer spirit'? In what sense can breath be conceived of in epistemological terms? What kind of metaphor is at work here? And is 'breath' a kind of 'spirit', or are the two intended to be understood as separate ways of conceiving knowledge? Wordsworth is undoubtedly exploiting classical accounts of inspiration in these figures, as well as alluding to more conventionally religious contexts. But what these figures fail to achieve or convey is any possibility that we might know what the 'breath' of knowledge or its 'finer spirit' would involve or how either would be constituted or conceived or achieved. In this respect, the phrase's figural force may be said to work *against* knowing. Where Milnes argues that Wordsworth's ambivalent

Romantic response to David Hume's philosophical scepticism – a kind of despairing 'indifference' to knowledge as such – leads stubbornly, if at times uncertainly, towards an assertion of poetry's epistemological force, towards its conflicted knowing, in this essay I want to suggest that what is at stake in some key moments in Wordsworth's poetry and poetics is a privileging of not knowing, of ignorance (in a context in which being concerned with ignorance is a very different matter from simply being 'indifferent' to knowledge).

In fact, from the first, the Preface engages with the question of not knowing, to the extent that it might be said to be governed by a poetics of ignorance. Indeed, inasmuch as the Preface as a whole is constituted as a defence and justification of Wordsworth's new, surprising, original, unique or singular poems, it can be understood to be concerned precisely with the question of the assumed, if not by the time of its composition actually proven, ignorance of the book's first readers. This has to do in particular with Wordsworth's assumptions about his readers' assumptions, about their embeddedness, as he sees it, within an inappropriate reading community. As Wordsworth sees it, his readers are likely to apply improper interpretative codes and conventions and to adhere to what Robert Scholes refers to as established 'protocols' of reading, protocols with which, for Wordsworth, they are only too woefully familiar.[5]

At the beginning of the Preface, Wordsworth suggests that the reader of his poems is likely to be faced with unfamiliar *kinds* of poetry (not just unfamiliar poems). He proposes that while a poet makes a 'formal engagement' to 'gratify certain known habits of association' (*PW*, 1:123), in the case of the poems collected in *Lyrical Ballads* that implicit contract is effectively deemed null and void. Instead, he argues in the 1802 version of the Preface (in a passage adapted from the 1798 Advertisement), the reader of this collection of poetry will be faced with something entirely new and therefore disturbing or 'awkward':

> They who have been accustomed to the gaudiness and inane phraseology of many modern writers, if they persist in reading this book to its conclusion, will, no doubt, frequently have to struggle with feelings of strangeness and awkwardness: they will look round for poetry, and will be induced to inquire by what species of courtesy these attempts can be permitted to assume that title.
>
> (*PW*, 1:123)

According to Wordsworth, the knowing reader will be brought up against the limits of his own preoccupations. His knowingness, indeed, will be challenged. Although the statement seems to suggest that there will be other readers, readers whose poetic sensibilities have not been blunted by their encounter with modern poetry, who will be able properly to read his poems, a comment added in 1802 makes it clear that the purpose of the poems is in fact precisely to induce such feelings, feelings of 'defamiliarization' as we now say, to make the ordinary seem extraordinary, strange, different, unfamiliar, newly unknown. In this sense, it seems that the proper response to the poems *is* precisely an experience of 'awkwardness'. While Wordsworth here declares that he is using 'language really used by men' to reflect on 'incidents and situations from common life', he also explains that he has attempted to 'throw over' those incidents a 'certain colouring of imagination, whereby ordinary things should be presented to the mind in an unusual aspect' (*PW*, 1:123). The principle of defamiliarization, of making familiar things 'unusual', that Wordsworth is developing here involves the possibility of making the reader *not* know his or her own world: it allows or invites the reader to be newly ignorant, newly unknowing, of those things, thoughts, feelings, ideas with which she is most familiar. Inasmuch as poetry may be said to be constituted by this effort to make strange, inasmuch as it is poetry *because* it makes things strange, poetry may be said to be a kind of ignorance machine, an uncanny linguistic contraption that makes us unknow what we (think we) know.

But it is not only through reading that ignorance may be said to operate in Wordsworth's poetics: although he is said to have 'a greater knowledge of human nature' than other people (*PW*, 1:138), the poet is also, at some level, necessarily unknowing. Wordsworth states this most clearly when he talks about the production of poetry in terms of spontaneity. In his initial declaration on the 'spontaneous overflow of powerful feelings' (*PW*, 1:126), Wordsworth acknowledges the 'outcry', as he calls it, against 'the triviality and meanness both of thought and language' which he claims, some of his contemporaries have 'occasionally introduced into their metrical compositions'. But he tries to distinguish his own poems from those of other modern poets by referring to what he calls the 'worthy *purpose*' of his own (*PW*, 1:124). In an important declaration he then qualifies this question of the purposefulness of his poems:

> Not that I mean to say, that I always began to write with a distinct purpose formally conceived; but I believe that my habits of meditation have so formed my feelings, as that my descriptions of such objects as strongly excite those feelings, will be found to carry

along with them a *purpose*. If in this opinion I am mistaken I can have little right to the name of a Poet.

(PW, 1:124, 126)

In effect, the very constitution of William Wordsworth as a poet is said to involve the fact that his poems have a 'purpose', but one that is not 'formally conceived'. The question arises why Wordsworth deems it necessary to declare that the purpose is not conceived but rather an effect of habitual meditation – why it is necessary to distinguish the poem and indeed the composition of poetry from a kind of background context of thinking, from his habits of contemplation. At this point, it is true, Wordsworth at least gives the impression that the purpose of a poem *might* be or indeed will normally be 'formally conceived': he has not *always* begun with a purpose, he states, as if at other times he has done so. But he is not in fact primarily concerned with those poems that are formally conceived. And in the next sentence, one that he is to repeat and qualify later on and one that is to become one of the key directives in the Romantic conception of poetry, of the poet, and of poetic composition, he suggests more forcibly that the proper poem should *never* be so conceived: 'For all good poetry', he contentiously declares, 'is the spontaneous overflow of powerful feelings' (*PW*, 1:127). Such an idea of poetry would seem effectively to rule out formal conception in the production of the poem: 'spontaneous' (however construed, whether as 'unpremeditated' or as 'arising without external stimulus' [*OED*]), 'overflow', 'powerful', and 'feelings', all conspire to reinforce the sense that poems are not in the first place, not in their origin, not in their essence, *conceived*, formally or otherwise. Poems, in other words, just happen. In this respect, the Preface appears to be pointing towards the conclusion that a 'good poem' is that kind of work that *cannot* be 'formally conceived'.[6]

When he repeats his proposition a few pages later, Wordsworth famously seems to equivocate further over the question of whether the poem is 'conceived' or not:

> I have said that poetry is the spontaneous overflow of powerful feelings: it takes its origin from emotion recollected in tranquillity: the emotion is contemplated till, by a species of re-action, the tranquillity gradually disappears, and an emotion, kindred to that which was before the subject of contemplation, is gradually produced, and does itself actually exist in the mind.

(PW, 1:149)

Wordsworth appears here to reintroduce some kind of conception and therefore some kind of authorial knowingness into the origin or production of poetry: by introducing 'recollection' into the process of poetic composition he thereby allows for delay and deferral, which in turn seems to allow for contemplation or conception, for thought, thinking, consciousness, for cognition or knowledge. But the passage equivocates over the question of whether the poem is in fact a function of 'contemplation', of thinking, and therefore something that can, in its composition, be consciously conceived, be something known. While such a reading would offer a forceful account of the sentence, we might also recognize that whereas contemplation is involved in the process by which the poem is produced, the poem itself is constituted *not* by contemplation but by 'emotion'. Poetry just *is* the 'spontaneous overflow of powerful feelings'. A poem is not contemplation and recollection but feeling, the feeling itself, or at least its overflow. Poetry is a kind of emanation of feeling. Recollection and contemplation, by contrast, constitute ways in which the original emotion is reimagined or reconceived: they are mechanisms of retrieval. What is retrieved and then re-experienced is, in a certain sense, the poem, the prior, originary, non-linguistic experience that *is* in fact, however paradoxically, a poem. And the end result of this reconception or retrieval is a return to the original condition: the 'feeling' or 'emotion' 'does actually exist in the mind'. In this respect, the experiences of recollection and conception are not themselves the poem. Instead, the poem is emotion or what flows out of it, the originary experience uncontaminated by recollection or contemplation, by conception, by thought or indeed by knowledge. Poetry, as Wordsworth puts it in his Note to 'The Thorn', is 'passion': inasmuch as it is history or science, it is, he says, the 'history or science of feelings'.[7]

2

What I am suggesting, then, is that one of the crucial questions in Wordsworth's poetic theory concerns the *relationship*, which means in effect and in the end not only the imbrications of but also the *oppositions* between poetry and knowledge, between the cognitive, the gnoseological, the sciential on the one hand and feeling, emotion, pleasure and poetry on the other. In the Preface, in fact, Wordsworth attempts both to argue for the intrinsic cognitive value of poetry and to distinguish the two realms of discourse, to both align poetry with and distinguish it from knowledge. But what I want to emphasize here is the conceptual importance, as well as the subsequent influence, of

Wordsworth's framing of poetry as in fact resistant to knowledge. The attempt to distinguish between the two is presented most explicitly in a footnote in which he argues that there is no significant difference between poetry and prose except in terms of 'metrical composition': 'much confusion has been introduced into criticism by this contra-distinction', he remarks, rather than 'the more philosophical one of Poetry and Matter of Fact, or Science' (*PW*, 1:135n). As this makes clear, Wordsworth is appealing to the sense of 'science' as knowledge in the widest sense, and the assertion raises the spectre of the ancient distinction between science as *epistemé*, concerned with truth, and art as *techné*, concerned with *praxis* or with effecting a certain result.[8] But what is at stake in this shifting of definitional pertinence from metre to epistemology is the very gnoseological status of poetry.

Wordsworth makes a number of points that in fact explicitly query poet-ry's epistemological power. The 1802 version of the Preface is particularly clear about this: as well as making a fundamental distinction between poetry and 'Matter of Fact, or Science', Wordsworth differentiates poetry from what he sees as the empirical discourses of biography and history, and he emphasizes his identification of poetry with the non-knowledge-yielding emotion of pleasure. With regard to the historicity or otherwise of poetry, Wordsworth alludes to Aristotle's well-known dictum that poetry is 'more philosophical' than history and attempts to develop the distinction between poetry and history in a way that seems to suggest that the factual-ness or otherwise of poetry is somehow beside the point, since poetry has an at best indirect take on knowledge:

> The obstacles which stand in the way of the fidelity of the Biographer and Historian, and of their consequent utility, are incalculably greater than those which are to be encountered by the Poet who has an ade-quate notion of the dignity of his art. The Poet writes under one restric-tion only, namely, that of the necessity of giving immediate pleasure to a human Being possessed of that information which may be expected from him, not as a lawyer, a physician, a mariner, an astronomer, or a natural philosopher, but as a Man. Except this one restriction, there is no object standing between the Poet and the image of things; between this, and the Biographer and Historian, there are a thousand.
>
> (*PW*, 1:139)

What seems to be at work in Wordsworth's statement is the idea that the poet is at liberty to invent without being concerned with the 'thousand' restrictions of empirical veracity and verifiability to which the biographer and historian are both bound. Wordsworth suggests indeed that mimesis or the kind of realism or fidelity with regard to empirical evidence required of biographers and historians leads inexorably to a 'slavish and mechanical' *reproduction* of the 'passions' of others (*PW*, 1:138). The primary function of the poet, by contrast, is liberatory: to give pleasure, not information (the 'information' is already assumed in the reader). If poetry yields knowledge, it is therefore the kind of 'knowledge' that has little need of empirically verifiable or indeed cognitively viable facts. Indeed, it is not knowledge in the conventional sense but knowledge redefined as pleasure. The point is also made a few sentences earlier, although in slightly different terms. Here, Wordsworth attempts to explain how the poet 'creates' things where he does not find them. He argues that the poet is someone who is 'affected more than other men by absent things as if they were present' and who displays an ability of 'conjuring up in himself passions, which are indeed far from being the same as those produced by real events' and yet which 'do more nearly resemble the passions produced by real events, than anything which, from the motions of their own minds merely, other men are accustomed to feel in themselves' (*PW*, 1:138). It is a difficult, if compelling, passage, but one in which it is clear that Wordsworth is attempting to discriminate the empirically verifiable knowledge of ordinary men from the knowledge that poets produce, to distinguish between foundational or empirical knowledge and creative or poetic ways of 'knowing'. Another way of thinking about this 'poetic' knowledge would be to say that it is not knowledge so much as invention – that the poet creates where the historian or biographer or scientist discovers.[9] As Wordsworth puts it in 1815, the poetic genius involves 'the introduction of a new element into the intellectual universe' (*PW*, 3:82).[10]

One of the most important and most heavily emphasized claims in the Preface concerns the idea that the kind of 'knowledge' that poetry produces or avows or institutes or constitutes must be defined in terms of pleasure.[11] For both the poet and the 'Man of Science', Wordsworth argues, 'knowledge ... is pleasure', the 'grand elementary principle of pleasure, by which [man] knows, and feels, and lives, and moves': 'We have no knowledge,' he declares, 'no general principles drawn from the contemplation of particular facts, but what has been built up by pleasure, and exists in us by pleasure alone' (*PW*, 1:140–1). According to this rather odd and rather un-philosophical reasoning, the poet is therefore even better placed than the Man of Science with regard to knowledge, since his knowledge, Wordsworth says, 'cleaves to us as a necessary part of our existence', whereas scientific knowledge is a 'personal and individual acquisition' which is 'slow' to arrive, indirect, and not part of our 'habitual' make-up (*PW*, 1:141).[12] This insistence on the link between pleasure and knowledge, and the associated idea that we can know *nothing* without pleasure (where the anatomist has 'no pleasure he has no knowledge', Wordsworth opines [*PW*, 1:140]), both reinforces and subtly undermines the claims concerning the epistemic power of poetry. If knowledge is pleasure and pleasure is poetry, then the conventional conception of knowledge – even in the most basic, colloquial sense of 'that which is known' – has been so radically redefined as to void it of the kinds of 'scientific' or 'philosophical' or 'biographical' or 'histori-cal' senses with which it is conventionally associated. Knowledge has been redefined in terms of emotion, in terms of the emotion associated with the pleasure that one experiences in relation to reading or writing a poem. By redefining knowledge as pleasure Wordsworth in fact manages to eliminate it from poetry. If poetry is a superior form of 'knowing', it is so not because it is more epistemologically precise, capacious, accurate, or inventive even, but simply because it is more pleasurable. And it is precisely this element of pleasure that, in a thinking other than Wordsworth's rather contorted reasoning, may more credibly be said to *distance* poetry from knowledge. Indeed, in the sense that what is pleasurable about poetry involves metre and rhythm and figuration and rhetorical complication, one might say that the 'knowledge' that poetry produces or constitutes amounts, in the final analysis, to a form of nescience: poetry allows one to not know, allows one to accept not knowing – a profoundly political point, one might add, link-ing poetry as it does to the foundation of democracy in an acceptance of both the principle of what Lorenzo Infantino calls 'gnoseological fallibility' and the principle of the final unknowability of, the privacy of, the 'subject' in democracy, with that democratic paradox whereby the individual both is and cannot be a political 'subject'.[13]

3

I want to suggest that the poetics of ignorance that Wordsworth begins hesitatingly to develop in the Preface is, in effect, a response to, or indeed a displaced articulation of, one of the primary thematic and technical con-cerns of those curious and sometimes alarming poems that they introduce, defend, and excuse. This is clear, for example, with regard to the use that Wordsworth makes of nescient, unknowing narrators in two of his most notorious poems, 'The Thorn' and 'The Idiot Boy'. In 'The Thorn', the speaker repeatedly assures his audience that he knows nothing, or next to nothing: 'No more I know, I wish I did, / And I would tell it all to you', he declares (ll. 155–6). Although he insists that he will tell us 'every thing I know' (l. 105) – 'I'll tell you all I know' (l. 114), he remarks – in fact he tells us far less than we might think we need to know and far less than he knows, rightly speaking, he should. 'I cannot tell', he repeats more than once in a way that manages to ambiguate a telling phrase: Is it that he cannot tell us what he knows or that he cannot tell us because he knows that he doesn't know? Or is it simply that he cannot 'tell' in the sense that he just doesn't know (ll. 89, 214, 243)? In fact, the latter would seem to be the case, since in stanza fifteen he repeatedly declares not only his own but the world's ignorance: 'There's no one that could ever tell' (l. 160), he says, because in fact 'There's none that ever knew' (l. 158), 'There's no one knows' (l. 162). Of course, the speaker knows some things, knows them only too well: he's good, notoriously good, on measurements in particular. He knows that the thorn in question is about the height of a 'two-years' child' (l. 5), that it is positioned 'Not five yards from the mountain-path' (l. 27) and three yards from a 'little muddy pond' (l. 30), which is 'three feet long, and two feet wide' (l. 33), and that close by there is a mound, a 'hill of moss' that is 'half a foot in height' (ll. 36–7). And he knows and tells us various things about Martha Ray and Stephen Hill – that they were lovers and engaged to be married, that Stephen Hill married someone else, that Martha Ray was distraught and that she was thought to have been pregnant by Stephen and thought to have had his child and possibly to have killed it, and that this happened twenty-two years earlier. And he knows, finally, as he asserts at the end in a resounding moment of epistemological confidence ('And this I know', he declares in line 247), that he has heard the woman's melancholy cry. But the precision of these details of measurement and the vacuity of the declaration that he *knows* that he has heard her cry only serve to reinforce our sense that the speaker does not know or cannot tell the important thing: what happened here? Was a child in fact born? Did it die? Was it killed by its mother?[14] Since these are the important questions, we might ask what the speaker is doing telling us this (non-)tale, why he's telling us when he doesn't know. In this respect, the poem is precisely about the condition of not knowing, about what it's like not to know.

A similar affliction – a refusal or an inability to 'tell', and the conundrum of whether this means that one doesn't know or that one knows and cannot communicate – defines the narrator of 'The Idiot Boy'. Like the speaker in 'The Thorn', the narrator in 'The Idiot Boy' is characterized by the fact that he is unable to tell what on the face of it we need to know. In effect, he cannot tell us the tale that he purports to be telling us. 'Oh reader!', the narrator says, 'now that I might tell / What Johnny and his horse are doing! / What they've been doing all this time, / Oh could I put it into rhyme, / A most delightful tale pursuing!' (ll. 322–6). The speaker's very existence as a narrator is constituted by this paradoxical inability to tell, and in fact this is just what the poem is about, his – and therefore our – ignorance of the boy's activities. 'Oh gentle muses!' he goes on, 'let me tell / But half of what to him befel' (ll. 349–50) – as if he could but can't; 'I cannot tell', he admits of Johnny's laugh, whether it expresses cunning or joy (ll. 388–9) – as if he would tell if he could. The reason that he cannot tell, in a fundamental epistemological sense, is of course that the poem is concerned for most of its 463 lines with an unanswerable question, the question of where the idiot boy has gone, or (once he is found) of where he has been. No one – not the boy's mother, Betty Foy, not the narrator, not the reader – is enlightened even at the end of the poem. Since Johnny himself is characterized by his idiocy, we can also take it that he too fails to be enlightened about his own whereabouts or about the significance of his wandering. So the poem is constituted by and constructed around ignorance and around ignorance within ignorance. With its peculiarly slow-witted narrator (who is still indentured after an unprecedented fourteen years) the poem, as Avital Ronell puts it, 'draws a blank'.[15] The search for the boy ends but we, the narrator, Betty Foy, and presumably the idiot boy himself still don't know where he has been:

> 'The cocks did crow to-whoo, to-whoo,
> 'And the sun did shine so cold.'
> —Thus answered Johnny in his glory,
> And that was all his travel's story.
>   (ll. 460–3)

Johnny's words involve what David Bromwich calls a 'derangement of sense'. But, as Bromwich observes, his answer is also – or therefore – a kind of poetry, involving the metaphorization of owl-calls as the crowing of cocks and of the moon as a cold-shining sun.[16] But if this is poetry, it is poetry as a form of idiocy.[17] Perhaps most importantly, 'The Idiot Boy', like 'The Thorn', involves a kind of mockery of narrative requirements, of story: it's a joke of a poem, premised precisely around its resistance to the 'knowledge transfer', as we have learnt to call it, involved in the traditional conception of narrative poetry, of narrative as sense-making, of narrative as cognitively productive. At the very least, the narrator of a poem or another tale is the one who, in accordance with the etymology of his designation, is supposed to know. But much of the force of these poems comes from the narrators' denial of their job description: these narrators are precisely those who, beyond certain very strict limits, do *not* know, *cannot* tell.

Both 'The Thorn' and 'The Idiot Boy', then, present us with the curious and curiously productive phenomenon of protagonists and narrators who are cognitively limited. But it is not only in narratives about idiots or in tales told by narrators who are stubbornly loquacious and (therefore) somewhat slow that Wordsworth explores the significance of nescience. In 'We are Seven', to take another perhaps rather obvious example, the rational, lucid and apparently intelligent speaker is nevertheless cognitively limited because of his lack of sympathy with the girl's understanding of the status of her dead siblings – because of his assumption that she is simply wrong, ignorant; and whatever else it does, in presenting the two incompatible and finally irreconcilable conceptions of death, the poem brings us up against our own ignorance of what it means, what it must mean, to be dead. In the companion piece to 'We are Seven', 'Anecdote for Fathers', the role of the father-as-teacher (the one who is supposed to know) and that of the son-as-pupil (the one who is supposed not to know) are overturned: the painful lesson that the father learns in this poem is the lesson of gnoseological humility. Not only is it the case that he has ignorantly insisted on an answer to his intrusive questions despite his son's protestations that he doesn't know ('I cannot tell, I do not know', the son replies, in line 39), but the very act of asking is premised on an inappropriate desire to know something, something that shouldn't or cannot be known. The father learns that not everything should or can be known, needs to be known, that there are ways of being, ways of relating to others, that are, or that should be, premised on mutual unknowing.

'Simon Lee', to take one more example, this time an example concerned neither with idiots nor with those miniature idiots, those ignoramuses that we call children (although it is, arguably, concerned with that other idiocy of old age),[18] might be seen as a kind of meta-poem on the problem of literary knowledge and ignorance. It is a poem about the refusal to provide the kind of tale that is expected, the kind that involves the recounting of significant events and the provision of a moral. Instead of providing us with any kind of information, the poem simply exhorts the reader to 'think', indeed to not know *because* she is thinking ('It is no tale; but should you think / Perhaps a tale you'll make it', declares the poet [ll. 79–80]). The poem suggests that knowing, in the form of being told a transparent, an easily legible tale, would in fact simply prevent or preclude such thinking, and that knowing is the enemy of thought, as it is of those other things the poem seems most to value: moral responsibility, human sympathy, fellow feeling.

There is a more subdued but nevertheless insistent concern with nescience in many other poems in *Lyrical Ballads*. In 'A slumber did my spirit seal', the narrator declares his own ignorance in the poem's first line: he, or his spirit, is 'sealed' in a 'slumber' that is constituted by his sense that the girl will not, cannot die. The poem seems to move around a veiled or absent moment of recognition, of anagnorisis – she seemed like someone who would not age or die but now, as a consequence of some moment or method of revelation to which we are not party, the narrator knows that she could die and indeed has died. But the understanding or knowledge gained by the second stanza is both limited and in fact seriously compromised. The speaker seems to know that she did die, but knows or reveals, at least, nothing more. And her death seems, paradoxically, even to *confirm* the state of ignorance in which the speaker began in the sense that, 'Roll'd round in earth's diurnal course' (l. 7) as she now is, she appears in death to have achieved the timeless quality he thought she had when she was alive. In this respect, the poem is itself 'rolled' cognitively or epistemologically round in the sense that moving from life to death the girl's existence seems hardly to have changed. In this sense – a rather perverse sense, to be sure, but a sense nevertheless – the narrator can be understood *not* to have been ignorant in his initial appraisal of the girl's immortality. But then it would seem that what he has learnt he has not learnt, that he *ends up* rather than begins in ignorance. In this poem, therefore, the moment of anagnorisis, of narrative knowing, the turn of enlightenment or recognition, is severely compromised if not entirely disabled. Moreover, the internal movement of nescience that the narrative provokes and constitutes is reflected in its reception, one that is inescapably caught up in this strange dynamic of unknowing. What is it, we might ask, that has been revealed or understood, that has come to be known in reading this poem? That the girl is dead? Perhaps – but even that (and even that there is a girl) we don't know for sure, can only 'construe'. That the narrator *was* ignorant but is now aware? Maybe – but as I have indicated, this is open to doubt, to question. More powerfully than either of these dubious narrative consequences, we are left with a sense of not quite knowing what we might make of the epistemological dynamic of such a short, allusive but almost entirely, almost perfectly baffling poem.

And then there are those others: 'She dwelt among th'untrodden ways' is about how people and events are known, come to be known, and how they are not known, or how they are when they are not known. 'Strange fits of passion' is concerned with the strange way that the thought of Lucy's death 'slide[s]' (l. 25) into the lover's mind as he approaches her cottage, and about the surprise of certain kinds of apprehension, certain kinds of thought, thoughts that the lover didn't know he could have and doesn't know why he has. In poems such as 'Lines Written at a Small Distance', 'Expostulation and Reply', 'The Tables Turned', and 'The Idle Shepherd-Boys', books, book-learning and more generally the 'meddling intellect' are rejected for 'brooks' and a 'wise passiveness' ('The Tables Turned', l. 26; 'The Idle Shepherd-Boys', l. 84; 'Expostulation and Reply', l. 24); the eponymous female vagrant tells an 'artless story' ('The Female Vagrant', l. 2); nature 'enter[s] unawares' the mind of the Winander Boy ('There was a boy', l. 22); 'The Brothers' relies fundamentally on the ignorance of one party to a conversation; like many other poems, 'Three years she grew' celebrates 'mute insensate things' (l. 18); the old cumberland beggar in the poem of that name is described as seeing 'and never knowing that he sees' (l. 54); 'Tintern Abbey' is in part about 'all this unintelligible world' (l. 41).

In these and in other ways, then, the poems that are guarded or explained or defended by the famous Preface are often concerned thematically and technically with various forms and conditions of not knowing. If poetry somehow governs knowledge, if it is the first and last of knowledge, its 'breath and spirit', that would mean, in the end, that poetry, the new kinds of poetry that Wordsworth is writing and defending, must engage with what knowledge is not – with narrators who cannot tell, with characters that do not know, with readers who must think but must equally have no firm epistemological ground, with authors or poets whose primary concern is to express pleasure, and to convey and indeed experience certain kinds of emotion free from the restrictions of conscious calculation, of epistemological certainty, of knowledge. If the 'haunt' and the 'main region' of Wordsworth's 'song' is to be the 'Mind of Man', then he must engage with that most pervasive, that most universal condition of the human mind: ignorance.[19] Writing in March 1798 to James Tobin, Wordsworth explains that he has 'written 1 300 lines of a poem in which I contrive to convey most of the knowledge of which I am possessed'. 'My object,' he goes on, 'is to give pictures of Nature, Man, and Society.'[20] He is referring, of course, to 'The Ruined Cottage' and more generally to his initial plans for *The Recluse*, the poem that was never written. Just at the time when he is busy at work on his first collection of lyric and short narrative poems, in other words, Wordsworth is also beginning an epic poem that will present most of what he knows. That poem, that failure of a poem, *The Recluse* (the poem that over a lifetime Wordsworth failed again and again to write), may be said to provide in its outline an alternative to the poems which at that time Wordsworth was writing for his most famous and most influential collection. *The Recluse* is supposed to present what the poet knows. Many of the poems in *Lyrical Ballads,* by contrast, are concerned with what the poet doesn't, what he cannot know: the collection and its Preface are largely concerned to present the democratizing, liberatory power of poems that work as, and as works of, poetic ignorance.

Notes

1. Percy Bysshe Shelley comes close, though, when in 'A Defence of Poetry' he declares that poetry is 'at once the centre and circumference of knowledge', that it 'comprehends all science', and that it is 'that to which all science must be referred'. *Poetry and Prose,* ed. Donald H. Reiman and Sharon B. Powers (New York: Norton, 1977), p. 503.
2. *The Prose Works* of William Wordsworth, ed. W. J. B. Owen and Jane Worthington Smyser, vol. 1 (Oxford: Oxford University Press, 1974), p. 141. Hereafter indicated as *PW* and cited by volume and page numbers in the text. All references to the Preface to *Lyrical Ballads* are to the 1802 version. As Maureen McLane observes, in these remarks, Wordsworth 'boldly assimilates "knowledge" to the category of "poetry"'. *Romanticism and the Human Sciences: Poetry, Population, and the Discourse of the Species* (Cambridge: Cambridge University Press, 2000), p. 6.
3. For a similar argument in relation to philosophy, truth, and the question of thinking in Wordsworth, see Simon Jarvis's analysis of Wordsworth's poetry as 'itself a kind of cognition, with its own resistances and difficulties'. *Wordsworth's Philosophic Song* (Cambridge: Cambridge University Press, 2007), p. 4.
4. Tim Milnes, *Knowledge and Indifference in English Romantic Prose* (Cambridge: Cambridge University Press, 2003), p. 92.
5. See Robert Scholes, *Protocols of Reading* (New Haven, CT: Yale University Press, 1989).
6. See James A. W. Heffernan's comment in *Wordsworth's Theory of Poetry: The Transforming Imagination* (Ithaca, NY: Cornell University Press, 1969), p. 43, that 'consciousness plays no part in the creative act itself'. Also see W. J. B. Owen, *Wordsworth as Critic* (London: Oxford University Press, 1969), pp. 68–9, on the 'automatism of the process' that Wordsworth is outlining here and the idea that it is 'aesthetically reprehensible for the poet consciously to interfere' with that automatism and that 'the authentic part of the utterance has ... a life of its own, and uses the poet only as a mouthpiece'. More generally, Donald G. Marshall argues that 'the collapse of neoclassical poetics ended the project of making poems the product of conscious art and left the field to the notion that they emerge from some unspecifiably elusive creative process'. 'Writing Criticism: Art, Transcendence, and History', in *The Wordsworthian Enlightenment: Romantic Poetry and the Ecology of Reading,* ed. Helen Regueiro Elam and Frances Ferguson (Baltimore: The Johns Hopkins University Press, 2005), p. 215.
7. *'Lyrical Ballads' and Other Poems, 1797–1800,* ed. James Butler and Karen Green (Ithaca, NY: Cornell University Press, 1992), p. 351. Hereafter indicated as *LB* and cited by page numbers in the text. Poems in this volume are cited by line numbers in the text. See Heffernan's comment that Wordsworth 'specialized in the study of feeling' and that 'if there is one thing that

dominates his critical thinking over the years, it is the vital importance of emotion in poetry'. *Wordsworth's Theory of Poetry*, p. 57.

8. This idea of the distinction between poetry and knowledge ('science' in its broadest sense) returns in 1815 even more forcefully and in an even more entrenched opposition that will later be taken up and developed by Thomas De Quincey when he makes his famous assertion of the difference between the literature of power (i.e. literature) and the literature of knowledge (i.e. other kinds of discourse). In the Essay, Supplementary to the Preface, Wordsworth argues that the 'ends' of literature are not 'to be attained by the mere communication of *knowledge*' and that the poet's ability to create the taste by which he will be appreciated (for Wordsworth the very definition of the true poet, the poet that will last), involves the ability to 'call forth and bestow *power*', of which, he says, 'knowledge is the effect' (*PW*, 3:81, 82; italics added). On this point, compare Owen, *Wordsworth as Critic*, pp. 194–216. It should be noted that when Wordsworth declares his hope, at the end of the Winander Boy episode in *The Prelude*, that children might take 'joy' from 'books and nature' as well as knowledge 'not purchas'd with the loss of power', what he expresses is the melancholy fear that knowledge, adult knowledge, *is* precisely accompanied by such a loss. *The Thirteen-Book Prelude*, ed. Mark L. Reed, vol. 1 (Ithaca, NY: Cornell University Press, 1991), p. 173 (5.447–9). Knowledge, for Wordsworth (and for Romanticism more generally), is, as Gerald Bruns puts it, 'a condition of separation'. 'Poetic Knowledge: Geoffrey Hartman's Romantic Poetics', in *Wordsworthian Enlightenment*, ed. Elam and Ferguson, p. 113.

9. This is what Milnes calls a 'kind of epistemic creation' (*Knowledge and Indifference*, p. 84). On invention (as an artistic practice) versus discovery (as science), see Dugald Stewart's comment in *Elements of the Philosophy of the Human Mind* (London: Strahan and Cadell, 1792), p. 310: 'The object of the former ... is to produce something which had no existence before; that of the latter, to bring to light something which did exist, but which was concealed from common observation' (quoted from Owen, *Wordsworth as Critic*, p. 140).

10. Perhaps more accurately, Wordsworth may be said to be moving towards the Derridean position, as summarized by Derek Attridge, that literature neither 'uncomplicatedly name[s] something in the world' nor 'uncomplicatedly bring[s] something into existence'. *The Singularity of Literature* (London: Routledge, 2004), p. 6.

11. 'Pleasure' and its cognates (pleasing, please/s/d, pleasurable) appear at least 55 times in the 1802 Preface. As Owen comments, this is 'one of Wordsworth's most firmly held tenets in documents connected with *Lyrical Ballads*' (*Wordsworth as Critic*, p. 77 n.). The link between poetry and pleasure is also made forcefully in chapter fourteen of Coleridge's *Biographia Literaria*, where Coleridge distinguishes poetry from science and knowledge: 'A poem is that species of composition, which is opposed to works of science, by proposing for its *immediate* object pleasure, not truth'. *Biographia Literaria*, ed. James Engell and W. Jackson Bate, vol. 2 (London: Routledge & Kegan Paul, 1983), p. 13.

12. See Milnes, *Knowledge and Indifference*, pp. 86–9, on Wordsworth's difficulties in transcending the didactic and utilitarian claim that poetry increases knowledge and therefore increases happiness.

13. See Lorenzo Infantino, *Ignorance and Liberty* (London: Routledge, 2003), esp. pp. 1–7.

14. All the man knows, as he repeatedly affirms in a kind of chorus, is that she cries '"Oh misery! oh misery! / O woe is me! oh misery!"' (ll. 65–6, 76–7, 252–3). See David Bromwich, *Disowned by Memory: Wordsworth's Poetry of the 1790s* (Chicago: University of Chicago Press, 1998), p. 109, on this point: 'Suffering is by ascription: it cannot be fully known, not even surely known to exist.'

15. Avital Ronell, *Stupidity* (Urbana: University of Illinois Press, 2002), p. 276.

16. Bromwich, *Disowned by Memory*, p. 101; see also p. 102 on Johnny as 'a type of the poet, though not himself a poet'.

17. See Ronell, *Stupidity*, p. 276: 'poetry is the idiot boy'.

18. See John Locke's argument at the beginning of *An Essay Concerning Human Understanding* on the equivalence of children and idiots (as well as savages and illiterate people) with respect to their proving the non-existence of innate 'Impressions' or 'Notions' because it can be demonstrated that such people have few if any 'general Maxims' and no notion of the 'universal Principles of knowledge'. *An Essay Concerning Human Understanding*, ed. Peter H. Nidditch (Oxford: Clarendon Press, 1975), pp. 63–4 (I.2.27). For a discussion of this passage in these terms, see Ronell, *Stupidity*, p. 267.

19. Prospectus to *The Recluse*, ll. 40–1, in *The Poems*, ed. John O. Hayden, vol. 2 (Harmondsworth: Penguin, 1977), p. 38. For a reading of Wordsworth's autobiographical poems in terms of not knowing (specifically in terms of forgetting), see chapter eight of my *Wordsworth Writing* (Cambridge: Cambridge University Press, 2007); for a development of the question of literary ignorance in the larger context of the Romantic and post-Romantic traditions, see my *Ignorance: Literature and Agnoiology* (Manchester: Manchester University Press, forthcoming 2009).

20. *The Letters of William and Dorothy Wordsworth: The Early Years, 1787–1805*, ed. Ernest de Selincourt, rev. Chester L. Shaver (Oxford: Oxford University Press, 1967), p. 212.

2
Poetic Objecthood in 1798

Stefan H. Uhlig

This brief essay mainly explores an even shorter text: the 1798 Advertisement to *Lyrical Ballads*. I seek to identify what strikes me as a telling analogy between Wordsworth's revisionary claims for poetry in the essays around *Lyrical Ballads* and aspects of Kant's account of aesthetic judgement in the third *Critique*. By way of this analogy I argue that Wordsworth's theory of poetry has, certainly in its early forms, a stake in the rejection of what I call 'poetic objecthood'. What I am describing here is, as it were, a twinned or twofold turning away from the idea that poems – or artworks generally – could be in essence understood like other crafted, well-made objects, and that a rule-based and predictive theory could capture a distinctive role for art.

In the prefatory note and essays which introduce Wordsworth and Coleridge's *Lyrical Ballads* first in 1798, and then in 1800 and 1802, Wordsworth begins what we may think of as his theory of poetry by suggesting that the reason why he has, reluctantly, decided to engage in criticism at all is that there is a particular problem about these poems. From the start, Wordsworth makes a strong claim for the status of the poems in *Lyrical Ballads* as genuine, and indeed uniquely authentic, poetry. Yet, by the same token, he seems forced to concede that there is one immediately apparent reason why this effort to communicate with readers may well simply fail. And his concern is that because these poems do not instantiate the familiar kind of object – because they fail to display the ostensibly 'poetic' properties which readers have long come to expect – these poems will not look like poetry. The presumed risk is that without such concrete, obvious markers readers simply will not recognize these poems as poetry, and will consequently disregard them. Wordsworth writes in the Advertisement:

> Readers accustomed to the gaudiness and inane phraseology of many
> modern writers, if they persist in reading this book to its conclusion,

will perhaps frequently have to struggle with feelings of strangeness and aukwardness: they will look round for poetry, and will be
induced to enquire by what species of courtesy these attempts can be
permitted to assume that title.[1]

For me, the point being made here is that these new pieces lack a range
of recognizably 'poetic' attributes. And it is only if readers cease to
look around for their familiar kind of thing, Wordsworth here begins
to explain, that poetry can make its claim as an experiential, affective
exchange within his quest for a discursively rehumanized community.

Wordsworth has already clarified that these poems are in a strong
sense 'experiments', in that they were designed to test how far the
language of the 'middle and lower classes' could be 'adapted' to 'poetic
pleasure' (*PW*, 1:116). And readers may well, therefore, find it hard to
grasp their style, as they present no elaborate metrical or stanzaic forms,
few recognizable conceits like the personification of abstract ideas, and
generally 'little', as the Preface summarizes, 'of what is usually called
poetic diction' (*PW*, 1:130).

For Wordsworth's project, though, our inability to mark up concrete
attributes should really turn out for the best, since rather than a set of
highly crafted works, poetry is, or is defined as such by, an occurrence
of what the Preface specifies as 'the spontaneous overflow of powerful
feelings' (*PW*, 1:126). 'The Reader', Wordsworth insists in his Note to
'The Thorn' in 1800, 'cannot be too often reminded that Poetry *is*', properly understood, 'passion'.[2] What defines poetry is not, in other words,
a craft – not even by analogy or metaphorical endorsement – with traditional rules, criteria and canonically established pieces. The relevant
criterion is instead some form of affective communication or exchange
(perhaps not then, or now, fully worked out) that has no definite, and
in that sense dependable, material analogue. Which is to say that part
of the founding gesture of Wordsworth's criticism is an explicit rejection of conventional, craft-based poetic objecthood. He begins, that is,
by insisting that, unlike ordinary objects in the world (like, say, a stool
that can be specified as having legs and a flat top to sit on), poetry and
poems are not defined by concrete properties, but instead by a kind
of experience or affective communication which they make possible.
Remarkably, Kant's third *Critique*, or *Critique of Judgement* of 1790, can, at
some distance from Wordsworth's own context, help us better to understand what has – since around 1800 – been at stake in this claim.

One way to describe the contribution of this founding text in philosophical aesthetics would be to say that for Kant the independent

interest of what we may call 'aesthetic judgement' rests not on a specific set of objects in the world (for instance, a museum of artworks, or a can- on of great literary texts on our shelves), but instead on a pleasurable interaction between the faculties with which – in ordinary or scientific cognition – we grasp and understand the world. In paragraph nine, Kant describes this pleasurable, affective engagement as 'the mental state in which we are when imagination and understanding are in free play'. This state of play is pleasurable, that is, 'insofar as' these faculties 'har- monize with each other as required for *cognition in general*'.[3] Now, unlike our regular, 'determinative' efforts to cognize the world, the playful or 'reflective' judgements of taste that are at issue here assign no attributes to objects (*CJ*, 18–19). Such judgements of the beautiful, to take just one of their main forms, do not determine through a set of properties whatever object may give rise to them. And while it is a fact of language that ascriptions of the 'beautiful' will seem to claim an actual predicate, beauty is not in fact determined as a concept under which particular, concretely given intuitions could be brought (see *CJ*, 54, §6). Aesthetic judgements are in no position to resort to such conceptual fixities: they work instead as if to find a universal that might match their play.

Having established that these judgments cannot but be singular, and have their basis solely in the subject's state of mind, Kant famously insists that 'when we make a judgment of taste, the pleasure we feel is something we require from everyone else as necessary'. This profound sense that such pleasure ought to generally communicate itself may sometimes make aesthetic judgements look like knowledge-claims – 'just as if', Kant writes, 'we had to regard beauty as a characteristic of the object, determined in it according to concepts'. Yet if forms of judgement, or experience, are in fact what make for the aesthetic, we must come to face the thought that 'apart from a reference to the subject's feeling, beauty is', strictly, 'nothing by itself' (*CJ*, 62–3, §9).

Beyond the claim that judgements of taste have no way of determin- ing objects, Kant moreover argues that they lack all 'interest' in their ordinary existence in this world. While our 'liking' for, say, chocolate involves the desire to possess or to consume the object, and thus a sensory interest that it actually be real, what we would call aesthetic pleasure is characteristically 'disinterested' in relation to all concrete things, and their fixed properties (*CJ*, 47–8, §3). So we can 'universally' conclude: 'whether it concerns beauty in nature or in art: *beautiful is what we like in merely judging it* (rather than either in sensation proper or through a concept)' (*CJ*, 174, §45). Right at the outset of the third *Critique*, Kant rehearses a number of thoughts we may have when faced with, say, a building so as to explain that if we were to take a structure like it as a work of art, we would inevitably disregard much of what is otherwise most real about it:

> Suppose someone asks me whether I consider the palace I see before me beautiful. I might reply that I am not fond of things of that sort, made merely to be gaped at. Or I might reply like that Iroquois *sachem* who said that he liked nothing better in Paris than the eating-houses. I might even go on, as *Rousseau* would, to rebuke the vanity of the great who spend the people's sweat on such superfluous things. I might, finally, quite easily convince myself that, if I were on some uninhabited island with no hope of ever again coming among people, and could conjure up such a splendid edifice by a mere wish, I would not even take that much trouble for it if I already had a sufficiently comfortable hut. The questioner may grant all this and approve of it; but it is not to the point. All he wants to know is whether my mere presentation of the object is accompanied by a liking, no matter how indifferent I may be about the existence of the object of this presentation. We can easily see that, in order for me to say that an object is *beautiful*, and to prove that I have taste, what matters is what I do with this presentation within myself, and not the [respect] in which I depend on the object's existence.
>
> (CJ, 45–6, §2)

It is quite true that when we are led to say things like 'this is beautiful', we talk as if we were in fact assigning concrete properties to things (*CJ*, 55–6, §7). Yet the kind of judgement that we need to ground such claims in fact occludes the object as an independent fact: to the point, Kant says, where even the existence of that object seems to us of no concern.

Clearly, this conception of aesthetic judgement has momentous implications for the study and the teaching of existing art, as much as for the training of practitioners, or indeed our predictions about future art and what forms it might take. Without aesthetic or poetic objecthood, things in art or nature may provide more or less powerful occasions for the experience we call 'aesthetic'. We will, however, have no firm grasp on a set of properties that could in perpetuity secure the status of these things as art. As a result, we can neither call on self-identifying legacies of artworks nor count on rational rules for creativity in different arts and genres. In sum, outside someone's experiences which, as it were, come off, there will be little chance for artists or for readers, viewers or listeners to pre-judge the kinds of thing that may turn out to matter or, specifically, to feel like works of art.

If we resituate this Kantian account, as I suggest we should, alongside Wordsworth's earliest components for a theory of poetry, the two may strike us as analogous in various related ways. To pre-empt his expectation that readers looking 'round for poetry' will simply fail to recognize the poems of *Lyrical Ballads* as such, Wordsworth shifts the ground of poetry from any range of works – however conventional or avant-garde – to a distinctive form of pleasurable interaction: first between experience, memory and writing and, as he hopes, a fortiori between poets and their readership. The point is not that better poetry has better properties than other, more conventional kinds, but that what makes it genuinely poetry can simply not be properties at all. Instead, what grounds poetic art are subjective relations that involve, diversely and in open-ended ways, what Kant would call a pleasurable 'mental state' (*CJ*, 62, §9).

In other words, what we have been tracing both in Wordsworth and in Kant towards the 1800s is a strong version of the thought that poetic or aesthetic objects cannot, like ordinary or regular things, be made and judged and reproduced according to the rules or the criteria of a craft. Not least because we can put the argument against objecthood in those terms, my case for an analogy between Kant and Wordsworth involves no conjecture about influence. The shared components of their theories decisively reject the expectation that poetry and other forms depend substantially on rules, apprenticeships and corresponding canons of the critic's expertise. And to this extent, Wordsworth and Kant both separately respond to antecedent, and gradually mounting eighteenth-century lines of scepticism about how useful even the most guarded, probabilistic rules and regular predictions could be in the fine arts – as they are accordingly rethought – of genius or originality. If craft or artfulness in no decisive fashion gives the rules to art, the artwork no longer forms part of a determinable class of objects in the world. Considered as a poem, or indeed as art, a work of poetry now seems not a conventional thing at all, but rather a suspended opportunity for affective engagement – or, as Wordsworth says, a 'passion' – which alone can make for poetry or the aesthetic.

In contrast to the ways in which the strands we have followed in the third *Critique* form part of a much larger enterprise, it is of course less obvious that Wordsworth's opening attack on objecthood in the Advertisement (or its reduplication in the Preface) remains consistently in line with arguments made even in those texts, or by extension with his subsequent additions and revisions to a theory of poetry which lead up to the essays of 1815. As part of his reluctant, wary truck with theory in prose, this proposition does, however, form a signal strand in Wordsworth's gambit to ward off resistance to poetic novelty. And in a cluster of related thoughts, this Kantian suspension of poetic object-hood remains one of his central starting-points for more productive views of poetry's real force as art.

To return to the Advertisement, some of its claims may now bear added weight as part of this deflection of predictable demands that poems represent – before they are even read – a reassuringly distinctive class of things. Those who have vainly mined the book 'for poetry' are warned that its appeal is not best brought under the conceptual fixities supplied by 'poetry' as a term. Again, it is not just that the received, albeit contested, sense of 'poetry' will point us in the wrong direc-tion. In the paths of affective exchange, and their more fundamental premises, between the poet and a readership any such general, and only speciously enabling, categories are seen to block the way:

> It is desirable that ... readers, for their own sakes, should not suffer the solitary word Poetry, a word of very disputed meaning, to stand in the way of their gratification; but that, while they are perusing this book, they should ask themselves if it contains a natural delineation of human passions, human characters, and human incidents.
>
> (*PW*, 1:116)

If readers find themselves drawn into this poetic tracing of impassioned selves and dispositions, there is no need at all for them to codify or even to determine their response: 'If the answer be favorable to the author's wishes', they simply 'should consent to be pleased in spite of that most dreadful enemy to our pleasures, our own pre-established codes of decision' (*PW*, 1:116).

We may finally turn to Wordsworth's very first suggestion that the fact, or better the phenomenon, of poetry should be re-thought out-side familiar glossaries and archives of accomplished works. One of his strongest gestures to defend 'attempts' at or 'experiments' in poetry is his peremptory claim in the Advertisement that it is not only a feature, but in fact the distinctive honorific, literally, of poetry that we can never forecast either what its themes might be, or what much broader forms of inquiry may feed into its making and inventiveness. 'It is', the Advertisement begins, 'the honourable characteristic of Poetry that its materials are to be found in every subject which can interest the human mind' (*PW*, 1:116). Of course the Preface goes on to pursue the interaction of such curiosity with characteristically affective states, and does so further in alignment with 'a worthy *purpose*' (*PW*, 1:125). Not only is the charge of poetry to relay 'influxes of feeling'; it is to inflect these affective exchanges as they are, in turn, 'modified and directed by our thoughts' – thoughts that come in a further synergy to represent 'past feelings'. Only in this sense can the poet actualize the variously connected ways 'in which our feelings and ideas' are generally 'associated in a state of excitement' (*PW*, 1:126).

However, as I have tried to sketch, this purposefully formal or – especially in interpersonal terms – relational scheme derives much of its impetus from Wordsworth's opening move: from his incisive and, in this or other contexts, rare attempt to theorize the work of poetry (or elsewhere, and analogously, art) without the reassurance of achieved collections, connoisseurship, and predictability. Just as poetic writing cannot tie itself to resources that are already known, Wordsworth suggests that poems cannot, as such, be conceived as a familiar kind of thing.

Notes

1. *The Prose Works*, ed. W. J. B. Owen and Jane Worthington Smyser, vol. 1 (Oxford: Clarendon Press, 1974), p. 116. Hereafter indicated as *PW* and cited by volume and page numbers in the text.
2. *'Lyrical Ballads' and Other Poems, 1797–1800*, ed. James Butler and Karen Green (Ithaca, NY: Cornell University Press, 1992), p. 351. Hereafter indicated as *LB* and cited by page numbers in the text.
3. Immanuel Kant, *Critique of Judgement*, trans. Werner S. Pluhar (Indianapolis, IN: Hackett, 1987), p. 62. Hereafter indicated as *CJ* and cited by page and paragraph numbers in the text.

3
What Is a Lyrical Ballad? Wordsworth's Experimental Epistemologies

Peter de Bolla

1 'The honourable characteristic of Poetry'

The Advertisement to *Lyrical Ballads, with a Few Other Poems* (1798) opens with the following sentence: 'It is the honourable characteristic of Poetry that its materials are to be found in every subject which can interest the human mind.'[1] No manuscripts of this 'Advertisement' are known to survive and we do not know with any certainty when it was written.[2] Although some of the phrases in it reappear in the later 1800 Preface, Wordsworth chose not to include this introductory text in any of the lifetime editions of his poetry. Was he unsure about the frame the Advertisement provided for the poems? Did he have second thoughts about its content? Or was it merely superseded by the later and considerably longer Preface he wrote to accompany the second edition? These are, of course, imponderables: there is no evidence in either letters or manuscripts that might help resolve them. But in opening them up to scrutiny, in asking what the force of that first sentence might be within Wordsworth's poetic corpus and his thinking, we can begin to understand some of the risks involved in reading *Lyrical Ballads*. One of those risks is the formulation of what might be called a 'poetics', if that word is taken to embrace within its meanings an attitude or stance towards knowing. This essay sees its contribution to this volume, then, as an exploration of what one might need in order to have or recognize a poetics. It outlines a set of conceptual architectures, the experimental epistemologies of my title, which may be thought of as necessary preparations for poetry, and therefore for life.

At first glance Wordsworth's opening statement, even if it has the air of a programmatic creed, appears to be plain enough: it sets out to alert us, give fair warning, that the poems we are about to encounter will

43

take for their 'materials' a wide range of subjects. But let us scrutinize it a little more carefully: why, for example, is the characteristic of poetry deemed to be 'honourable'? Who or what is being honoured in poetry's making? Why, in any case, is honour an adjunct of poetry at all? As if the opposite, or at least the counterweight to honour, let us say shame, might also be a possibility. Would it be, for instance, a shameful characteristic of poetry were it to find its materials in a very narrow seam? In, say, the life or, perhaps even worse, the ego of the poet? In emotion recollected in tranquility?

What is implied by, or at stake in, conceiving of poetry as seeking 'materials'? Does this suggest that *poesis* is a transformative operation, taking base materials and turning them into the thrill of poetic pleasure? And from pleasure into knowledge? Or, on the other hand, is it thinking of poetry's relation to *material* somewhat differently? Imagining that the building blocks of poetry – let us call them *poetic* materials – are out there in the world needing only due diligence for their discovery. In this second scenario the art of poetry is not transformative but forensic and accumulative. This distinction, which is broken across the issue of how one builds the dwelling place of poetry, and therefore for Wordsworth of being, is one of the ligaments of the epistemologies explored below, and I shall characterize one of the tasks of a 'lyrical ballad' as the exposure of that distinction.

The second part of Wordsworth's opening sentence raises still further questions. What is the weight borne by the word 'can' in the phrase 'which can interest the human mind'? Are we to take this as implying that the potential to interest the mind is in every subject in the world? And is 'subject' here to be read as standing for or as a representative of every *thing*? Or is the sense more restrictive: poetry finds its materials in those subjects which already excite interest? The first option suggests that poetry's task is to generate interest – perhaps pleasure or knowledge in other formulations which are more embedded in the Wordsworthian idiom of thinking about poetry. The second sees its task somewhat differently, as essentially identifying and locating 'interesting' subjects which are subsequently woven into the fabric of poetry.

It is the argument of this essay that all of the above questions raised by the opening sentence of Wordsworth's Advertisement to *Lyrical Ballads, with a Few Other Poems* are to greater and lesser extents addressed by the poems themselves. As the first word 'Advertisement' says: we need to advert to, in the sense of turn towards, the poems which follow. As so often in Wordsworth, however, the 'turn towards poetry' needs to be weighed in the balance of both experience and its relations to knowing as they are exposed, created, and attenuated by language. This is why the greatest imponderable, though not explicitly spoken by Wordsworth's Advertisement, is: What is a 'lyrical ballad'? It is a question that as yet has no answer.

It is clear, I think, that at the time of publication in 1798 Wordsworth did not know the answer to this question. He did not even, yet, know what his jointly authored collection entitled *Lyrical Ballads, with a Few Other Poems* achieved *as ways of making poetry*. The answer to the question 'What is a "lyrical ballad" a category *of?*', for example, was not immediately apparent in 1798. Although the commonsense answer – that it is a category of 'poetry' – would seem to be blindingly obvious, there are good reasons, some of which are explored below, to hesitate in making such a swift assumption.

By the time the third, 1805 edition of the collection was published with the modified title *Lyrical Ballads, with Pastoral and Other Poems*, Wordsworth – claiming sole authorship on the title page as he had done for the second, 1800 edition titled *Lyrical Ballads, with Other Poems* – was less interested in what a 'lyrical ballad' might be than in what *poetry* might do or reveal. There are two ways of seeing this: on the one hand, it can be understood as a failure. Giving up on the rather more opaque and difficult question – 'What is a lyrical ballad?' – Wordsworth turns instead to the matter or material of poetry. On the other hand, this turn towards poetry can be seen as a success, a solution to the problem posed, even if that turn involved a risk or wager in respect to the larger category 'poetry'.

The second sentence of Wordsworth's 1798 prospectus is, unfortunately, no less problematic. 'The majority of these poems', Wordsworth writes, 'are to be considered as experiments' (*PW*, 1:116). Which of these poems, however, are we to take as 'the majority' and which fall into the minority: those poems which are not to be considered as experiments? Are the 'experiments' supposed to be *only* the 'lyrical ballads', or are some of the 'other poems' also with the 'majority' which comprise the experimental? Furthermore, what is the force of the locution 'are to be considered as'? Wordsworth did not indicate that the 'majority' of the poems *are experiments*. Still less does he tell us what they are supposed to be experiments *in*. Moreover, if, as has been suggested, the use of the term 'experiment' in relation to poetry was common enough at the time of publication, the force of the sense of 'newness' or innovation that may accompany the use of the word must be attenuated.[3] An experiment need not, in itself, be innovatory: one can, of course, set out to repeat experiments as scientists often did and do.

It looks as if some help is at hand when we read on to the following sentence since it gives us an indication as to the general drift of the experiment: 'They were written chiefly with a view to ascertain how far the language of conversation in the middle and lower classes of society is adapted to the purposes of poetic pleasure' (*PW*, 1:116). But once again any careful examination of this observation raises as many questions as it answers. If the experiment was to 'ascertain' something, then what are we to conclude from the poems presented? That the experiment was a success or a failure (although this already queers the pitch since it imagines that experiments must either succeed or fail)? And what, in any case, is the relationship between the experiment to ascertain this 'adaptation' and the poems? Are the poems 'adaptations' of the language of conversation, as they have often been taken to be, or rather the distillate of the experiment? The thing which results once that adaptation has taken place?

Behind the questions of generic identification – Are the 'majority' of poems ballads at all?; Which of them are 'lyrical ballads'? – are others.[4] Why did the experiment take place, if indeed it did, *in verse*? Why, as Wordsworth asked himself, had he 'written in verse?' (*PW*, 1:144). Of course a blunt and simple answer is that he was, after all, attempting to make his career as a poet, but to leave it there would be to mistake this as a question of instrumentality. Something far more fundamental is at stake than Wordsworth's chosen career path. And in order to understand that and begin to see how the question might have been answered we need, as did Wordsworth, a sense of what the turn to poetry consists in, an assessment of the risks involved. We need, as he did, a poetics. It seems to me that one way of reading the Preface Wordsworth added to the second, 1800 edition is to see it as precisely articulating that poetics – but this is not the route I shall take.

2 'Each of these poems has a purpose'

One way of making sense of the Preface Wordsworth wrote to accompany the 'Poems in two volumes' he intended to publish in 1800 is to read it as an apology for writing in verse. This would be to ignore the manifest apology contained within it, namely Wordsworth's admission that were he to supply 'a systematic defense of the theory, upon which the poems were written' he would, in effect, be '*reasoning*' (*PW*, 1:120) the reader into finding felicities and pleasures in his verse. He does, nevertheless, have a shot at answering the question, 'Why have I written in verse?' by addressing what he calls the 'purpose' of his poems. Each of the poems within the two-volume 1800 edition has 'a worthy *purpose*' (*PW*, 1:124), and he continues:

> Not that I mean to say, that I always began to write with a distinct purpose formally conceived; but I believe that my habits of meditation have so formed my feelings, as that my descriptions of such objects as strongly excite those feelings, will be found to carry along with them a *purpose*.

> (*PW*, 1:124, 126)

This purpose, he claims in the following paragraph, is to 'illustrate the manner in which our feelings and ideas are associated in a state of excitement' (*PW*, 1:126). It does not say, as it is often read as saying, that the poems presented *are illustrations* of the associations of feelings and ideas in states of excitement. And although this paragraph of the Preface does point to specific examples in the collection – picking out 'The Idiot Boy', 'The Mad Mother', 'We are Seven' among others – it is also not the central claim that these poems are or contain *representations* of feelings and ideas in states of excitement. Wordsworth's aim is, in fact, targeted not at the poems but at the reader whom he hopes to place 'in the way of receiving from ordinary moral sensations another and more salutary impression than we are accustomed to receive from them' (*PW*, 1:126, 128). In other words, the purpose is to enable the reader to receive impressions, that is, to come into knowing. This is why the poems explore a number of different ways in which encounters between individuals – most commonly the poet/speaker, who is supposed to be the reader's proxy, and someone more marginal or less accomplished or mature than the poet/speaker, often a child or rustic – demonstrate the distances one must travel in order to understand knowledge as even approaching a common property.

3 'Is there ... no essential difference between the language of prose and metrical composition?'

Wordsworth does not, at least explicitly, see his task as a forensic inquiry into knowing. The drift of his own thought in answering why he wrote in verse is to turn towards the issue of metre. The weight and prominence given to the discussion of metre in the Preface is sufficient evidence for this.[5] And there is also the bald statement made in the second sentence of the Preface that the 'experiment' was to ascertain 'how far, by fitting to metrical arrangement a selection of the real language of men...' (*PW*, 1:118). Where this comment is not taken to be substantially concerned with the 'real language of men' – as if the purpose of *Lyrical Ballads, and Other Poems* was entirely focused on the artificiality (so perceived) of poetic language or diction – it is usually understood as indicating a concern with poetic form, as if the burden of the Preface is to justify the use of the term 'lyrical ballad' as a descriptor for the poems, or at least some of the poems, contained within the collection.[6] But the issue of metre is far more complex than is customarily thought, as two recent careful readings of Wordsworth's poetic making argue in considerable detail.[7] I shall not rehearse those arguments here, since I wish to highlight a slightly different aspect of the experience of being exposed to Wordsworth's language in its totality, to 'receiving impressions' in a slightly different register from sound.[8] My purpose here is to approach a narrower understanding of the *thingliness* of Wordsworth's poetry.

The answer that Wordsworth gave to the question posed at the head of this section – Is there a difference between prose and poetry? – was no. One way of understanding this, a way in which Wordsworth himself did, is to note the shared linguistic properties of poetry and prose, but the answer was also qualified since Wordsworth is at pains to point out how the other constraints of poetic form rein in the otherwise unruly power of language. This is to bring to mind the various tensions that are put into play by the coalescence of rhyme, accent, stress, metre and so forth.[9] It is not to say that tensions do not exist in prose, but according to Wordsworth the peculiar pleasure of poetry and its numbers lies in the sensation of perceiving 'similitude in dissimilitude'. Given that pleasure – perhaps the most overdetermined word in the entire Preface – for Wordsworth always raises the spectre of cognition, this particular capacity of poetry needs to be glossed with respect to knowing.

It would be hardly original to note that those people who 'devote [their] life to literature'[10] either have or develop particular sensitivities to language.[11] Wordsworth's ear, as is well known, was particularly attuned to the cadences and stresses of vocalization.[12] It is also well known that he composed, as it were, more in the mouth than on the page.[13] And the topos of speech is clearly one that provided strong resources for his thinking and making poetry. As Andrew Bennett points out, many of the poems in *Lyrical Ballads* are staged as scenes of speech and if we are to properly understand a distinctively Wordsworthian poetics we need to attend to the physical dimension of speech, how words are sounded in and by the body, to a phenomenology of poetic voice. But that phenomenology does not only comprise attention to the *sound* of verse; we also need to weigh within the balance of our own experience of language the forms of writing in their most material guises. In their look, shapes, and geometries. This phenomenology is directed equally at the bodily process of writing; the physical attitude we must adopt in holding an instrument of inscription; the feel of different writing instruments; our address to the surface of the thing we inscribe, the particular movements and gestures made by the hand and arm and the synergies between hand, arm, and eye which are set in motion by the physical act of writing; and at the visual experience of reading, at pattern recognition or shape identification. My claim here is that Wordsworth was not only attentive to the sound of language; he was also deeply attuned to the 'thingliness' of words, to their weight, texture, contour, and shape.

In the important Note Wordsworth appended to 'The Thorn' he states that words, 'a Poet's words more particularly, ought to be weighed in the balance of feeling'. This leads him to a defence of repetition since, he claims, experiences of intense excitement tend to break down our verbal capacities: we hold on to the words we have, repeating them without any sense of embarrassment or redundancy. The repetition of words, he says, can produce 'beauties of the highest kind', and the mind 'luxuriates in the repetition of words' partly out of a 'spirit of fondness, exultation and gratitude'.[14] If we turn to the poetry, we can begin to see how this pans out. The opening poem of the 1800 edition, 'Expostulation and Reply', for example begins with repetition: 'Why, William' (l. 1). How does this create the spirit of fondness? For the poet, or anyone named 'William', I suppose we might imagine there to be a certain kind of attachment to the name, let us say a fondness for the sound of one's self, but for others how does this repetition lead to our 'luxuriating' in it? Why, furthermore, might we feel gratitude? The answer to these difficult questions is to be found in what I earlier characterized as the exposure of the distinction between poetry as discovery and a transformation of materials. The repetition is a form of travel that shuttles between these different ways of making poetry: these words, now discovered as integuments of poetry, are in that discovery transformed into something else, topoi in which pleasure and knowledge are lodged.

We can see a similar thing happening at lower linguistic strata, within the elements of the word, its distinct sounds, shapes, and graphic architecture. Here I mean to draw attention not only to the repetition and modulation of sounds within and across words – say the travel between the 'eye/I' and 'ill' sounds in 'Why William' – but also to the repetition and modulation of the shapes of words and the letters within them. A good example in this opening poem of the 1800 edition can be seen in the fifth and sixth stanzas, where the word 'feel' is placed into a relationship of tension with the word 'feed', weighed in the balance of a fully material phenomenology of language. At least in the first instance I do not mean to highlight the semantic excitements generated by this relation, even though there is something of interest to say about this; rather I want to keep with the difference of a letter – the distance that must be travelled in the alteration of an 'l' into a 'd'.

Once one becomes sensitized to the materiality of language in the fullest sense, the *thingliness* of words, the immediate surrounding terrain of stanzas five and six both support and proleptically signal this transmutation of 'feeling' into 'feeding'. Thus the 'd' in 'bid', 'bodies', 'deem' and 'minds' creates a kind of pressure on and tension around the 'l' in 'feel' which is resolved once 'feed' arrives. That resolution is, in the first place, a *material* effect. It is the work of language in its full materiality. This does, of course, include the meanings of the words 'feel' and 'feed', but the motivations for the resolution of what I called the tension in the verse are not solely or indeed primarily semantic.

Such a reading, if indeed it is a reading in the standard sense – perhaps one should call this a *weighing* of the worth of words – encourages us to make the transformation both ways, as it were, so that the line 'that we can feed this mind of ours' might also be weighed as 'that we can feel this mind of ours'. We are here being asked to consider the differences and distances between feeling and feeding, and to notice how they are opened to each other, to the possibility of sharing their worlds. And this, at base, is to recognize that what is at stake here is epistemology, though not as an abstraction, as a theory or systematic account of knowledge but as a form of experience, a felt knowing that seems internal to the thing that is this language.

4   'To be affected … by absent things as if they were present'

Etched across the volume we have come to know as *Lyrical Ballads* is the thingliness of words.[15] In part the process by which absent things are brought into the immediate orbit of experience, and thereby within the enclosure of affect, is the process of speaking of such things – by using language. But I think Wordsworth also had another, perhaps more fundamental, process in mind: the exposure of the materiality of language and, weighed in the same balance, the transformation of words into things. And this, being affected by absent things as if they are present, is a form of knowing. One does not have to make an exorbitant

case in order to claim that a number of poems in *Lyrical Ballads* explore
questions of knowing. They take as their explicit subject matter issues
such as the following: How do we know what we take to be knowledge?
How and why are some things taken to be outside or eccentric to knowledge and yet known to us? Time and again the verse circles around
these issues: one can find it in the 'What should it know of death?'
(l. 4) of 'We are Seven', or the 'What, woman! should I know of him?'
(l. 270) asked by the doctor in 'The Idiot Boy', or the speaker's 'I'll tell
you all I know' (l. 114) in 'The Thorn'. The explicit engagement with
knowledge and knowing can be identified simply by turning to those
places – 38 in all in the 1800 edition – where the word 'know' is used.
But it would be unwise to imagine that the mere use of this word signals
a common purpose, theme, or understanding of what 'knowing' might
comprise. Still less would it be sensible to assume that where the word
occurs it is grounded in a simple or easily characterizable epistemology.
Just one example will suffice: the repetition in 'I'll tell you every thing
I know' (l. 105) and 'I'll tell you all I know' serves to render ever more
opaque what knowing might be here: What Martha herself understands
as knowing, how her interlocutor understands it and how the reader
interprets whatever is taken to be knowledge by both. One might
say that the speaker's 'all I know' turns out to be evanescent at best,
weighed in the balance of the moral of the poem which explicitly
engages with the process of coming into knowledge. And there, in the
final stanza, the speaker admits both that 'I cannot tell' (l. 243) and
at the same time that he has come into knowledge: 'And this I know'
(l. 247). But that knowledge is not a proposition, or perhaps it might be
more accurate to say that it is not amenable to being conveyed in the
form of a proposition. Still less is it a 'fact' or a quantum of knowledge.
It is a felt experience of knowing, an affective event in which an absent
thing is felt as if it were present.

As if these explicit occasions on which the topos of knowing colonizes
the centre of attention were not troublesome enough, there are many
more places where the surface of the verse is sealed up, protecting itself
from the intrusions of the weight of the word 'know'. It is these I mean
to highlight in turning to what I think of as Wordsworth's experimental
epistemologies. The poem that Wordsworth selected to open the two-
volume 1800 edition, 'Expostulation and Reply', is as good as any a place
to begin. Here Wordsworth asks us to consider what it might be to 'dream
[one's] time away' (ll. 4, 32). The interlocutor opens with this question,
and the poem closes with the character chastising his interlocutor for
asking the question at all: ' – Then ask not' (l. 29). I take this poem to be

inquiring not into what might be known to us or knowable in dreams but rather to be asking what is known in the activity of dreaming one's 'time away'. It is not asking for the content of a dream, nor even for a justification of dreaming as a useful way of spending time. Rather the poem seeks to sensitize the reader to a form of knowing that might be both costly and valuable in its use of the resource of time. Both giving time away and luxuriating in its displacements, dreaming *away*. Both cheating time's arrow, dreaming it into impotence, and being held to account for being unproductive. Both transforming the experience of temporality into the strange timescapes of the dream and discovering the otherness of dreaming.

The sense that we are here in the orbit of an experimental epistemology is strengthened by weighing 'Expostulation and Reply' against its companion, the poem which follows it in the 1800 edition, 'The Tables turned'. At first glance it appears to be a counterweight to the first poem, announced in its title, and proceeds by way of entering into an argument with its preceding companion. In contrast to the first poem, which attempts to make a case against dreaming time away in favour of the utility of book learning, the second poem opens with the encouragement of a 'friend' to 'clear his looks' (l. 1). This, as the balance of the rhyme informs us, is tantamount to the casting away, or clearing, of his books. In place of reading, the interlocutor suggests that there is great benefit to be had in simply opening oneself to nature: 'Let nature be your teacher' (l. 16). But things are not so clear cut, or at least so transparent since the alternative recommendation to dreaming time away is something described as 'com[ing] forth'. The fourth stanza has it as the activity of 'com[ing] forth into the light of things' (l. 15), later to be reinforced in the penultimate line's 'come forth' (l. 31). Although the general drift of this is clear enough – nature is being upheld as a more effective teacher than book learning – and the tenor of the phrase given by the use of the word 'light' is easily gauged – the Christian sense of revelation certainly hovers within it – it nevertheless remains incumbent upon the reader to ascertain what might be involved in coming into the light of *things*, where that word has a specific weight or force. Does, for example, the action of 'coming forth' involve anything transformative? Would such a process amount to the embrace of being thingly? And does that require giving up on something else, on being, say, human? This is, of course, the explicit terrain of one of Wordsworth's most beguilingly simple lyrics, 'A slumber did my spirit seal', discussed in conclusion below. And in the back of these questions we need to inquire into the form of knowing that replaces book learning, the 'spontaneous wisdom' and 'truth' of the fifth stanza and the 'impulse from a vernal wood' (ll. 19–21) of the sixth. It is this, the 'impulse', which the speaker claims 'May teach you more of man; / ... Than all the sages can' (ll. 22–4). In some conceptualizations of knowledge 'impulses' are close to 'intuitions' but here the sense does not comprise a human or agential quality: it is a property of the natural world, of a thing, of trees. If an impulse is, then, close to an intuition, it would share with the latter a turn away from the support of external corroboration: for an intuition to remain just that it must not be resolved into a shareable knowledge, a fact. This, perhaps, is the knowing that resides in coming into the light.

Other poems invoke still stranger epistemologies. 'Anecdote for Fathers' indicates in its title that its topic is to be how the 'art of lying may be taught' without providing a firm steer as to whether learning this might be a good thing or not. And in the process of the poem what we might reasonably expect to comprise a moral account of the inadvisability of telling lies turns out to be something rather stranger: an encomium to what is known in childhood, or by the child, but unknown or unknowable to the adult. Hence the child's inability, when asked for a reason in support of his choice of Kilve against Liswyn farm, to formulate anything that might be taken by his father to be knowledge: 'I cannot tell, I do not know' (l. 39) is his reply. Furthermore, when pressed five times to explain himself he offers something that is explicitly marked as a mere contingency, the presence of a weather-cock at Liswyn which is supposed to justify his preference for Kilve. In the terms of the poem's subtitle, are we to take this as a lie? In terms of its basis in fact, it is not one since we are given to believe that there is indeed a vane upon the house top near Liswyn, and once again we are led to assume that this cannot be said about Kilve. But can the father *know* this, as the child does, as either true or false? Within the terms of the exchange the child uses the fact merely as a contingent excuse, a means for satisfying his persistent father, thereby setting the reader up to judge it as a lie in respect to the *reason* for making the choice. Here the reader seems to know something different and distinct from the father, yet the drift of the moral seems to indicate that the father *does* come to know the child's truth – 'Could I but teach the hundreth part / Of what from thee I learn' (ll. 59–60) – and the reader is supposed to share in that revelation. Can we be so sure, however, that the child and the father know the same thing? Who, after all, is teaching the art of lying, the child or the father? And is the lesson that one can know something without knowing how or why one knows it (the situation for the child), or alternatively that the child must learn to match facts and knowledge without lying (the discipline imposed by the father)?

Moreover, the status of what is known, both internally within the world of the poem and externally within the context of our reading, is uncertain. The poem explicitly places the exchange between father and child within the context of truth and falsehood, thereby suggesting that the distinction between them is easily determined. But this turns out to be rather more tricky. The coercive father insists on there being a reason for stating a preference no less than he requires the child to state a preference. Are we so sure that the child does, in fact, have a preference? That he tells the truth 'in careless mood' (l. 33)? Or does that mood leave him indifferent to the question? Having committed himself to the preference (a lie), he is then forced to justify it with another lie, only this time the demands of the cross-examination require that he find a 'true' analogue in the world of things. Hence his opportunistically alighting on the fact of the weather cock. Does this answer satisfy the father? What if the lie comprises the statement about Kilve, that in fact there is a weather vane there too? This would suggest that the real lesson to be learnt is that adults ought not to require children to operate under the same conditions of truth and falsehood as their elders. This is a reading that certainly corresponds to Wordsworth's later description of the intent of the poem as 'to point out the injurious effects of putting inconsiderate questions to Children, and urging them to give answers upon matters either uninteresting to them, or upon which they had no decided opinion'.[16]

But there is another aspect to the exchange which concerns the finding of words: the child states 'I cannot tell' and follows this up with 'I do not know'. And when he does alight on the contingent fact of the weather cock this is described as 'unlock[ing]' (l. 53) his tongue. This leads one to the observation that knowledge in the sense of a commonly held belief entails the matching of things to words. The knowledge that is transmissible, knowable to others, to both the child and the father, is grounded in such matching. Seen this way, the poem dramatizes the fact that the adult can 'know' the truth of his son only in the form of the contingent explanation that it is a 'lie', thereby suggesting that the adult corrupts the truth by insisting on the child's finding words when he has already indicated that he lacks them. Is the lesson here, then, about the corruption entailed in 'finding words' for our experience? If, as noted above, the knowledge known to the child is that he does not, in fact, have any reason for a preference and may have no preference in any case, can that be transmitted only in the form of the lie? A lie, that is, which conveys a truth to the adult. Is the poem, therefore, asking us to revalue lying, as in some sense containing or expressing knowledge that would otherwise remain out of reach? Is it an experimental epistemology which tests the distinctions between truth and falsehood, or if not the distinction between them, then the discursive contexts in which that distinction is held to be constitutive of a form of shared knowing?

Such a reading is certainly encouraged when the poem is situated within the sequence Wordsworth gave to the second, 1800 edition of *Lyrical Ballads*, where it follows 'We are Seven'. If that poem sets out to investigate what is known in numbering, and how the process of counting is caught up in the transformation of beings into things via language or finding words for lived and living experience, this one, 'Anecdote for Fathers', investigates the limits of the knowable to those words we insist on using to tell the truth.[17] Perhaps one could call this an '*in*-epistemology' of the lie.

5 'As if [poetry] were a thing'

The most perplexing poems addressing these issues are those known as the 'Lucy poems', and in conclusion I shall take just one of them for my example.[18] Here it is in full:

> A slumber did my spirit seal,
> I had no human fears:
> She seemed a thing that could not feel
> The touch of earthly years.
>
> No motion has she now, no force;
> She neither hears nor sees;
> Rolled round in earth's diurnal course
> With rocks and stones and trees!

I have read this poem more times than I can count, yet even so I always stumble over the first line. It is a kind of immovable obstacle standing sentry at the poem's threshold that has to be dealt with each and every time I read these lines. A thingly presence that seems to function as a kind of block or barricade to my ever coming to be with the poem's knowing. Here I do not mean to draw attention to the ambiguity that has often been remarked on in the first line – should we construe it as 'a slumber sealed my spirit' or as 'my spirit sealed (a?/my?) slumber'? Nor do I want to highlight the uncertainty over the 'she' of the third line: are we to take this pronoun as referring to some female person extrinsic to the poem (a purported 'Lucy') or to its closest grammatical antecedent, the spirit of the first line. It is neither of these so-called ambiguities that causes me to stumble. My problem is with the persistence of the letter 't'.

One can get at that a little better by returning to the two proposed readings of the first line. The alternatives are essentially created through the ascription of agency to the concept of sleep, which leads one to ask whether slumber is capable of taking on the grammatical role of the subject. Can it govern the verb 'to do'? Since the other alternative subject of the verb, 'spirit', might also be in some uncertain position with regard to the same question – does a 'spirit' do? – the first possibility, that sleep sealed my spirit, has a greater attraction – it feels less awkward than it otherwise might. This leads one to ponder the difference it would have made if Wordsworth had written 'Her slumber did my spirit seal'. Such a locution taps into the sense of appropriation that lies deep within the poem and is, on that account, strangely satisfying. Reading along these lines gives one 'my spirit sealed her slumber', and I take this to mean by implication, it sealed what made her animate, human.

Does the sound of the opening also invite or at least allow us to hear a slightly different inflection: 'aslumber' for 'A slumber'? This gives us something like: 'while asleep my spirit was sealed', and once again there is a certain satisfaction here since it edges close to the sense of appropriation or even theft that flickers in the verse. It might be put like this: while I slept whatever it is that makes me human, that I feel as my being human, was taken away from me, removed to another, inaccessible place. Not dreamt away, but now sealed up.

The poem is clearly attuned to the sensation of agency, suggesting in its lyrical balm that a lack of human agency would seem to be, at the very least, a place of repose. Thus the absence of 'motion', 'force' and the senses of hearing and seeing are troped as being somehow comfortable. All of which conspires to intensify the thingliness of 'she': she seemed a *thing*. These attributes and the fact that the last two lines prompt one to read them as qualifying the 'she' of the sixth line lead one to understand this thingliness as the state of death. And of course this is how the last line is most often taken, as suggesting that through the Christian practice of burial our flesh returns to the earth from which we are deemed, in some curious way, to have originally sprung. The selection of the slightly uncommon word 'diurnal', since it contains the word 'urn' and sounds the word 'die', helps to promote the availability of this reading. But there is something else in this 'thingliness', a feature of its own materiality that is imprinted within the poem, which requires further comment.

Returning to the hesitation or gait of the first line – its capacity to trip me up each and every time I reread it – the persistence of the letter 't', for which this poem has a curious fascination or to which it is strangely attracted, now appears to be instrumental in the creation of this feature of thingliness. What I mean by this persistence is first announced in the word 'spirit', a word that appropriately enough contains in its last sylla-ble the pronoun 'it', used in English to refer to unmarked gender agents or to non-agential, inanimate objects. From this moment on the pres-ence of the letter 't' increasingly makes itself felt. It is there in 'thing', 'touch', 'earthly', 'motion' and perhaps most tellingly in the last line's 'stones' and 'trees' (which also sensitizes one to the difference a letter makes: the subtraction of the 'r' would give us 'tees'). But it is in the first line where the insistence of this letter 't' causes such disturbance.

I find it difficult, if not impossible, to avoid reading the opening line as 'a slumber did my spirit *steal*' since the pressure or pulsion of the 't' in the word 'spirit' seems to infect, colonize, or appropriate the word which follows, 'seal'. It is as if something has been stolen before the poem gets started. And that theft is required by the poem, a necessary architecture for poetry to happen at all. This is why the agency of the poet is so weak; it is not the poet, William Wordsworth, who steals any-thing, not *his* slumber that has acted in this way, but 'a slumber'.

Is this why the speaker seems so unperturbed by the claim that he has no human fears? Would such a claim not entail a damaging, perhaps even decisive loss of agency? If the answer to this question is affirma-tive, it indicates that the stakes of turning towards this poetry, to *poetry*, are considerable. To embrace being with and being as an object presents risks that must be weighed and negotiated. But the wager that this poem makes, along with many others in Wordsworth's oeuvre, is that being there need not also entail the loss or theft of knowledge. Or at least the sense or sensation of knowing. That sensation invariably accompa-nies my reading of the first line of this poem: it is the effect and affect of my stumbling over the letter 't'. With that sensation comes a very strong sense that something might be, even has been, stolen from me. Something has been lifted from me which causes a certain lightness – it is as if I have been divested of a part of what I had thought to be inalienably mine, what I think of as my being human – but that lightness of spirit also contains a shadow of sorrow, since to lose something that I hold dear entails my giving up on some forms of certainty. That I might know an other, say.

For many readers of this affecting lyric the object of its attention, the unnamed 'Lucy', provides the fulcrum around which the poem balances.

For most the tenor or register of its affect falls within the domain of love. This certainly connects with my own sense of the poem's presence but in a way that might be slightly out of the ordinary. For what this poem's knowing indicates to me is that the acceptance of love – to love someone to death – the acceptance *that* we love, are capable of love, and *whom* we love, entails the forgiveness for being human. To have no human fears is the reciprocal gift that love delivers in death.

The turn towards poetry that is signalled by Wordsworth's Advertisement to *Lyrical Ballads, with a Few Other Poems* must embrace the risk that some things are known to things. The poems in the collection are experiments in knowing conceptualized as an attribute of the world, as an effect of our interaction with or residue of our being in the world: what precipitates out of the action and reaction of man and the objects that surround him, as the Preface has it (see *PW*, 1:140). They are experiments in the sense that they do not know in advance the outcome of their work. We are in the same place and have as our guides, as Wordsworth had, only the poems themselves. For that we owe them honour.

Notes

1. *The Prose Works*, ed. W. J. B. Owen and Jane Worthington Smyser, vol. 1 (Oxford: Clarendon Press, 1974), p. 116. Hereafter indicated as *PW* and cited by volume and page numbers in the text.
2. The editors of the Cornell *Lyrical Ballads* point out that the text seems to have been added at a late stage in the printing. See *'Lyrical Ballads' and Other Poems, 1797–1800*, ed. James Butler and Karen Green (Ithaca, NY: Cornell University Press, 1992), p. 738.
3. See Robert Mayo, 'The Contemporaneity of the *Lyrical Ballads*', in *Wordsworth: Lyrical Ballads: A Casebook*, ed. Alun R. Jones and William Tydeman (London: Macmillan, 1972), p. 97.
4. Considerable ink has been spilt over this issue. For some critics the label 'lyrical ballad' is an unhelpful distraction. Wordsworth, in fact, seemed to be unhappy with it since there is evidence in the letters that he wanted to remove it from the title page of the second editions, preferring 'Poems in two volumes, by W. Wordsworth'. To Messrs. Biggs and Cottle, 2 October 1800, in *The Letters of William and Dorothy Wordsworth: The Early Years 1787–1805*, ed. Ernest de Selincourt, rev. Chester L. Shaver (Oxford: Clarendon Press, 1967), p. 303 (hereafter cited as *EY*). It is not, however, at all clear that his motives in this regard were transparent. In a letter Dorothy wrote to Mrs John Marshall on 10 and 12 September 1800 considerable ambiguity surrounds the selection of a new title. She writes: 'My Brother William is going to publish a second Edition of the Lyrical Ballads with a second volume. He intends to give them the title of "Poems by W. Wordsworth", as Mrs. Robinson has claimed the

title and is about publishing a volume of *Lyrical Tales*. This is a great objection to the former title, particularly as they are both printed at the same press and Longman is the publisher of both the works' (*EY*, p. 297). What is meant here by 'this is a great objection'? That Longman objected on account of the similarity of the titles, or that someone in the Wordsworth circle objected? It is possible, for example, to read this as indicating that Wordsworth's preferred title was 'Lyrical Tales', something that the poems themselves might have felt more comfortable with given the frequency of use of the word 'tale'. Kenneth R. Johnston makes a different case, claiming that the title 'Lyrical Ballads' as applied to the second and subsequent edition is a misnomer. 'Wordsworth's Self-Creation', in *1800: The New Lyrical Ballads*, ed. Nicola Trott and Seamus Perry (Basingstoke: Palgrave Macmillan, 2001), p. 97.

5. The words 'metre' or 'metrical' appear 48 times in the Preface of 1802.

6. Once again the argument over which poems count as 'lyrical ballads' remains inconclusive. See the introduction to the Cornell edition (*'Lyrical Ballads'*, ed. Butler and Green, p. 10), in which a case is made for 11 'lyrical ballads' among the 23 poems in the 1798 edition. In contrast, Zachary Leader counts 12 while Kenneth R. Johnston makes it ten. Zachary Leader, 'Lyrical Ballads: The Title Revisited', in *1800*, ed. Trott and Perry, p. 24, and p. 40 n. 10; and Johnston, 'Wordsworth's Self-Creation', p. 96.

7. See Brennan O'Donnell, *The Passion of Meter: A Study of Wordsworth's Metrical Art* (Kent, OH: Kent State Press, 1995), and Simon Jarvis, *Wordsworth's Philosophic Song* (Cambridge: Cambridge University Press, 2007).

8. Metre, of course, is but one of the architectonics of Wordsworth's *sounded* verse, as O'Donnell is fully aware, and, perhaps even more importantly, those other forms of the organization of vocal language – rhyme, stress, intonation, accent, pitch, volume – all bear upon metrical values. It is a curiosity of the English language and its poetic tradition that the metrical schemata adopted are far looser than in other poetic traditions and languages – say Latin or French – on account of these other features of the organization of vocal language. As has been pointed out by a number of critics working on prosody, metre is a far more inexact value in English poetry than is often credited. This is partly on account of the stressed nature of the language, and to that extent it can be said to be a resource within the language of which poets may or may not avail themselves. See, for instance, Derek Attridge, *The Rhythms of English Poetry* (London: Longman, 1982) and, for an examination of what this observation entails in respect to how we might know the world, Simon Jarvis, 'Poetry as Cognition', *Critical Quarterly*, 40:3 (1998), 1–14.

9. For attentive readings of his verse with this in mind, see O'Donnell, *Passion of Meter*, especially pp. 48–67, and Susan J. Wolfson, 'Wordsworth's Craft', in *The Cambridge Companion to Wordsworth*, ed. Stephen Gill (Cambridge: Cambridge University Press, 2003), pp. 108–24.

10. '[I mean], if my health will permit me, to devote my life to literature.' Wordsworth to Anne Taylor, 9 April 1801, in *EY*, p. 327. Such an intention, whatever one might understand by it, could have been expressed only once the concept of literature was fully formed in its modern guise. The most extensive account of its formation is to be found in Stefan Hoesel-Uhlig, 'The Historical Formation of the Modern Concept of Literature', Ph.D. diss., University of Cambridge, 2001.

11. This ought not surprise us since a carpenter, say, develops a particular set of cognitive attitudes to wood. A painter learns to smell, touch, and see paint in particular ways. Not all writers want or need precisely the same attentive modes; some, of course, deliberately neglect to develop certain sensitivities, others resist their development, still others attempt to refine certain forms of attention to the highest possible degree. It is not my intention here to calibrate where Wordsworth may have stood in relation to other writers but rather to highlight the fact that he seemed to be particularly sensitized to the *materiality* of language.

12. In reading his own verse aloud Wordsworth adopted a form of singing. See David Perkins, 'How the Romantics Recited Poetry', *Studies in English Literature, 1500–1900*, 31 (1991), 655–71.

13. For an outstanding recent investigation into the consequences of this fact, see Andrew Bennett, *Wordsworth Writing* (Cambridge: Cambridge University Press, 2007), esp. pp. 23–31.

14. *'Lyrical Ballads'*, ed. Butler and Green, p. 351. Hereafter indicated as *LB* and cited by page numbers in the text. Poems in this volume are cited by line numbers in the text.

15. I do not mean to claim that this is a unique feature of *Lyrical Ballads*, but equally I do not wish to assume that it is a common property of Wordsworth's oeuvre. The test of this observation could be made only by turning to the larger corpus and examining the claim at some length.

16. To unknown correspondent, 17 October [1826?], in *The Letters of William and Dorothy Wordsworth: The Later Years. Part I, 1821–1828*, ed. Ernest de Selincourt, rev. Alan G. Hill (Oxford: Clarendon Press, 1978), p. 486.

17. I have written at length on 'We are Seven' in terms that complement this account. See my *Art Matters* (Cambridge, MA: Harvard University Press, 2001), Chapter four.

18. I am not here interested in whether there is a group of poems best read as 'Lucy poems', or indeed in the relations between them and others either within the two volumes of *Lyrical Ballads* or among Wordsworth's poetry in general. The most profound account of them as a group remains Frances Ferguson, *Wordsworth: Language as Counter-Spirit* (New Haven, CT: Yale University Press, 1977), pp. 173–94, to which my own reading is indebted.

4
Words Worth Repeating: Language and Repetition in Wordsworth's Poetic Theory

Alexander Regier

> On ne montre pas sa grandeur pour être à une extrémité, mais bien en touchant les deux à la fois, et remplissant tout l'entre-deux.
>
> —Pascal, *Pensées*, no. 323[1]

1 Introduction

This essay departs from the seemingly simple and obvious observation that language plays a major role in Wordsworth's poetic theory. It needs little argument to claim that Wordsworth thinks very hard about language, about how he uses it, its origins, its status, and its effects. His thinking about poetry and his thinking about the building blocks of poetry, about words, sentences, and linguistic structures, are two activities that are deeply wedded. My contribution to this volume scrutinizes an important aspect of this thinking. The essay discusses the Note to 'The Thorn' and a selection of passages from the *Essays upon Epitaphs* in some detail to show that in these writings Wordsworth positions language as a medium which lies between the material and the immaterial. Language in fact renegotiates the difference between the two, and points towards a poetic principle of non-resolution that lies at the heart of Wordsworth's poetic theory.

Wordsworth's theoretical pronouncements on language have always attracted widely divergent commentary. From Coleridge's *Biographia Literaria* (1817) until today, critics have deemed it one of the most fertile, puzzling, and productive aspects of Wordsworth's oeuvre. Most of these commentaries insist that his interventions on language are significant, whether they agree with their content or not. As with other parts of Wordsworth's prose, a few sceptical readers intuit that Wordsworth's thinking does not amount to a theory of language, or poetry, at all. This assessment is only really accurate, though, if we understand 'theory' as a systematic or holistic account of a linguistic, or poetic, sphere that is articulated in openly propositional forms. Given the richness of Wordsworth's critical corpus, this view seems a capitulation before its complexity and its often illuminating awkwardness. Most recently, Andrew Bennett's excellent study, *Wordsworth Writing* (2007), shows convincingly that the image of Wordsworth as a poet who does not consider the status of language and words is an ungrounded myth.[2] Wordsworth's refusal to formulate an openly systematic account of language (or, in fact, of poetry) does not distinguish him from most poets. He does, in fact, offer us more extensive reflections on language, and how it forms part of both creative and critical principles, than most. They certainly amount to a sustained critical engagement with the assumptions and principles of his poetry. The following exploration therefore understands the 'theoretical' in the more generous and loosely etymological sense of 'contemplation' and 'thinking'. And Wordsworth undoubtedly spends a considerable amount of his career thinking about language in this manner. Naturally, the present essay directly builds on the long genealogy of scholarship that has engaged with Wordsworth's thinking and writing on matters linguistic. While I believe that the sustained engagement with Wordsworth's oeuvre is unusually rich, I also want to draw attention to an important dimension of his thinking about language that has been surprisingly underestimated.

For Wordsworth, understanding the status of the word is central to an understanding of the world, and combines with its unique status in mediating between the material and the immaterial. His views often challenge current orthodoxies in a powerful way. They invite a reappraisal of his authorship but also a reconsideration of some cornerstones of our contemporary understanding of language. Wordsworth rethinks the relation between objects, ideas, and words in a radical way that leaves language to redefine the material and the immaterial. This has significant implications for the way we read Wordsworth as well as for how we might examine our own linguistic prejudices which we bring to such readings. Hence my essay proposes that it is productive to engage with Wordsworth's theoretical statements in terms that recover some of his own assumptions, even though they might seem initially alien or historically overdetermined. This process of renewed consideration is not to be done naively. Neither is it to capitulate before the historical or hermeneutic impossibility of such a task. Assuming that it is performed with care, this approach allows us a new way of understanding how language is central to both Wordsworth and our own critical practice. This includes shedding the critical habit of thinking about questions of poetics in a manner we might best term 'dialectical' – that is, via an analytical approach that defines a poetological problem in a conceptual way and offers an analytical method (or solution) to grapple with (or solve) it that proceeds through contrast and juxtaposition. Wordsworth does not see such an approach as the most promising solution to the historically determined impasse that our own critical position, and Wordsworth's, must always be caught up in. This essay suggests that it is possible and indeed productive to engage, at least temporarily, with such an approach. So, my discussion does not propose a dialectical solution to the contradictions uncovered in Wordsworth's writing. Rather it attempts to show that he makes a powerful case that thinking in contradictory oppositions is often, though not always, unhelpful. Wordsworth is very astute at uncovering false oppositions, and I believe we can learn something from attending closely to his argument. The way that he configures the status of materiality in language, for instance, is an illustration of a larger outlook on poetic representation that promises to be more finely grained than a dialectically progressive one. As I mentioned, it seems to me worthwhile to consider this outlook, not only as a moment to be surpassed in literary history (or Wordsworthian criticism), but also as an instance of how resisting such a model of history in literature might make us reconsider whether we adopted too narrow a version of literary history to begin with.

2   Repetition

As part of the second edition of the *Lyrical Ballads* in 1800 Wordsworth adds a note to his notorious poem, 'The Thorn'. Only a perusal of the whole volume leads the reader to stumble upon it, as the main body of poems does not indicate its presence at the very margin of the book. In later editions, such as in 1815, the commentary disappears again. The Note to 'The Thorn' is a curiously condensed version of the conundrum we so often face when confronted with Wordsworth's prose. According to him, the explanatory Note at the end should, in fact, have been an 'introductory Poem'. It remains in explanatory prose because Wordsworth was 'prevented from writing [the introductory poem] by never having felt [him]self in a mood when it was probable that [he] should write it well'.[3] The failed poem turned Note begins with a commentary on the specific structure of 'The Thorn' which elucidates the status of its poetic persona. However, soon after, the Note expands on larger issues.

Wordsworth uses the 'occasion' of the Note to 'add a few words closely connected with ... many other Poems in these volumes' (*LB*, 351). In typically Wordsworthian fashion the recovery of the introductory frame leads him to theorize about a specific poem, which in turn pushes him to make much more general claims about the nature of the *Lyrical Ballads* as a whole. In the end, as we will see, the Note grows from an aborted poem into a description and theorization of the nature of words and language.

The most prominent general concerns of the Note are the rhetorical devices of tautology and repetition. Given the context, this does not seem surprising: after all, 'The Thorn' abounds in repetitive structures. However, as we have already observed, Wordsworth's comments seek to encompass a much wider perspective. He states that:

> There is a numerous class of readers who imagine that the same words cannot be repeated without tautology: this is a great error; virtual tautology is much oftener produced by using different words when the meaning is exactly the same.
>
> (*LB*, 351)

Wordsworth explains why and how tautology and repetition are quite distinct from one another (thereby contributing to a long history of philosophy, theology, and poetics that reflects upon the status of repetition and difference).[4] His philosophical distinction centres on the relationship between equivalence and difference. The repetition of the same word does not necessarily imply equivalence of meaning or signification. Repetition often highlights difference rather than equivalence. Correspondingly, variation in vocabulary does not reflect variation in thought or meaning. By widening his claim in the Note he puts considerable pressure on the rhetorical device of repetition. Wordsworth then goes further than claiming that repetition in poetry is not equivalent to tautology. Repetition, in fact, highlights our linguistic limitations:

> now every man must know that an attempt is rarely made to communicate impassioned feelings without something of an accompanying consciousness of the inadequateness of our own powers, or the deficiencies of language.
>
> (*LB*, 351)

Poetry reminds us that language is never quite enough. For Wordsworth, this awareness of a deficiency includes our understanding of language as well as our inability to express ourselves successfully in it. The most condensed linguistic expression, poetry, is the site of a constant reminder of its own necessary failing. Understood as such, its shortcomings are part of language's positive definition: that language cannot but fail to communicate imperfectly is what makes it distinctive, what makes it 'language'. The melancholy associated with realizing such shortcomings is not altogether negative. While it might be deficient, language is still the best we have. In fact, despite its failings, we can celebrate it as the medium that makes poetry distinctive. Once language's limitations are grasped as a necessary part of its employment (and, in fact, the understanding of this structure in the first place), it becomes clearer why Wordsworth continues to engage in language despite its inevitably frustrating shortcomings, its futility. The poet goes on to describe and analyse the peculiar character of that ever-failing engagement with language concentrated by repetition:

> During such efforts there will be a craving in the mind, and as long as it is unsatisfied the Speaker will cling to the same words, or words of the same character.
>
> (*LB*, 351)

Repetition is a symptom of an unsuccessful communication (we are aware of our 'inadequateness'); this failure results in a visceral appetite that haunts the mind. Wordsworth highlights the strangely counter-productive move of hanging on to the same words despite knowing that they are unsuccessful. Although we are aware of its inadequacy, we continue to repeat precisely the word which we know does not capture what we mean to say. Wordsworth likens this mechanism of impossibility to a violent bodily reaction. Our mind feels a 'craving' for fulfilment, which, however, will never be satisfied because we keep 'cling[ing] to the same words'. Repetition enacts the 'inadequateness' of language, and in this is much more eloquent than any empty tautology. With each repetition the intensity and awareness are enforced; far from mechanically reiterating, repetition illustrates a linguistic principle of lack at the heart of poetry. After all, the unsuccessful 'craving' does not result in a refusal to repeat the attempt to communicate impassioned feelings.

Suitably unsatisfied with his discussion, Wordsworth has another go at explaining the role and significance of repetition. And he follows his description of the 'craving' and dissatisfaction with a surprising explication:

> There are also various other reasons why repetition and apparent tautology are frequently beauties of the highest kind.
>
> (*LB*, 351)

This is a remarkable non-sequitur, which, to my knowledge, has not been much commented upon. Repetition is not only a sign of inadequacy and shortcoming. It is also a frequent beauty of the highest kind. Repetition in poetry, it seems, is the sign of lack *and* of beauty. This sequence of statements presents a rich and complicated account of repetition, language, and poetry that repays close attention. How do we understand the word 'also' in the last quotation? Is the state of dissatisfaction and 'craving' a state connected to beauty? Or is Wordsworth suggesting something completely separate from his earlier statement about repetition, perhaps even contradicting it? Assume the repetition of words reminds us not only of the shortcomings of language, but also of why these themselves are reasons for beauty and visceral responses. One way of reading Wordsworth's statement is that he presents us with a poetics of lack: we enjoy repetition as it always allows us to defer fulfilment. We always come back for more because repetition is, apart from dissatisfaction, also a beauty of the highest kind. This strand of Wordsworth's poetic theory may seem reminiscent of melancholy or masochism.[5] We enjoy the lack repetition enacts and allows: the longer we can put off the satisfaction of our craving, the longer we can enjoy the power of repetition. Clinging to the same words allows us to defer, allows us to enjoy our craving, which turns out to be a beauty of the highest kind. Just as in masochism, repetition here 'is characterized by its "frozen" quality and the suspense' (*Deleuze*, 34) of waiting. We know plenty of examples from the world of philosophy, psychoanalysis, or literature which illustrate such an intimate connection between repetition and the beauty of lack and frustration.

Aptly enough, however, there is another aspect to Wordsworth's qualifying 'also' in his description of the 'various other reasons' for perceiving the beauty of repetitive structures. Further to (as well as instead of) a potential beauty of lack, there is a second side to repetition. The reason Wordsworth introduces here with his 'also' seems to stand in opposition to the limitations and frustrations indicated by the 'craving' he mentioned earlier. What follows is one of the reasons Wordsworth gives for why repetition can be a beauty of the highest kind:

> from a spirit of fondness, exultation, and gratitude, the mind luxuriates in the repetition of words which appear successfully to communicate its feelings.
>
> (*LB*, 351)

This presents an obverse side to repetition. It is certainly not a celebration of lack, and quite separate from the description of a craving. Opposing it to the latter seems the intuitively more straightforward meaning of Wordsworth's statements. However, we can adopt this reading only if we highlight the tension and seeming incompatibility between the two aspects of repetition even more. In Wordsworth's second account, repetition is a sign of lack *and* a sign of fulfilment. Most vividly the mind 'luxuriates' in linguistic repetition here rather than expressing a 'craving' through it. It feels 'exultation, and gratitude' rather than dissatisfaction. Repetition even appears to 'successfully communicate' the feelings of the mind. It celebrates the richness and depth of poetry by intensifying repetition. In other words, it is seemingly opposed to what Wordsworth describes two sentences earlier as the unsettling awareness of the 'deficiencies of language'. Significantly, however, he uses the same verb in both cases. He describes the mind's unsuccessful attempts to 'communicate impassioned feelings' as well as its luxuriating in appearing 'successfully to communicate its feelings'.[6] This reading of Wordsworth's Note leaves us with two seemingly incompatible versions of repetition and their significance side by side, one after the other. They relate two different sides of linguistic experience. Intuitively, both accounts ring true: we repeat our words in situations of linguistic frustration, desperately seeking to communicate a specific term (we 'look' for a different word, and repeat the same). Equally, it is pleasurable to repeat words over and over again when we feel that they successfully capture what we want to say (we repeat refrains, exclamations). We know many examples that illustrate both these dimensions, from King Lear's 'Never, never, never, never, never!' to any number of biblical passages or the tune we enjoy singing over and over again. What we are left with here is an account of two seemingly incompatible versions of the same phenomenon. However, rather than dismissing this passage of the Note as a confused or contradictory account I believe its non-sequitur points towards a larger aspect of Wordsworth's poetic theory.

It seems that, according to Wordsworth, repetition can be both craving and luxury, failure and success, lack and fulfilment. The difficulty is evident. Prima facie there is no way of telling whether a poetic repetition we encounter is a sign of frustration or luxury. In 'The Thorn', do Martha Ray's words 'Oh misery! oh misery! / Oh woe is me! oh misery!' denote a successful or an unsuccessful articulation of her passion? On the face of it, we have no discriminating tool to adjudge the potential success or failure of the character's utterance. We could diagnose this as a stifling contradiction hidden in Wordsworth's prose. However, its phrasing also offers a potentially more productive way to approach this problem analytically. Wordsworth not only says something about repetition; his argument also concerns the conceptual category of opposition and its often mistaken invocation in our thinking about poetry. This is how repetition, because of its double quality, becomes a way to uncover and illustrate a larger poetic principle of non-resolution. As we will see, Wordsworth's principle does not ignore contradiction per se but rather uncovers many contradictions as false oppositions. The Note goes further than illuminating the rhetorical figure of *repetitio* or pleonasm. It invites the reader to reconsider two fundamental components of Wordsworthian poetical and lyrical composition, language, and thought. Hence, the two seemingly opposed accounts of repetition might be described in a more complex manner than to simply pitch them against each other. While they appear to be indistinguishable but incommensurable, they illustrate the multivalent quality of lyrical language that contains two extremes without allowing them to contradict each other. Pain and pleasure, communication and frustration, are not contradictory contrasts at the extremes of language. They are poles whose containment without resolution, for all their tension (in fact because of it), creates the material of poetry. Repetition turns out to be a very good example of this dynamic because it looks deceivingly similar (empty) or incommensurable (contradictory). Its apparent tautology turns out to be enriching, and it accommodates and enacts its seemingly incompatible tensions in such a way as to reveal them to be interdependent pillars of poetic composition.

Wordsworth reflects on the power of non-resolution or, better, the detection of false oppositions, throughout his theoretical writing. The essays gathered in this volume offer several deep and knowledgeable discussions of his challenges to orthodox and seemingly self-evident distinctions between antithetical categories. The claim that there 'neither is, nor can be, any *essential* difference between the language of prose and metrical composition' (*PW*, 1:135) is certainly one of the most prominent. Another relevant example is the false distinction between poetry and philosophy. As part of this context, I want to draw attention to a further incisive moment in the Wordsworthian corpus dealing with false oppositions. It occurs in the first of the *Essays upon Epitaphs*. Discussing a paradigmatic genre of his own poetics, the epitaph, Wordsworth presents two different attitudes to burial, the human body, and the belief in the soul. Wordsworth contrasts the common story of Simonides encountering a stranger's corpse on the shore with an identical situation occurring to 'another ancient Philosopher'. The first, Simonides, buries the body and is 'honoured' for this act. The second leaves the body behind, disregarding the material corpse as the mere 'shell' of a more essential substance, the soul (*PW*, 2:52–3). However, neither of them acts objectionably, according to Wordsworth; in fact, both actions are commendable – although the poet does not express a preference. He explains the divergence in attitudes between the two figures as two different ways of appealing to a fundamental set of values that is common to both men, namely the immortality of the soul. While they might look very different, or contradictory, they turn out not to be. Significantly, Wordsworth goes further than claiming that they have a common denominator, thereby also questioning their incompatibility. Against appearances, the attitudes of Simonides and the unnamed philosopher are in fact not even opposed. Rather, Wordsworth states:

> Each of these Sages was in sympathy with the best feelings of our nature; feelings which, though they seem opposite to each other, have another and a finer connection than that of contrast.
>
> (*PW*, 2:52–3)

Much can be and has been said about this complex and important passage.[7] What is most significant in the present context is how Wordsworth emphasizes that, while the different figures seem to exhibit incompatible attitudes, they are in fact not as opposed as we might think. It is crucial that this qualification occurs at a central moment in Wordsworth's explication of his poetic theory. As many others have pointed out, the *Essays upon Epitaphs*, and this passage in particular, represent one of the most important moments in Wordsworth's straightforwardly theoretical discussions. Thus this passage concerns more than the immediately relevant discussion of immortality and poetry.

There is an implicit approach to Wordsworth's comments that is instructive to a reading of his own oeuvre. According to him, the attitudes of the two Sages are only seemingly opposed. They are actually akin in an important and sophisticated way. Their link is not constituted by dialectical opposition, but rather by a connection 'finer ... than that of contrast'. This 'finer connection' is both subtler and more desirable than an attempted resolution or synthesis of the oppositions. It is a way of describing the relation between two seemingly incompatible poles that in fact stand in a productive tension without necessarily advancing each other. They can be likened to the force-fields of two magnets holding them up against each other and maintaining a space between them. In this case, the type of connection allows us to discover an unsuspected similarity. In another case, as we shall see, it might help us to see a difference when things look too alike. What it does in both cases, as I have suggested, is point towards a larger principle within Wordsworth's reflections on poetry. In order to illustrate this more general claim I will return to the Note to 'The Thorn' and show how Wordsworth advances his claim that language itself encompasses and contains precisely such a 'finer connection than that of contrast' in a peculiar way.

3   Wordsworth's *Things*

We remember that, in the Note, Wordsworth presents two seemingly incompatible descriptions of repetition. Repetition is the sign of language's shortcoming. And it is also a moment of delight and luxury. These two poles have, I want to suggest, a finer connection than that of contrast. Wordsworth hints at this when he explains that there are various reasons why repetition is a beauty of the highest kind:

> Amongst the chief of these reasons is the interest which the mind attaches to words, not only as symbols of the passion, but as *things*, active and efficient, which are of themselves part of the passion.
>
> (*LB*, 351)

Repetition unfolds its pleasure when we contemplate and use words in a variety of particular ways. Wordsworth presents us here with a moment of careful yet ambiguous classification and qualification so characteristic of his prose. Out of the potential variety of 'chief' reasons he focuses on how repetition triggers a mental and linguistic process that ultimately influences the way we contemplate language and poetry. Given the various effects of repetition it is not surprising that he qualifies the particular attraction he highlights as the 'chief', not the only, reason for our interest. With this in mind, we can turn to a main aspect of this principal reason, namely 'the interest which the mind attaches to words, not only as symbols of the passion, but as *things*, active and efficient'. Wordsworth here is insistently coy in his negotiation of a poetic theory that is both historically aware of its sources and wanting to be deeply original. He knows he is placing himself in a long-standing tradition of theorizations about how the mind 'attaches' interest to words, as well as classical and biblical criticism that has engaged in a number of long-standing discussions about the ontology of words. William Keach rightly describes Wordsworth's passage as 'Perhaps the best known of all Romantic claims that "words are things"'.[8] As many commentators have pointed out, the phrasing in the Note directly echoes Coleridge's 1810 notebook entry, where he writes 'that words are not mere symbols of things & thoughts, but themselves things'.[9] The most obvious and common sources for this discussion, including Wordsworth's, are the book of Genesis and the Gospel according to St John, either directly or through a myriad influences (such as St Augustine, Thomas Aquinas, and all the commentary their writings on linguistics generate). The Judeo-Christian insistence on the ontological power of the word invariably forms part of the frame of reference in which Wordsworth operates. While this is undoubtedly a strong influence on Wordsworth, the Note also seems to allude to the classical background that informs the particular Judeo-Christian framing of the *res/verba* distinction. The mind attaches interest to words as '*things*, active and efficient'. The qualifying sub-clause Wordsworth inserts here seems a not-so-covert reference to Aristotle.[10] Words, as *things*, the Note seems to suggest, act according to what Aristotle would describe as material (in Wordsworth's terms 'active') and efficient causes. In the first case, words are the material cause of poetry, these *things* are what poetry is constructed, or made, of. The second imagines words as *things* working under the efficient cause, a process that may be likened to an attempt to answer the question, 'What makes poetry happen?' Both cases demand a consideration of the status of words as *things* that might fit Wordsworth's description. They also, however, encourage us to rethink whether words as *things* successfully challenge the way we think about causation and language. At the same time, Wordsworth maintains that the '*things*, active and efficient' come to form part of the passion (rather than just a representation, a symbol, of it). The Note seems to suggest, at least in an oblique way, that language performs, enacts, one of its deep characteristics by presenting itself as built by and through *things*, active and efficient.

Wordsworth's references back to classical as well as to Christian theorizations of the ontology of language contextualize the Note as a conscious intervention in this debate. While it is not a technical commentary or a scholarly treatise, the Note does invoke the wider question of the ontology of language in a pointed and direct way by insisting that words can be *things*. The phrasing of the allusion suggests, amongst many other aspects, a particular interest in the material status of the word. It allows a chance to reflect on how the division between the sphere of the material and that of the immaterial determines our understanding of language. Thus, despite its familiarity, or perhaps because of it, the assumptions bound up with Wordsworth's elliptical sentence are worth some further scrutiny. As we will see, the question of language's materiality becomes a particularly effective angle of analysis to evaluate the importance of words understood as *things* for his wider poetic theory. It turns out that the status of Wordsworth's *things* is two-fold; and that contemplating the link between their two aspects reveals a connection finer than that of contrast. First, these *things* are material: words become linked to objects in a more than figurative way. Secondly, they are immaterial: words are *things*, mental and spiritual.

Wordsworth believes in the ontological power and presence of words; they are *things* that have a material dexterity that goes beyond the figural. Words not only structure material reality; they also create it. In this sense they have a material presence that is inextricably bound up with their status as linguistic signs. Words are graspable, tangible, in a variety of different ways. Our body reminds us that language is always bound to the material of a linguistic subject. Rhythmical breath, necessary for any language, insists on a material presence that is kept alive. According to the Note, our minds take an interest in words as *things* when we understand that they are not only symbols but also actual objects whose presence makes a material difference to us. These *things* are in turn again represented and thus become 'themselves part of the passion'. Passion becomes both the subject and the medium of representation. And Wordsworth's simile of 'words as *things*' insists that these two spheres of the material and the immaterial overlap, blend into one another, rather than emphasizing their categorical difference. Thus, the Note goes beyond a description of the materiality of the signifier alone. Wordsworth believes in the creative power of words and that their tangible existence structures our material reality – a view, incidentally, that far exceeds a post-structuralist recovery of a linguistic trace within the material.

However, words, just as *things*, are also elusive, ungraspable, and immaterial. Words as *things* are immaterial signs, detached from the immediate physicality of the world they describe. We find this account intimately familiar as most contemporary linguistic theory is predicated on this immaterial aspect of the word. Signs are conceptually determined, and their theorization follows similar lines. Words are *things* in the same way in which thoughts or problems can be understood as things; they are in a realm that is already detached from the physical materiality of the word, describing its structure rather than materially participating in it. In this sense, words as *things* are precisely non-material.

Words as *things*, it turns out, can be many different things. The Note to 'The Thorn' presents language as possibly torn or confused between the material and the immaterial aspects of its description. However, it has already transpired how we can read Wordsworth as attempting to profit from this seeming difficulty. Might we not reconfigure the categories through which the perceived tension within the *things*, here between the material and the immaterial, is constructed? Rather than confusing two incommensurable extremes, can we understand language as occupying the gap between two spheres? Does that not illustrate that they have a connection finer than that of contrast as well as showing the initial division to be misguided? Understood in this way, Wordsworth's *things* make us think again, about both language and materiality. Given his wider poetical thrust, we can read the formulation in the Note as alerting us that the words we read lie in the space between the spheres of the material and the immaterial, so often understood as incommensurable. These *things* are not committed to the extreme dialectical poles that make up many other models of thinking about language, including our own. Read in tandem, the Note and the *Essays on Epitaphs* allow us to question the accuracy of thinking in such exclusionary terms. By following a finer connection than that of contrast, language fills up the space between the extremes. It thus becomes both the texture and the theme of poetry. Wordsworth's sentence urges us to think of words as containing two different elements, which are equivalent but not the same. Their ontology is predicated on mediating between two spheres that seem incommensurable but that are in fact deeply connected with each other. Language opens up a space at the fault line between the material and the immaterial; and it is this space between the two spheres which becomes crucial for Wordsworth's poetic theory. Words are *things* in the sense that they are neither the same (the statement is not tautologous) nor incompatible. Language contains the material *and* the immaterial, and its thingliness is predicated on accommodating the space between two seemingly exclusionary aspects. They are neither and they are both at once.

Wordsworth's simile alerts us to how words are precisely *both* material and immaterial, how they are immaterial symbols and material objects. This highlights the complexity of the connection between symbol, language, and passion offered in the Note. Remember that, when we attach an interest to words, we meditate about them 'not only as symbols of the passion, but as *things*, active and efficient, which are of themselves part of the passion'. In the same paragraph Wordsworth reminds the reader that 'Poetry is passion' (*LB*, 351). The passionate language of poetry, then, illustrates in a condensed way that words, in incorporating both material and immaterial, become the subject and the texture of poetry. Contemplation allows us to perceive (and enjoy) that words can be, as *things*, part of the passion rather than limited to the sphere of a representation ('only as symbol'). Over and above being the building blocks of poetry, words become part of lyric expression ('a part of the passion') in their power to perform and encourage a reconsideration of materiality. Poetry, passion, is formed out of *things*, active and efficient. Language exhibits its own internal connections, subtler than of contrast, by making the relation between the material and the immaterial part of its pleasurable experience in poetry. It thereby makes its own internal tensions an integral part of its representations.

We all know that Wordsworth grapples with the complex representational structure of language throughout his work. The different ways in which he approaches linguistic issues theoretically illustrate his continuous engagement with the material aspect of words. Wordsworth uses the third of the *Essays upon Epitaphs* as a platform to encourage the potential reader to appreciate how language inhabits and produces a connection between the spheres of the material and the immaterial. It includes his most notorious pronouncement on the matter, namely the warning that

> If words be not … an incarnation of the thought but only a clothing for it, then surely will they prove an ill gift.
>
> (*PW*, 2:84)

We learn that words can be terrible *things* indeed if we do not attend to their various qualities. The word as 'incarnation of the thought' is another not-too-covert reference to a Christian history of negotiating the relation of materiality and language. The desired incarnation contains both immaterial thought and material presence in the body of the word. If we concentrate only on their dimension as arbitrary signs ('clothing'), they become an 'ill gift', a coat of Nessus, lethal to our perception of the world. Wordsworth appreciates the power of the scheme that divides the sign into 'garb' and 'body'.[11] However, he strongly objects to such an understanding of either thought, words, or language. According to him, it is based on a number of false oppositions (here between thought and word), which cloud our understanding of language and materiality in serious ways. It should perhaps give us food for thought that Wordsworth's warning, for all the commentary it has provoked, has hardly ever been read on its own terms; a sign, perhaps, of its deadly accuracy. In Wordsworth's alternative account, words are not stable entities that belong to the particular sphere of either the material or the immaterial. Their status as incarnations or *things* avoids such a dichotomy.

The Note to 'The Thorn', then, suggests that an attempt to understand language allows us to reconsider the spheres of materiality by establishing what kind of *things* words can be. As Frances Ferguson points out, in 'the Note to "The Thorn", the whole question of poetic language becomes highly elusive, because Wordsworth's explanations of the power of repetition do not submit themselves easily to the subject–object dialectic which is the basis of most justifications of the literary symbol'.[12] In following Wordsworth's argument, we discover that the poles of materiality and immateriality exhibit a connection finer than that of contrast in the linguistic. Considering his wider writings and concerns, scrutinizing the Note's approach to uncovering connections without setting them into dialectical oppositions is fruitful. Language exhibits and illustrates a tendency that is at the heart of Wordsworth's thinking about poetry. Or, rather, Wordsworth's poetical practice leads him to discover the connections finer than of contrast that fill language and his own poetry with productive tension. The experience of these linguistic tensions is part of how poetry delights. However, it is not always the tension between two opposing extremes that the reader enjoys. Often it is their ability to perform the connection finer than that of contrast, by exhibiting 'the subtle progress by which ... qualities pass insensibly into their contraries, and things revolve upon each other' (*PW*, 2:53).

In how far do these claims translate back into Wordsworth's poetic practice? Our immediate reference must be 'The Thorn', given its proximity to the selection of Wordsworth's wider statements here presented. The narrator of the poem arrestingly presents the story of Martha Ray, her initial happiness, her disappointment at being left upon her wedding day, her supposed madness and seeming restoration, and, most importantly, the assumed death of her child, buried next to the thorn which gives the poem its title. Of the many memorable lines in this lyrical ballad the narrator's direct report of Martha Ray's wailing is particularly haunting. Every reader of 'The Thorn' will remember how she returns to the spot that marks her child's unmarked grave and utters the words:

> 'Oh misery! oh misery!
> Oh woe is me! oh misery!'

These lines illustrate well the value of Wordsworth's differentiation between repetition and tautology. Rather than being empty and endlessly self-stating, the exclamations evolve and intensify the expression of the character's misery. Their repetition illustrates their difference. This has an immediate relevance to how we read the poem, both in literary–historical terms and in relation to the issues of repetition and materiality discussed before. While I want to focus mainly on the latter aspect, it is helpful to mention a relevant historical dimension of these lines. The four exclamations of 'Oh' (five if we include 'woe') are an example of how this poem draws on what J. H. Prynne, discussing Hazlitt's lectures 'On Poetry in General', terms an 'emphatical language'. As Prynne shows, the use of 'Oh' is 'notable in the impassioned utterance of much Romantic poetry' as well as 'marking and performing moments of culminative emphasis of poetic speech'.[13] Exclamatory lines such as 'Oh misery!' or 'Oh woe is me!' effectively remind us how language is tied to a material body that utters each emphatical word. Prynne eloquently traces the history of these moments and, while I will not be able to situate 'The Thorn' in this account, it is important to acknowledge the larger chronological context to which the poem draws attention. It certainly intimates that Wordsworth's lines are highly poetical in their linguistic concentration. Here are Martha Ray's words once more:

> 'Oh misery! oh misery!
> Oh woe is me! oh misery!'

Any reader who reads these lines aloud will immediately understand, and perform, why they are not an empty tautologous statement. The differences each time she exclaims 'Oh woe is me! oh misery!' point to the line's potential as a concentrated example of a larger linguistic condition. It illustrates the double nature of repetition, ultimately making us reflect on the material status of words.

Considering the tension we earlier uncovered in the Note, is this line of the poem an example of frustration at not being able to communicate? Or does the mind luxuriate, however painful this might be? It is both; and we begin to see how these two poles exhibit a connection finer than that of contrast. On the one hand, the words, and their repetition, are quite clearly about the shortcomings of language. It is an example of why we 'know that an attempt is rarely made to communicate impassioned feelings without something of an accompanying consciousness of the inadequateness of our own powers, or the deficiencies of language' (*LB*, 351). Martha Ray's lines are never quite enough to express the event, or her grief. No narration is possible (remember, all the events surrounding her child's death are conjecture) and there can be no eloquent closing gesture. However often we read the lines, they remind us of the deficiencies of language. Importantly, and as we will discover, this relates to our language as much as Martha Ray's. She cannot put the event into words, and repeats her frustration in the face of both her misery and her inability to express it.

On the other hand, we can, and do, read the repetition as a successful communication of the character's grief. It has a soothing or therapeutic function, and we partly believe that it 'successfully communicates' her feelings. While not born out of pleasure itself, the linguistic repetition creates a dirge that successfully articulates Martha Ray's grief. Just as she returns to the beauteous spot, she comes back to these lines as they capture the melancholy beauty:

> 'Oh misery! oh misery!
> Oh woe is me! oh misery!'

Reading these lines again, we are struck by the second repetition, the variation and difference of the phrase 'Oh woe is me'. It seems to be at once a variation of the misery invoked as well as allowing us to read its surrounding invocations as address. In between the different versions of misery, and their repetitions, these four monosyllables powerfully illustrate Martha Ray's fixation with language and its power to conjure up entities, *things* even. Now, 'Oh woe is me' is a phrase with a long literary history. It is the English version of a turn of phrase familiar to the reader through Greek tragedy, the Latin *o me miserium*, or, in its anglicized incarnation, as an interjection since early English literature.[14] Martha Ray's incantation in 'The Thorn' reflects on this usage, as well as representing a direct statement in relation to the Note that accompanies the poem. The continuous invocation of this line during 'The Thorn' not only shows the double-sided nature of repetition; the phrase also begins to go beyond the representation of passion becoming part of the passion itself. We can understand this process in a variety of ways. The poem shows a character who internalizes woe to a degree that she and that passion become inseparable. When Martha Ray says 'Oh woe is me', she is not only invoking a phrase or symbol of the passion. She also *is* woe, she is part of the passion. And she is so, and becomes woe, through the word. This is an ancient poetical device. Again, in this context, it is important to see its dimension as a linguistic commentary in relation to the Note. The character in the poem 'is' also the word that expresses the passion. She is 'woe' the word, she has merged with the sign she utters.

Martha Ray is, in other words, both immaterial woe and material 'woe'. Martha Ray is a *thing*, a word, as well as a poetic character who comes to stand for a passion. That is not to say that 'The Thorn' is allegorical or its characters personifications of abstract ideas. It means, rather, that the poem thematizes ontology by allowing for the possibility of collapsing the difference between the representation of a passion and the existence of that passion itself. Hence the epitaphic dirge of the poem confronts us with far more than a standard literary reference or invocation. The phrase 'O woe is me' is also about the ontological force of words, how words can become and create things. The word here also *is* the thing (an abstract entity, a passion) and it simultaneously becomes linked to the existential presence of the speaker.

The refrain of Martha Ray consists of a repetition that is both a successful and an unsuccessful communication of a passion. This does not mean we need to conceive of the character's (or Wordsworth's) statements as confused. We have seen the power of invocation these lines possess. The repetitions they represent allow us to see one of the ways in which words can be *things*, and how that might enact a connection finer than that of contrast. The word, through her, and alongside her, becomes a *thing*. 'Woe is me', the passion and the word, are a living material reality in and through the poem, not only for Martha Ray. They are also such as part of the poem we encounter as contemporary readers. We therefore should attach a related interest to these words, including how their repetition in the poem might make them *things*. The words 'Woe is me' become a way of reconsidering how we negotiate our relationship with language. This concerns the poetic persona as well as ourselves as readers. For Martha Ray the words are tied to the spot to which she needs to return in order to repeat her dirge. Each time she does so she reaffirms the power of words to bridge the gap between a passion and its representation. As readers we are in a comparable position. We return to the poem as to a mysterious spot, repeating our experience of seeing its words reconfigure our sense of material reality. Every time we read the poem this happens anew. In reading 'The Thorn' over and over again we understand that words not only denote, pass on information, narrate, and are symbols of the passion. We also attach an interest in how they perform the frustration and pleasure of words, and how words become *things*, not only for the fictional Martha Ray but also for us. The poem allows us to perform, repeat, and vary this insight by reading it over and over again. By reading closely and attentively, with a sense of the power of how language can change material reality, we see how the words of 'The Thorn' could become *things*, active and efficient. The way in which the poem forms and interacts with reality is not only limited to the actual physical existence of 'The Thorn'. In a related fashion, Keach subtly traces the claim that 'words are things' to our contemporary 'transformation of poems into commodities'.[15] Could we go even further? I want to suggest that the Note can dissolve the way we think about materiality in the first place. The language of 'The Thorn' and that of its accompanying Note exhibit the power to explore a connection finer than that of contrast that sidesteps the division between the material and the immaterial. In this, they allow us to see that the importance of words as *things* not only lies with limiting their sense to either of these spheres. In effect, both the poem and its accompanying commentary make us reconsider the distinction between words, objects, and thoughts. Our reading, and the interest that we attach to the words of Martha Ray, or Wordsworth, allows us to see how language can reconfigure our sense of materiality.

Notes

1. Blaise Pascal, *Œuvres Complètes* (Paris: Gallimard, 1954), p. 1169. 'We show greatness, not by being at one extreme, but by touching both at once and occupying all the space in between.' Blaise Pascal, *Pensées*, trans. A. J. Krailsheimer (Harmondsworth: Penguin, 1966), p. 243.
2. Andrew Bennett, *Wordsworth Writing* (Cambridge: Cambridge University Press, 2007).
3. *'Lyrical Ballads' and Other Poems, 1797–1800*, ed. James Butler and Karen Green (Ithaca, NY: Cornell University Press, 1992), p. 350. Hereafter indicated as *LB* and cited by page numbers in the text. Poems in this collection will be cited by line numbers in the text. All references to the Note are to the first published version.
4. Thinking about repetition begins with Heraclitus and is still an extremely fertile field in many disciplines. While its philosophical (Søren Kierkegaard, Gilles Deleuze), literary (Gertrude Stein, Samuel Beckett), and psychoanalytical (Sigmund Freud) aspects all form part of the background for this analysis, I want only to gesture towards them here and concentrate on Wordsworth.
5. See Gilles Deleuze and Leopold Sacher-Masoch, *Masochism* (New York; Cambridge, MA: Zone Books, 1989), pp. 116–21. Hereafter indicated as *Deleuze*.
6. This also is a reference to language at large, and the men who 'hourly communicate with the best objects from which the best part of language is originally derived' *The Prose Works*, ed. W. J. B. Owen and Jane Worthington Smyser, vol. 1 (Oxford: Oxford University Press, 1974), p. 125. Hereafter indicated as *PW* and cited by volume and page numbers in the text. It is precisely not the transmission of information but of passion, of poetry, that is at stake for Wordsworth in this passage.
7. A recent and fruitful discussion can be found in Simon Jarvis, *Wordsworth's Philosophic Song* (Cambridge: Cambridge University Press, 2007), pp. 16–21.
8. William Keach, *Arbitrary Power: Romanticism, Language, Politics* (Princeton, NJ: Princeton University Press, 2004), p. 27.

9. Samuel Taylor Coleridge, *Notebooks*, ed. Kathleen Coburn and Merton Christensen, vol. 3 (New York: Pantheon Books, 1957), p. 3762.

10. Wordsworth's debt to Aristotle, especially the *Poetics*, is somewhat of an under-researched topic. As a notable exception, Umberto Eco speaks of 'references to the *Poetics*, however vague and even at times polemical' that he finds in Wordsworth and Coleridge. However, unfortunately, he does not discuss these allusions in much detail. See Umberto Eco, *On Literature* (Orlando: Harcourt, 2004), p. 237. Also see Paul H. Fry, 'Classical Standards in the Period', in *The Cambridge History of Literary Criticism*, ed. Marshall Brown, vol. 5 (Cambridge: Cambridge University Press), pp. 7–28 (p. 18).

11. The model of presenting the sign as the 'dress of thought' has a long history that includes John Locke, the most prominent target contemporary to Wordsworth.

12. Frances Ferguson, *Wordsworth: Language as Counter-Spirit* (New Haven, CT: Yale University Press, 1977), p. 15.

13. J. H. Prynne, 'English Poetry and Emphatical Language', *Proceedings of the British Academy* 74 (1988), p. 136. In connection to Wordsworth, see J. H. Prynne, *Field Notes: 'The Solitary Reaper' and Others* (Cambridge: J. H. Prynne, 2007).

14. The earliest date for an interjection equivalent to 'woe is me' recorded by the *OED* is *ante* 1200 (see entry on 'wumme'). Also see the entry on 'woe'. The expression has been the subject of a number of academic and non-academic commentaries. Mostly these discussions revolve around the question of the grammatical correctness of the translations of *o me miserium* to 'Oh woe is me', 'Woe is I', or 'Woe am I'. See Roy Flickinger and Clyde Murley, 'The Accusative of Exclamation: Seneca to Juvenal', *Classical Philology* 18 (1923), 162–9. William Safire, 'Woe Is Not Me', *The New York Times*, 17 October 1993, sect. 6, p. 10. My own reading will veer away from the issues of history or of a grammatical discussion in the technical sense. There is a philological investment to my interpretation. However, here I have to postpone a further discussion of the grammatical correctness of 'Woe is me' (as opposed to 'Woe is I' or 'I am woe'), both in itself and as a translation from earlier sources. Like any other analysis of language and ontology, my reading has to acknowledge the power and importance of grammar. However, all available versions of the phrase make similar general assumptions about the link between existence and language, which is the focus here. Hence it will transpire why the exact transliteration of the phrasing is less important in this context than a brief survey of secondary literature might suggest.

15. Keach, *Arbitrary Power*, p. 23.

5
The Poetic Structure of Complexity: Wordsworth's Sublime and 'Something Regular'

Claudia Brodsky

In the Preface to *Lyrical Ballads* (1800 and 1850 editions), Wordsworth describes the 'sublime notion of Poetry which [he has] attempted to convey' as follows:

> What then does the Poet? He considers man and the objects that surround him as acting and re-acting upon each other, so as to produce an infinite complexity of pain and pleasure; he considers man in his own nature and in his ordinary life as contemplating this with a certain quantity of immediate knowledge, with certain convictions, intuitions, and deductions, which from habit acquire the quality of intuitions; he considers him as looking upon this complex scene of ideas and sensations, and finding every where objects that immediately excite in him sympathies which, from the necessities of his nature, are accompanied by an overbalance of enjoyment.[1]

The 'complexity' of experience this extraordinarily complex definition describes derives immediately from its origin in two separate but inextricable sources: 'man' and 'the objects that surround him' or 'man in his own nature' and 'in his ordinary life'. 'Acting and re-acting upon each other', these internal and external seats of experience alternate as subject and object of the activity the poet considers, just as the actions of man, while pertaining to one overarching process, themselves appear alternately subjective ('contemplates') and objective ('looks') in kind. As if this definition of the changing object that 'the Poet' 'considers' were not inherently sufficiently difficult to parse, Wordsworth repeats its terms later in the Preface when describing another action and its effects. The notion of 'an infinite complexity of pain and pleasure' and 'overbalance of enjoyment' 'produce[d]' by our 'interact[ion]' with the world finds its echo in the poet's description of 'an overbalance of pleasure' and 'complex feeling' occasioned not by the 'nature' of man in view of the 'objects' that 'surround' him but by the effect upon a 'Reader's mind' of poetry itself. The natural complexity of empirical experience the poet 'considers' is re-enacted, Wordsworth suggests, in the poet's recounting of that experience. In reading poetry we encounter the verbal 'construction' of our encounters with the world and thus experience a 'complex feeling of delight' analogous to that experienced in living. Turning the 'painful feeling' that accompanies the reading of 'powerful descriptions' (*PW*, 1:151) into one of mitigated delight, the 'construction' of the poem in fact not only re-enacts experience, it allows us to surpass it and continue reading. Poetry thus *represents* experience in both senses of the word, on the one hand making it appear present by objectifying or describing it and, on the other, standing in for it, substituting for its immediacy that of its own continuous medium. For, as Wordsworth states in his contemporaneous Note to 'The Thorn', the 'interest' of 'the mind attaches to words, not only as symbols of the passion, but as *things*, active and efficient, which are of themselves part of the passion'.[2]

Just as poetry and the non-verbal subject of poetry share a common descriptive language in the Preface, empirical experience and the experience of reading poetry so closely resemble each other in Wordsworth's poetic theory that they prove, if not theoretically identical, at least highly difficult to keep conceptually apart, and any attempt to describe Wordsworth's theory of poetry will fail to describe its own object if it 'considers' what the 'Poet' 'does' in independence of those actions his poetry is about. For the interactions of man with the world and with language, the life of 'intuitions', 'ideas and sensations', and of verbal 'expression' and encounter are presented by Wordsworth as not only analogous but as themselves interactive: perhaps more explicitly than for any other English-language poet in history, for Wordsworth theory of poetry equals philosophy of mind.[3]

Still, in its attempt to represent the 'complexity' of experience, to render its 'infinite' nature legible, poetry, Wordsworth states, invests 'powerful description' with a powerful, added distinction. Not unlike Kant's key stipulation in the *Critique of Judgement* of the unlimited effect of the mind's ability to recognize its own inability to form a cognition of the infinite – the recognition of the representational limits of the senses resulting in our supersensory capacity instead 'to think' such things as number, dimension, and power beyond measure – Wordsworth ascribes to poetry a singular, verbally produced power, that of recording, naming, and so proceeding beyond the point at which consciousness falters, making the activity of representation exceed the representational limits of experience in language that is not limited to experience, the 'construction' of poetry he calls 'sublime'.[4] While the true subject of the sublime in Kant is the subject that 'judges' 'sublime' its own failure to know through objective representation that which reason prompts it to imagine, sublime poetry in Wordsworth uses representational language to make something infinite its very subject – a kind of action whose complexity exchanges the identities of subject and object, like those of lived and represented experience, in the course of its own dynamic progression.[5] Whereas in Kant the sublime is another name – considered from the vantage point of aesthetic analysis – for the 'spontaneous act' of thinking without representation that must 'accompany' all acts of representational intuition and knowledge, in Wordsworth it names the continuous difficulty of distinguishing thinking from representation, a difficulty both historical and immediate in quality.[6]

What is *not* difficult to distinguish, however, is the marked contrast drawn in Wordsworth's poetic theory between the nature of the subject of poetry and its means. Accompanying the affirmation of the 'infinite complexity' of experience the poet 'considers' is the very different argument Wordsworth makes regarding the non-complex nature of the language of the poet's 'powerful descriptions', the single thesis, regarding poetic language, for which the Preface is best known. That thesis is memorable not only for its own directness of exposition but because, appearing in a 'Preface' to poems its author has already written, it articulates and re-represents critically the thinking immediately accompanying the acts of representation committed in them. Giving a second intellectual life to the 'complex feeling' effected by the poems' particular verbal 'construction', it recasts an apparently idiosyncratic style of authorship into a watershed event in poetic history.[7] For, in making an analysis of the qualities of poetic language the central thrust and substance of a 'Preface' to his own poems, Wordsworth, writing as critic, not only calls attention to the specificity of the historical moment in which, as poet, he himself has written, but suggests that the break with the contemporary poetic landscape the *Lyrical Ballads* enact stems less from any passing personal predilection than from a general truth about poetry, a permanent theoretical necessity extending beyond individual authors and poems because it originates in language as such.

Defying the critically enshrined styles of Donne, Dryden, and Pope, the theory of poetic language contained within the larger theory of poetry presented in the Preface proceeds, like Wordsworth's analysis of the subject of poetry, along both internal and external lines. In the process it redefines at once the language constitutive of poems and the contours of the history of their reception, and lays the groundwork for the scathing narration of fads and frauds exposed, in the later Essay, Supplementary to the Preface (1815), to constitute popular 'taste' (*PW*, 3:80), even as it takes the ground out from under all familiar and accepted doctrine of poetic form. Famously 'reject[ing]' the special 'use', or abuse, of language assumed to identify the presence of poetry – the codified rhetoricization of language he calls 'poetic diction' (*PW*, 1:131) – in favour of the language he variously, and always – if necessarily – inadequately calls the 'language really used by men' (*PW*, 1:123), 'the very language', or, simply, 'the language of men' (*PW*, 1:131), Wordsworth defines poetic language in the Preface as ultimately having no defining characteristics at all, nothing that would distinguish its individual words as inherently different from those composing the language employed by all:

> If in a poem there should be found a series of lines, or even a single line, in which the language, though naturally arranged, and according to the strict laws of metre, does not differ from that of prose, there is a numerous class of critics, who, when they stumble upon these prosaisms, as they call them, imagine that they have made a notable discovery, and exult over the Poet as over a man ignorant of his own profession. Now these men would establish a canon of criticism which the Reader will conclude he must utterly reject, if he wishes to be pleased with these volumes. And it would be a most easy task to prove to him, that not only the language of a large portion of every good poem, even of the most elevated character, must necessarily, except with reference to the metre, in no respect differ from that of good prose, but likewise that some of the most interesting parts of the best poems will be found to be strictly the language of prose when prose is well written.
>
> (*PW*, 1:133)

Attacking those 'Critics' who would canonize what counts as poetry by enforcing what, in the Advertisement to the first edition of the *Lyrical Ballads*, Wordsworth had memorably dubbed 'that most dreadful enemy to our pleasures, our own pre-established codes of decision' (*PW*, 1:116) setting poetic language apart from that of prose, Wordsworth denies to poetry-writing all the accoutrements of a specialized 'profession': exclusionary status, rules of procedure, an added professional 'class' exercising authority to oversee these, and, for its practitioners, approved access to specialized tools. Citing, verbatim, a sonnet by Gray, he italicizes the only lines in it he deems 'of any value' so as to demonstrate that, just as the diction of those lines does not, 'the language of every good poem can in no respect differ from that of good Prose'. From this observation of the interchangeable quality of poetry and prose, Wordsworth proceeds to formulate a premise of non-distinction between the two genres, equating them not only as they appear in individual instances and prescribed forms (as words assembled into the textual shape of a sonnet, for example, or not) but as in all instances, or in essence, they are (as words employed in any context whatsoever): 'We will go further. It may be safely affirmed, that there neither is, nor can be, any *essential* difference between the language of prose and metrical composition' (*PW*, 1:135); 'they require and exact one and the same language' (*PW*, 1:164).

Even the single distinguishing feature Wordsworth at first grants poetry – that of its accommodation and conveyance of 'metre', the linear number and natural inflection with which its verbal sequences are composed – is undermined in the Preface immediately upon being stated as Wordsworth 'go[es] further' still, redefining the absence of any '*essential* difference' between poetry and prose to encompass, in addition to their common verbal forms, the given, extra-lexical rhythms he had ascribed to the 'metrical composition' of poetry alone. In a footnote to the word 'Poetry' – the only note appearing in the Preface – Wordsworth criticizes the fallacy of understanding the term (itself cited between quotation marks by Wordsworth) to be uniquely 'synonymous with metrical composition', noting that 'passages of metre' not only routinely 'occur' in prose but do so 'so naturally' 'that it would be scarcely possible to avoid them'. Thus any theoretical attempt to distinguish the language *and* composition of poetry from those of prose as if these differed in, rather than were two of a, kind (much as Wordsworth admits that, 'against [his] own judgment', he himself had just cursorily done) will contribute no helpful knowledge to the 'criticism' of poetry but, rather, only cause further 'confusion' as to its real nature and effects. True knowledge of what constitutes poetry depends instead, Wordsworth suggests, on our ability to identify that to which poetry is neither lexically, nor sensuously, but rather 'philosophical[ly]' opposed – not prose writing but any writing intended to establish 'Matter[s] of Fact':

> * I here use the word 'Poetry' (though against my own judgment) as opposed to the word Prose, and synonymous with metrical composition. But much confusion has been introduced into criticism by this contradistinction of Poetry and Prose, instead of the

more philosophical one of Poetry and Matter of Fact, or Science. The only strict antithesis to Prose is Metre; nor is this, in truth, a *strict* antithesis, because lines and passages of metre so naturally occur in writing prose, that it would be scarcely possible to avoid them, even were it desirable.

(PW, 1:135)

Reviewing and revising his own previous statement, Wordsworth replaces the sensuous aspect of poetry he now no longer considers 'strict[ly]' opposed to that of prose with an opposition between poetry and that discourse concerned with other sensuous forms, the 'Matter' not of 'contemplation' but 'of Fact', i.e., 'matter' whose very existence is independent of language itself. Unlike the discourse of poetry *and* prose, the discursive observations of science, bent on recording the weight of physical reality, bear with them no relation to the natural inflection and force of articulation, and the different nature of their involvement with matter – the natural verbal stresses inhering in metrical text and the externality of matter to constative science – proves, as Wordsworth suggests in the Preface, and as we shall examine further below, central to his own poetic practice. By contrast, the only possible line of distinction between poetry and prose is, according to Wordsworth's theory of poetry, just that – the cadence and number of linear metre – and the presence of metre is not solely such a dividing line between the genres, but also a line or link between them. Re-evaluating the material–metrical criteria for distinguishing prose and poetry while drawing a 'philosophical' distinction between the infinite complexity of man's empirical experience and empiricist 'matter[s] of fact', Wordsworth paradoxically anchors his theory of poetic complexity in the very 'prosaisms' conventionally condemned by critics of poetry, denying to the identity of poetry precisely those complex lexical figures conventionally identified with 'poetic diction'.

Wordsworth's general aversion to the 'mechanical' use of 'figure[s] of speech' and early exclusion of them from his own poetic practice are well known. Its influence on the course of English literature is as widely acknowledged as it is welcomed or deplored, the poet's pointed critique in the Preface of the 'family language' *(PW*, 1:131) of poetic 'ornaments' *(PW*, 1:137) that 'from father to son have long been regarded as the common inheritance of Poets' *(PW*, 1:133) – those generic linguistic forms defining the poetic genre by tautology that his own purposefully prosaic poetic language rejects – provided and remains the source of legitimation from which the diction of most English-language

poetry written over the past two centuries directly descends. Yet what
Wordsworth frankly, if opaquely, describes as 'Poems so materially
different from those upon which general approbation is at present
bestowed' (*PW*, 1:121) are not merely the result of a theory of poetry
aimed at deflating the vanity of figurative displays or confined in their
own content by the sole goal of stylistic effrontery. The language of
Wordsworth's poetry is often characterized pejoratively as resembling
that of the least verbally varied speakers in his poems – the 'simple
Child' reiterating a single arithmetic sum differently to an interlocutor describing himself as 'throwing words away' in the effort to have
her distinguish the living from the dead numerically in 'We are Seven'
(ll. 1, 67);[8] his 'happy, happy, happy John', or eponymous 'Idiot Boy',
responding to the question of what he 'had seen' (ll. 96, 454) while
lost beyond knowing by mimicking with his own voice the sounds of
a rooster crowing. However, the excess of simplicity, in all its senses,
that Wordsworth's poetry represents for many readers remains in direct
opposition to the thesis of poetically rendered 'complexity' which
Wordsworth repeatedly articulates in the Preface.

Having defined the content of what the poet 'considers' as a compound
of empirical, intellectual, and reflexive experience – that of a 'complex
scene of ideas and sensations' itself 'look[ed] upon' by 'man', a scene
staged as much by his directly 'contemplating' the world as by the
'habit[s]' formed by such contemplation – Wordsworth's theory of poetry
must define the language that can convey such a multiply mediated and
yet immediate relation to the real. In order to render with commensurate
complexity that already 'complex scene', poetic language cannot resort
to the mere mannerism of complexity, inherited conventions of empirically gratuitous artifice. Instead, just as the complexity upon which man
'looks' is itself both product and component of his interaction with
reality, for Wordsworth the language of poetry must maintain relations
with the reality it names: only 'a language arising out of repeated experience and regular feelings' can constitute the 'more permanent' and 'far
more philosophical language' of poetry, i.e., a language which, remaining true to man's desire to speak of experience, 'communicates with the
best objects from which the best part of language is originally derived'
(*PW*, 1:125). Esteeming that the conventions of 'poetic diction' destroy
exactly such subject–object 'communic[ation]', Wordsworth declares his
intention 'to avoid' verbal artifice and approximate as closely as possible
'the language of men' (*PW*, 1:131). Only if communicated in such language will the 'powerful description' of man's interaction with objects
in 'poetry' resemble the 'scenes' of man's experience in reality; only by

representing rather than disguising or replacing those 'objects' in the interaction with which 'the best part of language is originally derived' can a theory of poetry give rise to a 'real' theory of experience, the account of experience as it is lived internally and externally, at which, according to Wordsworth, poetry aims.

In the context of Wordsworth's definition of 'what...the Poet [does]', the question raised by the thesis of the common language of poetry and prose is thus, inevitably, the following: how can words presented and read as semantically non-complex – as intentionally lacking in the logical complications, verbal 'abuses' (*PW*, 1:161) and inter- and intra-linguistic conceits which Wordsworth condemns[9] – represent, on the one hand, the complex *empirical* experience that every man knows, and, on the other, take part in the *verbal* 'construction' of that experience such as every poet worth reading composes? For the unifying insight tying the world to man and man to words in the Preface is that the experience of everyday, circumstantial 'objects' *and* of the 'description' in poetry of the 'feelings', 'ideas' and 'sensations' which such experience incurs entails not simplicity or simplicity only but rather the kind of complexity which poetry alone can represent. And yet, if this is so, what is it, in the absence of recognizable figural language, that can constitute such complexity; what, in Wordsworth's theory of poetry, *does* distinguish prosaic simplicity ('Seven are we' [l. 18]) from sublime complexity ('Nay, we are seven!' [l. 69]), prose from poetry, the experience of the poet's 'real language' from the experience either of reality *or* of language overall?

For the achievement of complexity, Wordsworth repeatedly contends, depends not on the presence of rarified verbal figures detached *per force* from all lived experience, but on the presence, indeed the omnipresence, of the prosaic, the objects and language of lived experience itself, and this attention to the prosaic must include the language composing the theory of poetic language itself. Declining, at the outset of the Preface, to write 'a systematic defense of the theory upon which the Poems were written' (*PW*, 1:121), Wordsworth develops a theory of poetry whose understanding of complex interaction is such that it could only ever be rendered in 'systematic' terms at the double price of the 'real language' of poetry and the reality of experience it would defend. For, in direct contrast to their joint presupposition by all structural approaches to language throughout history, the prosaic elements and systematic organization of language are not aligned by Wordsworth but, rather, are theoretically opposed. His understanding of the 'objects' and experience of poetry requires the efficacy and immediacy of their everyday description just as it stymies, in theory as in poetic practice, the separation of objects and the words that name them as naturally necessitated by their subordination to any conception of language as a signifying or semiotic system.

If the diction of Wordsworth's poetry, like that of the poetry of Chaucer and Milton he most strongly commends, is marked by its prosaic nature, its immediate availability, and literal sense, and if poetic rhetoric and theoretical systematicity are both set aside in the Preface, and the prosaic is put in their place, then the question that arises regarding Wordsworth's definition of poetry returns, from a theoretical perspective, redoubled: what is the source of the complexity of the reading experience, like that of empirical experience, that poetry both sets into motion and represents? 'Complex feeling', in Wordsworth's view, results from neither the systematic nature of language nor a rhetorically produced state of ambivalence but from the condition of becoming unbalanced in perceiving, whether in words or in the world, the 'complex scene' of experience itself. Just as experience simplified of its complexity would be experience missed, poetry amenable to systematic theoretical defence would not be poetry in any real, practical sense, and certainly not the necessary mode of reflecting on experience Wordsworth suggests. For '[t]he end of Poetry', he states, 'is to produce excitement in co-existence with an overbalance of pleasure' (*PW*, 1:147).

Yet in the course of producing such excitement, poetry, like experience, may well put complexity of experience at risk. Wordsworth recognizes that the composition of complexity may also occasion its demise, that '[i]f the words ... by which this excitement is produced be in themselves powerful, or the images and feelings have an undue proportion of pain connected with them, there is some danger that the excitement may be carried beyond its proper bounds'. Thus if poetry is to work towards the 'end' of considering the experiential course of the complex, then poetry must add to that common experience of complexity, something unthinkably simple. Rather than offer a systematic theory of poetry, or sacrifice to inherited, experientially empty 'poetic diction' the immediate power of 'the language really spoken by men', Wordsworth asserts that such complexity in poetry as mirrors the complexity of experience must be submitted to something in addition, something that immediately underlies our sensuous perception of poetry. As proximate to us as the objects perceived by our senses, that something is no substantial thing but the 'co-presence of something regular' (*PW*, 1:147), the 'laws' and 'charm' exercised upon our minds by the 'greatly underrate[d] ... power of metre in itself' (*PW*, 1:145).

It is metre that, already described by Wordsworth as distinguishing *and* conflating poetry and prose, is also said to join poetic formulation to the actual experience of the world, and it is at this point that what is probably the most familiar, and most mangled, quotation in the history of English poetic theory – the apparent non-sequitur beginning, 'For all good poetry is' – deserves a longer and closer look. In the case of Wordsworth's most famous (and infamous) definition of poetry, most well-known is also worst known, or, as Wordsworth might have written, most complex. For the opening of the single definition of poetry by Wordsworth, or indeed any poet, that English-language readers are most likely to recognize – to embrace for its welcome, apparent anti-intellectualism, reject as deeply ideologically mystified, or dismiss as dramatic evidence of wishful 'romantic' simplicity – the introductory statement, 'For all good poetry is the spontaneous overflow of powerful feelings:', is, as its punctuation indicates, only part of a longer thought, and, moreover, one which, after its initial full colon, directly contradicts what has come before.

Routinely cited only up to and excluding the full colon mark, Wordsworth's two-part definition of poetry also contradicts the argument regarding the necessary aim of poetry which immediately precedes it.[10] Just before stating his bifurcating definition, Wordsworth affirms that it was not 'powerful feelings' but, rather, 'habits of meditation' which first endowed the *Ballads'* 'descriptions of such objects as strongly excite [my] feelings' (*PW*, 1:127) with the sole attribute allowing for the definition of such descriptions as poetry. This attribute regards not the origin or genesis of poetry – how poetry derives from emotion – but the guiding aim or reason for its words' being poetry, the object named, nearly eponymously, by the poet named 'Wordsworth', 'a worthy *purpose*' (*PW*, 1:125). Instead of an overabundance of personal feeling, it is the ability of poetry to convey an impersonal objective – an aim that could not be 'formally conceived' in the absence of the poem itself – which Wordsworth, just previous to his definition of poetry, proffers as practical proof of every poem, implying that, if they do not 'carry along with them a *purpose*', his own poems, too, should not be considered poems at all, by asserting that the calling of a poet be denied even to him if his theory of poetry be flawed: 'If this opinion be erroneous, I can have little right to the name of a Poet' (*PW*, 1:125–7).

Following, thus, upon a categorical notion of poetic 'purpose' extending to his own work, and descriptions of reflective and habitual mental processes that spontaneity can neither eradicate nor contain, the full statement of Wordsworth's most frequently and least completely quoted definition of poetry proceeds as follows.

> For all good poetry is the spontaneous overflow of powerful feelings:
> and though this be true, Poems to which any value can be attached
> were never produced on any variety of subjects but by a man who,
> being possessed of more than usual organic sensibility, had also
> thought long and deeply.
>
> (PW,1:127)

In this internally divided definition of those 'Poems to which any value can
be attached', Wordsworth enacts the very notion of complexity that is at the
core of his poetic theory, combining spontaneity with an opposing length of
time, feeling with thinking, overflow with depth. Small wonder that such an
apparently self-cancelling definition, so inherently difficult to summarize,
has been regularly, if misleadingly, abbreviated in the course of its repetition,
and that, despite – or because of – its now nearly rote transmission, it has
rarely been analysed as written. This is a definition that begs definition, and
still more disturbing to the attribution to Wordsworth of a derisory concept
of poetry of unthinking simplicity is the explanatory sentence that, following
directly upon this one, seeks to do just that, i.e., to define what Wordsworth's
paradoxical definition cannot. Composed of a series of complete verbal
clauses, all of which run counter to the self-contradictory definition they
succeed, this extraordinarily extensive sentence delineates in specific verbal
detail the 'act[s]' of representation, repetition, mental habit, and abstraction
which together produce poetry, discrete, non-interchangeable acts taking
place over time in the mind alone:

> For our continued influxes of feeling are modified and directed by our
> thoughts, which are indeed the representatives of all our past feelings;
> and, as by contemplating the relation of these general representatives to
> each other, we discover what is really important to men, so, by the rep-
> etition and continuance of this *act*, our feelings will be connected with
> important subjects, till at length, if we be originally possessed of much
> sensibility, such habits of mind will be produced, that, by obeying blindly
> and mechanically the impulses of those habits, we shall describe objects,
> and utter sentiments, of such a nature, and in such connection with each
> other, that the understanding of the Reader must necessarily be in some
> degree enlightened, and his affections strengthened and purified.
>
> (PW, 1:127; emphasis mine)

In this thoroughly internalized version of the representational subject of poetry, that of 'man' and 'objects' 'acting and reacting upon each other', the 'objects' poetry 'describe[s]' and the 'sentiments' it 'utter[s]' arise in a manner as removed as any imaginable from a 'spontaneous overflow of ... feeling'. These come into being not as feelings that (catachrestically) 'flow' 'over' and out of us alone, but rather as being in general 'of such a nature, and in such connection with each other, that the understanding of the Reader must necessarily be in some degree enlightened'. Furthermore, rather than feelings as such (even assuming these could be isolated and defined), it is the transformation and direction of feeling by thinking that makes possible the making of poetry – thinking that is here considered distinct from, but definitely not opposed to, emotion. 'Thoughts' are instead what Wordsworth now calls 'the representatives of all our past feelings', and it is in our 'contemplating' such representatives in their 'relation' to each other, in the 'repetition and continuance of this act', and, ultimately, in our 'blind' and 'mechanical' obedience to the 'impulses' of 'habit', or non-thought, which the preceding series of acts has 'produced' over time – 'impulses' as continuous and unthinking in ourselves as is the rhythmic beat in poetry of metre – it is in these, Wordsworth specifies, that poetry of any value can come about. Wordsworth's definition of poetry, then, begins with a premise whose development leads – still within the scope of that definition – to its obliteration, as 'mechanical' obedience to the 'habit' of forming 'thought' intervenes in 'spontaneous feeling', the 'continuance' of the one transforming the 'continued influx' of the other. This is not to say that feeling and thinking, or immediacy and habit, cancel each other, any more than the experience of continuous temporal extension can overrule the experience of spontaneity. It does suggest, however, that in describing poetry as a complex kind of action rather than a recognizable kind of complex language, Wordsworth defines an experience unilaterally unattributable to either the first or the second part of his definition.

The complexity, then, of Wordsworth's most widely circulated definition of poetry, when that definition is read in its entirety, matches that of the subject of poetry he describes. In both there is an interaction of the sensuous and empirical with the reflective and internal that produces not an inarticulate outpouring of feeling but a 'poem', which is to say, language that does not merely register the occurrence of feeling or communicate empirical data but represents givens already shaped by our experience of them and of our own minds' activity: a 'complex scene'. Several other definitions of poetry in the Preface summarize the detailed mental processes preceding and succeeding Wordsworth's reference to 'powerful feelings', and the subject at which these summary definitions aim, the 'worthy *purpose*', as Wordsworth writes, that defines all poets worthy of the name, is what Wordsworth repeatedly calls neither 'feelings', nor even 'the representatives of feelings', 'thoughts', but 'knowledge'. In contrast to the extensive, self-contradictory definition of poetry just discussed, these brief references to knowledge are, like the poetic language Wordsworth commends, strikingly direct, non-complex. Yet the kind, subject and object, of 'knowledge' Wordsworth has in mind he just as clearly leaves undefined. It is these apparently simple definitions and, finally, their complex representation in defining passages of prosaic language in Wordsworth's poetry that an analysis of Wordsworth's poetic theory must address if it is to 'carry along' if not 'enlighten' the Reader's 'understanding' of the unstated – or, as stated – 'formally' unknown 'purpose' at which Wordsworth's theory of poetry and poetry both aim.

Unless one were to consider feeling and knowing to be indistinguishable, it is difficult to harmonize the (partially) familiar definition discussed above with such statements in the Preface as the following:

> What is a Poet? ... He is a man speaking to men: a man, it is true, endowed with more lively sensibility, more enthusiasm and tenderness, who has a greater knowledge of human nature.
>
> (*PW*, 1:138)

> Poetry is the breath and finer spirit of all knowledge. ... Poetry is the first and last of all knowledge – it is as immortal as the heart of man.
>
> (*PW*, 1:141)

> I have said that poetry is the spontaneous overflow of powerful feelings: it takes its origin from emotion recollected in tranquillity: the emotion is contemplated till, by a species of re-action, the tranquillity gradually disappears, and an emotion, kindred to that which was before the subject of contemplation, is gradually produced, and does itself actually exist in the mind.
>
> (*PW*, 1:149)

Finally, when, in the Essay, Supplementary to the Preface, Wordsworth expounds the pitfalls of the public's falling in with decided habits of 'taste', proving by repeated historical example that such habits will only conceal lasting poetic merit not *because* taste changes but because it must *be made to change* by literature itself – 'every author, as far as he is great and at the same time *original*', Wordsworth states emphatically, 'has had the task of *creating* the taste by which he is to be enjoyed' (*PW*, 3:80) – the unspecified notion that poetry is 'first and last of all knowledge' is linked in addition to the unnamed 'power' produced by the creation of 'taste', yet in a manner that Wordsworth does not or cannot elucidate. Speaking of the need of the 'reader', too, to 'exert himself' in reading, to take part in the communication of creative 'power' rather than 'be carried' by the efforts of the poet 'like a dead weight', he states: 'Therefore to create taste is to call forth and bestow power, of which knowledge is the effect; and *there* lies the true difficulty' (*PW*, 3:82).

One can say that the 'true difficulty' of Wordsworth's poetic theory and '*purpose*' of his poetic practice lie '*there*' as well, in the difficulty of indicating what and where that elliptical '*there*' is. For the main burden of Wordsworth's complex poetic theory, a burden consistently, one might say almost 'naturally', misread, owes to its attempt to elucidate and represent the 'true difficulty' of producing in language at once 'philosophical' and 'real' a 'power' whose own immediate effects – disproportionate 'feeling', 'excitement … carried beyond its bounds', and the 'pain' that therein results – and whose media – 'the language really spoken by men' and the 'the co-presence of something regular', 'the power of metre' allowing such an 'irregular state of the mind' to persist – are *not* presented by the poet as identical with the defining purpose of poetry, the very different object of its action: 'knowledge'. It is not the new old axiom that 'knowledge' is 'power', whether in the liberatory or the cynical sense, but the absolutely critical and far more 'difficult' transit *from 'power' to 'knowledge'* that guides the '*purpose*' of poetry according to Wordsworth, permitting us indeed to *read* rather than reject the disturbance to our habits of reading by such 'power', and granting, in so doing, impersonal endurance to its verbally produced effects. How and whether one can go '*there*' from a here composed as much of 'feeling' as its 'recollection' and 'representatives, thought', as much of 'act[ion]' as of 'react[ion]', of 'sensations' as of 'ideas', is the question Wordsworth's difficult theory of poetry raises by implication, and its answer, outlined in practical rather than purely theoretical terms in the Preface, may find its best, if not only, 'real' formulations in the complex experience regularly represented in his poetic work.

Spatial constraints prohibit extensive analysis of Wordsworth's poetry in the present context. Still, the complexity of Wordsworth's theory

and heterogeneous definition of poetry, the explicitly delineated,
and unresolved, contradiction they compose between overpowering
experience and the 'co-presence of something regular' – a 'something'
that may itself consist in categorically different things: the natural
occurrence of 'metre', mindful 'continuance' of '*act[s]*' of contemplation, or involuntary, 'blind' and 'mechanical', 'habits' of mind – may
reflect nothing so much as the 'true difficulty' of deriving 'knowledge'
from 'power', the power that writing and reading poetry first bring to
light. Since the poet who 'does' as Wordsworth's theory describes must
'create' rather than inherit 'taste', 'call[ing] forth' and 'bestow[ing]'
power' by returning poetry first to 'the language really used by men',
it is finally to the language of Wordsworth's own poetry that we must
turn, however briefly, in considering the 'difficulty' to which his theory
of poetry openly admits. Of the many great passages in Wordsworth's
poetry that demonstrate 'the true difficulty' of his poetic principles even
as they put these to the test, a well-known 'experiment' (*PW*, 1:119) – as
Wordsworth calls these poems – from the *Lyrical Ballads* (1800) may
help tell us how the poet arrives 'there' and where the poet gets.

In 'Strange fits of passion I have known' the passage to 'knowledge'
from 'power' is represented as an interruption of experience, a stark dis-
juncture between two interwoven forms of sensation and the mind. The
speaker pursues a familiar course to Lucy's cottage, the forward motion
of his journey provided by the horse that carries him while the moon
provides the point of focus for his sight:

> When she I lov'd, was strong and gay
> And like a rose in June,
> I to her cottage bent my way,
> Beneath the evening moon.
>
> Upon the moon I fix'd my eye,
> All over the wide lea;
> My horse trudg'd on, and we drew nigh
> Those paths so dear to me.
>
> (ll. 5–12)[11]

Inclined in motion, 'bent' towards one goal, the rider 'fix[es]' his 'eye' on
an object whose apparent movement takes place as an inverted mirror
image of his own: 'And now we reach'd the orchard-plot, / And, as we
climb'd the hill, / Towards the roof of Lucy's cot / The moon descended

still' (ll. 13–16). The combination of motion and 'fixed' vision produces a kind of unconsciousness of experience in the traveller, as if the two, very different sensations were indeed and would remain naturally continuous with one another, until, by the force of motion itself, the traveller's visual object vanishes. The poem continues:

> In one of those sweet dreams I slept,
> Kind Nature's gentlest boon!
> And, all the while, my eyes I kept
> On the descending moon.
>
> My horse mov'd on; hoof after hoof
> He rais'd and never stopp'd:
> When down behind the cottage roof
> At once the planet dropp'd.

> (ll. 17–24)

Even as the unceasing movement of the horse carries the traveller closer to his chosen goal, Lucy's home, 'hoof after hoof', it makes the traveller's purely visual point of reference appear to disappear, or rather appear to fall so abruptly as to seem to 'drop' precipitously from the visible scene. The cottage and not the moon is the traveller's destination, yet it is the moon, appearing apart from the external movement that carries him, and to which his body is joined, that provides the counterpoint to the ongoing nature of that motion, its 'never stopp[ing]'. Constant in that it is *not* his goal, neither brought closer to him nor left behind him as he continues on, the movement of the 'descend[ing]' moon is as separate from the traveller's ascent as is the imperceptible motion of the earth upon which he rides. The result of its sudden falling from view is the traveller's equally sudden, internal passage from 'one of those sweet dreams' induced by the senses – 'Kind Nature's gentlest boon!' – to equally exclamatory 'thoughts' of death: 'What fond and wayward thoughts will slide / Into a Lover's head— / "O mercy!" to myself I cried, / "If Lucy should be dead!"' (ll. 25–8).

If the steady hoofbeat, the 'something regular', of riding with his eye focused on the moon provided the traveller with a dream-like sense of Nature's beneficence, in allowing him to apprehend simultaneously the sense of the infinite communicated by the power of motion and the sense of finitude communicated by the visually fixed identity of a distinct thing, the abrupt contradiction of the one by the other that the very coordination of these incommensurables brings about provides instead the opening or angle of another kind of inclination, the bent of 'wayward thoughts'.

They is not feared dead because the traveller sees her in the fallen moon; rather he sees his own seeing as dead, as an act no longer at one with the activity of nature. It is his common *and* essentially poetic ability to be carried forward by movement while otherwise engaging his mind, keeping his eye 'fix'd' on something stable outside the continuing path of motion, that creates the ocular appearance of the moon's disappearance, and 'slide[s]' into its place the 'thought' of Lucy's death.[12] That 'place' is now in the 'Lover's Head', rather than the heavens, and just as the speaker prefaces the poem by stating he 'will dare to tell, / But in the lover's ear alone, / What once to me befel' (l. 4), true to Wordsworth's poetic theory, the objective event retold in 'Strange fits of passion' is at once enacted as subject by the poem itself: the 'wayward thoughts' described to enter 'in the Lover's Head' have now entered the ear of anyone so impassioned by the path of interactive experience the poem powerfully describes. Similarly, that 'thought', being not of Lucy but of her possible death, is the thought of the disappearance from the face of the earth of that which only those who see the earth either as face or surface, cognitive object or plane of movement, can envision, a finite object they join, in the act of moving, with infinity. He who sees or in any way senses the world in an articulate fashion is the locus of intersection between constancy and motion, and when the latter obliterates the former it is also he who notices. Human sense perception adds to the world the perspective from which we, at any given moment, sense as in a 'dream' its unification of things with motion; and *because* it is added to the world, that same perspective forces upon perception unwanted knowledge of the world's disunity. As the locus of the relation between contradictory natural powers that it alone coordinates, and that only the power of coordination can also discover in time to be severed, it is man, the speaker, traveller, and knower of relations of his own making, who, in seeing relation vanish, 'should be dead' by the poem's end. Instead, as his poem relates, the 'representatives' of 'feeling' now 'past', 'thoughts' of what is no longer living, enter into his head. The poet calls that something 'Lucy'; and, 'Lucy' having been the conscious goal that first set him upon 'familiar paths' now turned inward and 'wayward' with contradiction, when it comes to naming what has been lost and gained in his disconcerting journey 'there', he may just as well.

For what dies for Wordsworth in this poem is his theory of poetry, the theory of the continuous 'co-presence of something regular' able to 'throw a sort of half-consciousness of unsubstantial existence over the whole composition', the very sort of absence of thought to which the horse's metred or measured hoofbeats calamitously bring the traveller.

And what lives for Wordsworth is that theory as well, the theory of 'thoughts' that 'will' enter any man's head who lives to experience, whether in the world or in words, the interaction between a continuous and enabling state of 'half-consciousness' and the disabling eruptions of 'powerful' feeling to which such dream-like states unknowingly but inevitably tend: 'thoughts' that do not 'temper' or replace the 'pain' (*PW*, 1:147) of the loss of articulation but occur when, in the very course of 'something regular', the interactions that compose articulation are instead broken, the production of their poetic complexity interrupted.

'Strange fits of passion' presents as a story of experience the impassioned fit of 'something regular' and continuing and something singular and 'fixed'. In the inevitable but always unforeseeable – the 'spontaneous' – severing of these, the poem presents a sublimity joined not to the world but to the complex structure of poetry itself: the 'thought' of 'power', of knowledge regularly overwhelmed, and the 'thought' of the 'knowledge' which is the 'purpose' of poetry' 'first and last of all', its 'difficult' composition of itself, power's 'wayward' 'effect'.

Notes

1. *The Prose Works*, ed. W. J. B. Owen and Jane Worthington Smyser, vol. 1 (Oxford: Clarendon Press, 1974), p. 140. This edition hereafter indicated as *PW* and cited by volume and page numbers in the text. Unless otherwise noted, references to the Preface are to the 1850 text.
2. *'Lyrical Ballads' and Other Poems, 1797–1800*, ed. James Butler and Karen Green (Ithaca, NY: Cornell University Press, 1992), pp. 350–1. Poems in this volume will be cited by line numbers in the text. In defending 'The Thorn' from the criticism that its language is repetitive, Wordsworth includes the status and effect of words as *'things'* among the 'various other reasons why repetition and apparent tautology are frequently beauties of the highest kind' (ibid., p. 351).
3. The interaction of language and mind, noted at the opening of the Preface, logically extends the confluence of philosophy of mind with poetic theory to literary and social theory. Describing his decision not to proffer 'a systematic defense of the theory upon which the [Lyrical Ballads] were written', Wordsworth notes that any such defence would have first to be prefaced by 'a full account of the present state of the public taste', and that, in turn, such an account itself could not be given 'without pointing out in what manner language and the human mind act and re-act on each other, and without retracing the revolutions, not of literature alone, but likewise of society itself' (*PW*, 1:121). Recalling Rousseau's analysis (in *Lettre á d'Alembert* [1758]) of the spiralling social and moral corruption that would be visited upon Geneva by the introduction into its republic of paying theatrical spectacles, Wordsworth describes poets who 'indulge in arbitrary and capricious habits of expression' as producing and enforcing the public expectation for

such expression, furnishing food for fickle tastes, and tickle appetites, of their own creation' (*PW*, 1:125) and, echoing Rousseau's critique of the kind of entertainment popular in Paris, attributes to 'the increasing accumulation of men in cities, where the uniformity of their occupations produces a craving for extraordinary incident', the popularity of 'frantic novels, sickly and stupid German Tragedies, and deluges of idle and extravagant stories in verse' (*PW*, 1:129). The best analytic treatment of the complex cognitive effects of Wordsworth's verbal renderings of experience remains C. C. Clarke's *Romantic Paradox: An Essay on the Poetry of Wordsworth* (London: Routledge & Kegan Paul, 1962), in which the combination of transparency and opacity created both on the lexical and syntactic levels of the poems is examined for its exact representation of the 'paradox' of 'sense perception' itself. In Wordsworth, Clarke argues, '[t]he visionary power ... comes into being through the refinement of a more familiar and pedestrian power, a power manifest in everyday acts of sense-perception'. Yet what emerges with the poems as perception is hardly pedestrian in the commonplace sense: 'distinctions between thought and the objects of thought, things and the feelings that things evoke are (at one level) suspended', and 'it becomes difficult for the reader to sustain without radical qualification a normal, common-sense distinction between the living and the lifeless' (pp. 41, 48–9).

4. See Kant's 'Analytic of the Sublime' in *Werkausgabe*, ed. Wilhelm Weischedel, vol. 10 (Frankfurt am Main: Suhrkamp, 1974), pp. 177, 189, 193, 194: 'In order *to be able merely to think* the given infinite without contradiction, one needs a capacity in the human mind which is in itself supersensory' (§26, B 92); 'Sublimity is not contained in any thing of nature but – insofar as we can become conscious that we surpass the nature that is in us and also thereby (insofar as it influences us) the nature outside us – only in our mind' (§28, B 109); 'One can describe the sublime thus: it is an object (of nature), *whose presentation determines the mind to think to itself the unattainability of nature as a representation of ideas*' (§29, B 115); 'Literally taken and logically considered, ideas cannot be represented. But, when we widen (mathematically or dynamically) our empirical capacity for representation for the purpose of the intuition of nature, reason, as the faculty of the independence [from representation] of absolute totality, unavoidably intervenes, bringing to the fore the futile striving of the mind to make sensory representation commensurate with these [ideas]. This striving, and the feeling of the unattainability of the idea through imagination, is itself a representation of the subjective purposiveness of our mind in using the imagination to determine itself in a supersensible way, and compels us subjectively *to think* nature itself in its totality as the representation of something supersensory, without being able to bring this representation into being *objectively*' (§29, B 116). Original emphases; translations mine.

5. Ibid., p. 179: 'One thus also sees that true sublimity must be sought only in the mind of the one who judges, not in the natural object whose judgement this disposition occasions. Who would want to name unformed masses of mountains, towering above each other in wild disorder, with their pyramids of ice or gloomy roaring sea, etc. sublime? Yet the mind feels itself raised in its own judgement when, in considering these without consideration of

their form, and giving itself over to imagination and to reason which, set into relation to it without specific purpose, merely extends it, it finds the entire power of imagination incommensurate to its ideas' (§26, B 95).

6. See Kant's 'On the Synthetic Origin of the Unity of Apperception' in *Critique of Pure Reason*, quoted from *Werkausgabe*, ed. Wilhelm Weischedel, vol. 3 (Frankfurt am Main: Suhrkamp, 1974), p. 136: 'The: *I think*, must *be able to* accompany all my representations; if not there would be something represented in me which could not be thought, which is as much as to say as: the representation would either be impossible or at least nothing for me. The representation, which can be given before all thinking, is called *intuition*. Thus the entire manifold of intuitions has a necessary relation to the: *I think* in the same subject in which the manifold is encountered ... [A]n act of *spontaneity*, it cannot be viewed to belong to sensuousness. I call it *pure apperception*' (§16, B132–3). Original emphases; translation mine.

   In the unfinished manuscript posthumously entitled 'The Sublime and the Beautiful', published by Owen and Smyser as Appendix III to *A Guide through the District of the Lakes*, and probably written around 1811, Wordsworth, discussing the sublime in relation not to poetry but to the 'visible object[s]' presented by 'forms of Nature' (*PW*, 2:353, 350) partially incorporates Kant's thesis regarding the real location of the sublime in describing it as an experience of 'intense unity' between the 'mind' of the 'Spectator' and an 'external power' (*PW*, 2:354): 'To talk of an object as being sublime or beautiful in itself, without references to some subject by whom that sublimity or beauty is perceived, is absurd' (*PW*, 2:357). Despite his repeated disclaimers of ever having read it, Wordsworth's familiarity with the interrelated premises and overarching structure of Kant's *Critique* is most clearly indicated in this later work by his own repeated relation of the sublime to 'the moral law': 'it may be confidently said that, unless the apprehensions which [the Power contemplated] excites terminate in repose, there can be no sublimity, & that this sense of repose is the result of reason and the moral law' (*PW*, 2:355; cf. 356, 357). On Wordsworth's avowed ignorance of Kant's writings, see Duncan Wu, *Wordsworth's Reading 1800–1815* (Cambridge: Cambridge University Press, 1998), pp. 261–2.

7. In *Wordsworth's Theory of Poetic Diction* (New Haven, CT: Yale University Press, 1917), Marjorie Latta Barstow argued early for the consonance of Wordsworth's view of poetic language with that which characterized English poetry before the seventeenth century. While Barstow also astutely remarks on Wordsworth's endeavour 'to make his syntax reflect the movements of impassioned thought', her equation of Wordsworth's 'interest in words' with an interest in 'metaphors' capable of 'substitut[ing] imagery for language' (pp. 126, 177) seems particularly misplaced. For a contrasting view of Wordsworth's 'simplicity' of style as a devaluation of the verbal in itself, see John F. Danby, *The Simple Wordsworth: Studies in the Poems, 1797–1807* (London: Routledge & Kegan Paul, 1971 [1960]), p. 16: 'Wordsworth, at heart, we might say, was profoundly uninterested in poetry as words.' Observing, at the same time, that Wordsworth was 'committed ... to the public necessity of utterance', the non-verbal proclivity Danby attributes to this inordinately voluminous poet underscores, however perversely, the proximity of the experience of language to the experience of experience in Wordsworth's poems.

8. Whether or not his own writing attempts to mime the mind of the 'simple Child' to which it gives voice, it is clear that 'throwing words away' – whether in single-minded questioning or gratuitous 'poetic diction' – represents an unreflective relation to language that neither Wordsworth nor his 'simple' speaker has in mind. The child's confounding of the first-person speaker's (and by extension, the reader's) expectations of what counts at any moment in time, her inability or refusal to discount the presence of the dead ('How many *are* you') on the sole basis of their visible corporal absence, and her uncanny verbal incorporation instead of number itself in the slightest of syntactic reversals (from 'Seven are we' to 'We are Seven') effectively shift the burden of simplicity (much like that of life and death) from the child to her adult questioner. What Wordsworth demonstrates in the meantime is that such thoroughly prosaic accounts as the child's of her siblings' ongoing existence – their known presence not in heaven but in prosaic places marked and frequented – effortlessly presents to the unaccustomed narrator/reader just such a 'complex scene of ideas and sensations' regarded by the common man as poets, according to the Preface, consider.

9. First among these 'abuses' in the Preface are 'personifications of abstract ideas' (*PW*, 1:131). In the Appendix to the Preface adumbrating 'what is usually called Poetic Diction', Wordsworth goes on to excoriate all 'invented' 'modes of expression', the 'unusual language' and 'adulterated phraseology' that, severed from experience and 'imported from one nation to another', 'became daily more and more corrupt', i.e., less like the 'real language' of men contemplating the 'complex scene' of their interaction with the world than the false currencies of the suppositious sideshows distracting them from it: a 'motley masquerade of tricks, quaintnesses, hieroglyphics, and enigmas' (*PW*, 1:161–2).

10. The truncation of this quotation in Wordsworth criticism is nearly coextensive with that criticism itself. Its pervasiveness is perhaps best indicated in small by a fine recent study unusually questioning its claim on Wordsworth himself. Suggesting that, though he 'became famous for equating the best poetry with a spontaneous overflow of feeling', Wordsworth, some 14 years after writing the Preface, expressed 'second thoughts about this expression', Susan Wolfson still adheres to the traditional partial transmission of Wordsworth's two-part definition, omitting to mention the long second half in which such 'second thoughts' are already both stated *and* declared necessary. Wolfson instead cites a letter of 1814 in which, in markedly less detailed terms, Wordsworth states the same view yet again: 'My first expressions I often find detestable; and it is frequently true of second words as of second thoughts, that they are the best.' 'Wordsworth's Craft', in *The Cambridge Companion to Wordsworth*, ed. Stephen Gill (Cambridge: Cambridge University Press, 2003), p. 123.

By contrast, James A. W. Heffernan's study of Wordsworth's poetic theory offers a baseline indication of how little the full definition is read. For Heffernan, while quoting Wordsworth's complex sentence in its entirety, simply ignores the explicit meaning of its second half, commenting that, for Wordsworth, 'consciousness plays no part in the creative act itself', and obliterating thereby Wordsworth's explicit assertion that any poetry worth reading is the 'product' of 'long' and 'deep' 'thought'. *Wordsworth's Theory of Poetry* (Ithaca, NY: Cornell University Press, 1969), p. 43.

In attempting to account for the curtailment of Wordsworth's complex definition of poetry by its reception, one should note that, towards the end of the Preface, the poet himself quotes his own previous statement only in part, stopping at the full colon mark that punctuates its internal division. Once again, however, he immediately contradicts the content of that opening, apparently unilateral assertion, reiterating, in the words that follow, the necessity to poetry of non-spontaneous mental activity also specified in the prior utterance.

11. A helpful and insightful investigation of the centuries of criticism devoted to and recent critical debates centred upon the 'Lucy poems' is offered by Mark Jones in *The 'Lucy Poems': A Case Study in Literary Knowledge* (Toronto: University of Toronto Press, 1995). While noting that it was Margaret Oliphant, before Arnold, who first established the five poems, written in Goslar, Germany, from 1798 to 1799, as a group (see p. 71), Jones reminds us that despite Wordsworth's unusual 'silence' (p. 6) on their subject, 'he still placed the poems in a way that suggested the grouping he did not create' (p. 9).

12. For a similar view of the speaker's 'thought' as taking the place vacated by the moon, see Robert Marchant, *Principles of Wordsworth's Poetry* (Swansea: Brynmill, 1974), p. 45.

6
Dying into Prose: The Standard of Taste in Wordsworth's *Essays upon Epitaphs*

Soelve Curdts

1

> His Muse (it cannot be denied, and without this we cannot explain its character at all) is a levelling one. It proceeds on a principle of equality, and strives to reduce all things to the same standard.[1]

Hazlitt defines the quality of Wordsworth's Muse in ways that are crucial to the present argument both literally and figuratively. On the literal level, Hazlitt is one of the first critics to recognize the revolutionary quality of Wordsworth's poetic endeavour both in political and in aesthetic terms. Wordsworth's poetry, he suggests, 'is one of the innovations of the time. It partakes of, and is carried along with, the revolutionary movement of our age: the political changes of the day were the model on which he formed and conducted his poetical experiments.'[2] The figure of 'levelling', moreover, implicitly links Wordsworth's revolutionary aesthetics with the 'great leveller' explored in *Essays upon Epitaphs*.

In what follows, I shall argue for the critical significance of this linkage of death and its perceptions, on the one hand, and Wordsworth's poetics, on the other, as it unfolds from the Prefaces to the *Essays upon Epitaphs*. These liminal reflections, to which the epitaphic mode gives rise, bring to the fore a manner of thinking which is structurally constitutive of Wordsworth's deeply prosaic theory of poetry, and whose formal levelling inextricably binds together poetry and prose in the universality of 'every subject which can interest the human mind'.[3] Where Wordsworth's explicit poetics reflects on the lyric from beyond the limits of prose, as in the Preface to *Lyrical Ballads*, the *Essays upon Epitaphs* fully unfold the workings of liminal reflection as such.

Wordsworth's epitaphic reflections, by their unavoidable wider consideration of limits *qua* limits – of death as the precondition of all liminality – form a critical precondition of our understanding of his theory of poetry. The epitaphic mode gives rise to reflections on death as the limit of life, while at the same time it prompts an inquiry into how we reflect upon limits. Wordsworth's epitaphic reflections expand across time on multiple layers, until they have reached the hypothetical limit of timelessness – death – beyond which the time-bound living cannot venture. The 'whence' and 'whither' of the first *Essay upon Epitaphs* imply such liminal explorations: into the past, 'whence', and into the future, 'whither':

> For, if we had no direct external testimony that the minds of very young children meditate feelingly upon death and immortality, these inquiries, which we all know they are perpetually making concerning the *whence*, do necessarily include correspondent habits of interrogation concerning the *whither*. Origin and tendency are notions inseparably co-relative. Never did a child stand by the side of a running stream, pondering within himself what power was the feeder of the perpetual current, from what never-wearied sources the body of water was supplied, but he must have been inevitably propelled to follow this question by another: 'Towards what abyss is it in progress? what receptacle can contain the mighty influx?'
>
> (*PW*, 2:51)

Transposed onto the figure of the child these reflections gain several speculative layers. To begin with, the adult writer of the essay imagines reflections on past and future, on origin and telos, in the child. At the same time, however, the child is taken as an originary validation of these very reflections. Futurity, moreover, is farther removed still, as it is drawn out as an implication of the child's inquiry into origins. To the layer of transposition onto the child is added the farther remove of a futurity that is merely implicit in questions about the past. Finally, the image of the child reflecting on the 'whence' and 'whither' is itself supplied with an image of the stream symbolizing the child's inquiry into 'origin' and 'tendency'. In their very form, then, these liminal reflections are aware of their own liminality. They probe the limits of our existence both in their content and in the form they seek. It is precisely the tension of this form, and the limits it engages, which makes the interpenetrations of the language of prose and the language of poetry an integral part of Wordsworth's epitaphic inquiry.

The subject of epitaphs raises the question of how, in what form, to respond to the last finality of death. It posits an extreme with which human language must come to terms, for which forms must be found that contain their own inevitable inadequacy. In Wordsworth's theorization, the epitaphic mode counterbalances the radical rupture it confronts in death with simplicity, regularity, even a formulaic quality. Thus the language of epitaphs does not claim adequately to render the extreme pain to which it bears witness by means of hyperbolic figures and expressions. For Wordsworth, the epitaph is at its most convincing where such linguistic excesses are absent. Where the things to be represented are excessive – grief and mourning after death – this is not an obvious argument to make. Wordsworth is therefore in need of a theory of poetry and language which can account for his conception of the epitaphic mode.

In its encounter with the great leveller, as we shall see, Wordsworth's poetics levels hierarchies of poetry and prose at the same time as common language is made to confront time's passage and decay. It is in his reflections upon epitaphs that Wordsworth reveals this linkage of poetry and prose to be constitutive of his theory of poetry. Where the Prefaces assert the linkage of poetry and prose, the *Essays upon Epitaphs* unfold a theory of language which renders this linkage significant, indeed constitutive of any inquiry into the workings of literature. Ultimately, Wordsworth predicates his theory of making, *poiein*, on transience and decay.[4] To recall Paul de Man's incisive observation, the imagination in Wordsworth's poetry is in tension not so much with nature as with time.[5]

The 'levelling' of poesis and the 'levelling' of the graveyard are further intertwined if we consider Geoffrey Hartman's linkage of the graveyard and nature.[6] While Hartman reads this convergence in a move towards increasing directness, it is also possible to view it as an indication of the 'topicality', and the constructed monumentality, of nature in Wordsworth's poetry. In this sense, 'nature' becomes part of the poet's engraving mind, thinking – as Hartman goes on to argue – the ephemerality of its own presiding spirit. This points up the inquiry into 'origin' and 'tendency' in its privative implications. As immortality renders thinkable finality and death, the image of infinity cannot but take forms that are consciously ephemeral. If such 'inscriptions' are 'on' the ephemerality of the spirit of poesis, they can be read not as 'nature poetry', but as 're-marking' the indeterminacy between language and semantics, between word and referent, between tropes and meaning, as Cynthia Chase has richly demonstrated.[7] Significantly for the present context, in Wordsworth's epitaphic reflections such indeterminacy comes to inhabit the very interpenetrations of poesis and critical judgment.

2

Wordsworth's poetic theory insists that epitaphs give an accounting: they must gauge the limits of experience via death, even as they put life in the past – one human being at a time. They engrave the temporal and chronological limits of a life, and yet by their very existence as epitaphs they are gestures which point beyond the chronology they inscribe towards a remembering and commemorative future. As mere gestures, epitaphs in this sense necessarily fail to give full expression to the encounter with death of which they are a trace. And yet, precisely to the extent that no adequation is thinkable to the finality (or infinity, Wordsworth might add) which presents no living experience to adequate, the epitaphic gesture is the more adequate the more it points up the emptiness of any attempt at adequation.

Cognizance of this problematic leads to a mode of critique that expands Wordsworth's poetics as a whole in so far as it generally under-mines the delimitability of an ornate, elevated style. The more ornate, elevated, and strenuous the attempt of any epitaph to find adequate terms to circumscribe a past life, the more fully inadequate the epitaph becomes. Conversely, to produce an image of adequacy in the face of death, the epitaph must work with a kind of emptiness or generality:

> The first requisite, then, in an Epitaph is, that it should speak, in a tone which shall sink into the heart, the general language of humanity as connected with the subject of death – the source from which an epitaph proceeds – of death, and of life. To be born and to die are the two points in which all men feel themselves to be in absolute coincidence.
>
> (*PW*, 2:57)

This stipulation follows upon the discussion of 'refinements' to be avoided. Its admonition concerns a kind of judgement and discrimina-tion. For the writer of an epitaph, the means of production lie in the ordinary, the habitual, in language common to all men. The epitaphic generality to which Wordsworth refers, however, uses the ordinary as a deliberate outgrowth of aesthetic judgement. Like 'poetic diction' in the Preface to *Lyrical Ballads*, the sense of elevation, of discrimination and 'refinements' in the epitaphic mode points to possibilities of adequation which cannot but turn out to be delusional in the face of death; a tone too high to sink into the heart would strike a definite false note.[8]

Death, the passage quoted seems to suggest, requires universality. Or, to be more precise, it recalls 'all men' to their 'absolute coincidence' in birth and death. Thus not only the universal, but also its recalling, its recollection in the face of death, must be articulated in the epitaph, which cannot be elevated beyond the limits of a memento. Sublimity, beauty, even the imagination – all these aesthetic categories are here brought to a determined scope. Outweighed by the urgency of 'sincerity', which the *Essays upon Epitaphs* go on to treat at length, these conventional ingredients of aesthetics give way to 'the general language of humanity', whose commonplaces are individual, universal, and elusive enough to approximate the effects of death's decomposition.

The Wordsworthian epitaph retains just as much particularity as is necessary to enter the universal. Without its expression in the particular, the universal would in itself become particularized. Foregoing any trace of the particular, the universal would not, so to speak, be universally accessible, 'all men' would not be recalled to it. The epitaph therefore generalizes the individual, forming the universal through a particular trace at each inscription. The 'general language of humanity' recalls each individual to the universal in the face of death, recalls to each individual this universal finality. Such double 'recalling' intricately binds the reader and writer of an epitaph to its referent. It creates for the epitaph a universal 'subject': the subject reading, the subject writing, and the subject of the epitaph. This last, being dead, is presumably recalled to death's universality in the sense inscribed by the epitaph. To its reader and writer, on the other hand, the epitaph recalls their eventual partaking of the same: 'Pause courteous Stranger!' (*PW* 2:89).[9]

In keeping with this unique entanglement in the universal, the epitaph replaces a nuanced balance of an individual biography with the commonplace chronology of birth, death, and perhaps a few dates in between. Its general topoi universalize the individual, apparently without losing it – or the sense of loss – in abstraction. The *Essays upon Epitaphs* endow the laconic uniformity with which loss is expressed on tombstones in country churchyards with critical significance in such a way as to pose the question of 'sincerity', of the uniqueness of each individual act of mourning, on an entirely new plane:

> Enter a Church-yard by the Sea-coast, and you will be almost sure to find the Tomb-stones crowded with metaphors taken from the Sea and a Sea-faring life. These are uniformly in the same strain; but

surely we ought not thence to infer that the words are used of course without any heart-felt sense of their propriety. Would not the contrary conclusion be right?

(*PW*, 2:65)

The 'contrary conclusion' implies that the uniformity with which the 'general language of humanity' concretely manifests itself on tombstone after tombstone not only does not detract from its 'heart-felt sense', but in fact adds to this sense in ways unattainable by conventional strivings after originality. Originating solely with the individual, the language of epitaphs, as it emerges from Wordsworth's *Essays*, would become either trite (the false note analysed above), or altogether unintelligible, hence forgoing its status as language. For, if the radicality of each individual loss produced a true utterance of its own, such an utterance would increasingly forego the commonality inherent in all language, to the extent that its expression of grief would become more and more specific to the individual, more and more 'original'. Where common language is likely to render it false, the 'original' utterance of this most individual loss brought by death must have recourse to expressions completely and exclusively its own. Whatever such expressions might be, they would leave the realm of language.

Each individual radical loss in this sense, then, is truly unspeakable. So, to render itself intelligible at all, to provide measure where the outer limit of human measure has been reached, the language of epitaphs stands in need of laconicity of expression, and of the topical, perhaps formulaic recurrence of metaphors drawn from the ordinariness and uniformity of human life.

Like the language of the lyric, the language of epitaphs has recourse to what is repeatable, even predictable, to provide measure and hence articulability to the 'heart-felt sense'. In such recurrence, repeatability, and predictability, both the language of epitaphs and the language of the lyric remain suspended in the universal tangle analysed above. They forego direct adequation to any sense, thing, or being, only to forge all the more fully out of its ostensibly threadbare, used, hand-me-down topical repertory the sense of sense, thing, being, or loss – perhaps to outlast their reality.

Where identical topoi recur as expressions of grief, their repetition makes visible their formulaic character, the more so, the more unique, individual, and 'heart-felt' each grief expressed is imagined to be. The more frequently topoi recur in the same contextual setting, the more predictable they will become, until they are completely clichéd. Wordsworth notes this both in the *Essays upon Epitaphs* and in the

Prefaces. At the same time, the subject of the epitaph, presumably an eruption of grief as radical as the loss that caused it, throws this ossifying process of the 'heart-felt sense' into particularly stark relief. Where correspondence is expected between the uniqueness of each grief and its articulation, we find, instead, Wordsworth suggests, the same predictable formulae. The very enormity of what is to be articulated seems to induce this ostensible lack of correspondence, while the very absence of a linguistic corollary to the excess of grief that comes with death approximates the inarticulability of the matter with which each epitaph is concerned. In this sense, the simple repeated formula marks a deeper correspondence between each epitaph and its subject matter.

Used again and again, the epitaphic formula reinforces the 'absolute coincidence' that makes of every individual loss mourned the occurrence, recurrence, of death as the most universal human phenomenon. The recurrence of topoi in epitaphic writing partially mirrors the recurrence and predictability of death. Thereby epitaphs forego more immediate correlations with any particular instance of death, the overwhelming and ineffable nature of which is marked by this very absence. The language of the epitaph leaves a trace of this tension between the particular and the general.

It is no coincidence that we find 'the very language of men' (*PW*, 1:131) that Wordsworth links to poetry in a role not unlike that of the epitaph's 'general language of humanity' (*PW*, 2:57).[10] Before returning to the latter, the former should be analysed closely for its critical and theoretical significance.

3

In the Preface to *Lyrical Ballads*, Wordsworth transposes a universal claim, made in the Advertisement, from 'every subject which can interest the human mind' (*PW*, 1:116) to poetic form itself:

> There will also be found in these volumes little of what is usually called poetic diction; as much pains has been taken to avoid it as is ordinarily taken to produce it; this has been done for the reason already alleged, to bring my language near to the language of men.
>
> (*PW*, 1:131)

The absence of 'poetic diction' irredeemably entangles the lyric in 'the language of men'. Herein lies the possibility of the complete autonomization of the aesthetic as well as the total risk of its coming to naught: where poetry and prose are indistinguishable, where the whole universe of 'the language of men' can partake of poetry but where, conversely, the poetic project is laid open to all the incisions of language and its universality, the poetic disappears as an expression of conventionally set linguistic confines. In its place, the possibility of the poetic lurks at any linguistic juncture. However, such potential poetic omnipresence carries with it the privative implication that the lyric, at any given temporal or linguistic juncture, runs the risk of falling – to be more precise, of having fallen – unawares into the quotidian, hackneyed, and clichéd. The universality gained by poetry in the process of 'levelling' its language with the language of prose creates the same formal condition of possibility for the lyric and cliché. Its diction unlimited, poetry can either elevate the 'language of men' or fall into its most quotidian uses.

Recurrence and repetition can be the mark of both the lyric and the cliché, of careful poetic construction or simple overuse. While the status of the lyric differs radically from that of the cliché, Wordsworth's conceptualization implies a challenge constantly to justify why this should be so. Neither conceptually, in his universalizing of the aesthetic realm, nor in the concrete formal descriptions of his own working process do we find a clear demarcating line between the quotidian and the poetic. Indeed, it is precisely the absence of any line of demarcation between these realms which Wordsworth draws out to the fullest. It is the radicality of his own aesthetics which propels Wordsworth to speak of cliché:

> I have also thought it expedient to restrict myself still further, having abstained from the use of many expressions, in themselves proper and beautiful, but which have been foolishly repeated by bad Poets, till such feelings of disgust are connected with them as it is scarcely possible by any art of association to overpower.
>
> (*PW*, 1:133)

As the previous analysis indicates, this critique of cliché is inextricably bound up with Wordsworth's new, prosaic conception of poetry. Clichés in the lyric can be critiqued as such, precisely because the delimited realm of 'poetic diction' no longer safeguards it from the incisions of prose and the reading of its language. Wordsworth's revolutionary 'levelling' here operates both on the level of the literary work itself and on the level of critical thinking. Like the language of prose, the language of poetry is now exposed to being read *qua* language, with all its ordinary expressions. While this means that prose can be read poetically, it also implies that the hackneyed and quotidian in poetry can no longer escape its recognition as such by means of recourse to 'poetic diction', and that critique likewise must continue to come to terms with the formal equivalence of the lyric and cliché laid bare by Wordsworth's theory of poetry.

For Hegel, the 'ordinary' (*das Gewöhnliche*), that which has lost all freshness by repeated use, transitions into prose:

> For much that in earlier times had as yet been fresh, by repeated use and the habit that is thus formed, gradually itself becomes ordinary, and makes its transition into prose.[11]

But whereas for Hegel the ordinary, the habitual, the used or clichéd, constitutes a move away from poetry, for Wordsworth it forges both a new poetic project and a revolution of aesthetic judgement, the radicality of which comes into its own where it might least be expected: in the upholding of metrical composition, arguably the quintessential mark of poetry. For if indeed 'there neither is, nor can be, any *essential* difference' (*PW*, 1:135) between metrical and prosaic language, why would metre be at all necessary? The answer to this question bears quoting at length, as it will eventually elucidate the epitaphic mode, and the 'contrary conclusion', which valorizes uniformity, repeatability, even predictability, to give expression to the 'heart-felt sense':

> But various causes might be pointed out why, when the style is manly, and the subject of some importance, words metrically arranged will long continue to impart such a pleasure to mankind as he who proves the extent of that pleasure will be desirous to impart. The end of Poetry is to produce excitement in co-existence with an overbalance of pleasure; but, by the supposition, excitement is an unusual and irregular state of the mind; ideas and feelings do not, in that state, succeed each other in accustomed order. If the words, however, by which this excitement is produced be in themselves powerful, or the images and feelings have an undue proportion of pain connected with them, there is some danger that the excitement may be carried beyond its proper bounds. Now the co-presence of something regular, something to which the mind has been accustomed in various moods and in a less excited state, cannot but have great efficacy in tempering and restraining the passion by an intertexture of ordinary feeling.
>
> (*PW*, 1:147)

At first glance, this seems to be an almost neoclassical aesthetics of balance, which takes 'metrum' at its most literal. The 'measure' furnished by its regularity appears to keep in proper bounds any excess of pleasure or pain which might result from the representation of powerful passions. Intimately connected, however, with the process of thus counterbalancing potentially unwieldy subject matter which in prose, it would appear, would leave the domain of aesthetic form for the unbounded production of excess and measurelessness, there is a deeply prosaic sense of metre itself. Any measure which is invoked as negation of its potential absence implies what it is to negate. Measure here is not posited in and of itself, but as a counterpoint to excess, or 'excitement carried beyond its proper bounds', and it thus partakes of a negative dialectic by which regularity is intelligible and necessary to the extent that the possibility of its absence is realized in the prosaic. Number itself, upon which metre depends, is a boundless measure: infinite in the possibility of its additions, infinitely repeatable in constellations.

Metre is 'ordinary' because its recurrent rhyme and rhythm create a sense of what might be expected. Like the cliché or commonplace, it is predictable, and the fact that it shares this quality with the quotidian, the habitual, the ordinary, takes it out of any special realm of 'poetic diction' and into the realm of the prosaic. The aesthetic quality of metre, Wordsworth's poetics suggests, depends not upon its extraordinary elevation, but upon the regularity of the measure it provides: the principle of finding 'similitude in dissimilitude' is, amongst other things, 'the life of our ordinary conversation' (*PW*, 1:149).

We are now in a position to return to the epitaphic mode, which is in sore need of a dose of the ordinary in the sense of Wordsworth's aesthetic justification of metre.

4

Epitaphs do not – or not necessarily – rhyme in the literal sense. They do, however, partake of the interplay of similitude and dissimilitude which Wordsworth associates with metrical language, as their larger rhythm consists in the recurrence of certain metaphors and topoi, 'uniformly in the same strain' (*PW*, 2:65). Punctured by such recurrence, epitaphic writing is likewise measured, both within the text of each epitaph and across different epitaphs. Wordsworth's deeply prosaic justification of metre, then, holds for the epitaphic mode as well, perhaps even more fully than for other modes of writing. All the thematic risks that contribute to the formal necessity of metre are present – even gaining the greatest possible force – in each epitaph.

Regarding metrical composition, Wordsworth refers to the possibility of measure being undone by 'excitement … carried beyond its proper bounds', and an 'undue proportion of pain' (PW, 1:147) There are risks of measurelessness which inhere all the more profoundly in the epitaph's attempt to level the thresholds at which it stands: the threshold of experience and its absence as discussed earlier, but also the temporal threshold of past, present, and future. The former threshold embodies both fullness and depletion to excess. It marks the most absolute of human experiences, beyond which – almost at the same time – living experience comes to an end. The remains of this transition are perceptible only from the outside, which is precisely the problematics captured by the epitaphic mode and its topoi.

Externality, however, also engages the threshold of time. The past life, of which the epitaph is a memento, has become external to the present. Since the epitaph also gestures towards a commemorative future, it necessarily begins to externalize the present as well, which will have become past to the very futurity for which the epitaph is left. The epitaph demands a memory which projects its continuing possibility into the future, whilst thereby pushing any given instance of its present occurrence into the past. Such memory, which gives the epitaphic sign of dismantling its present for the mere possibility of continuing in the future, is well served by the mechanics of recurrence.

Like rhyme schemes in a metrical composition, images and other commonplaces recur in epitaphic writing in variations of what is expected or transformed, of similitude and dissimilitude. As Paul de Man notes in his allegorical, temporalizing reading of Hegel's aesthetics, formal recurrence in poetry, precisely because of its very mechanicity and externality, lends itself to being learned by heart.[12] In the *Essays upon Epitaphs*, Wordsworth carries this realization one step further, from the realm of reading and memorization into processes of writing and poetic production. The formal preconditions of learning by heart furnish the very means to express the 'heart-felt sense' (*PW*, 2:65).

Thus, the epitaphic mode gives rise to a critique which binds together an interpretation of the object of reading, and of reading or judgement itself. It exposes the truly common grounds of critical perception and poetic production, without thereby equating the two. Their commonality lies in the search for measure in the full consciousness that the medium of both production and perception – language – has been demeasured. Since, as we have seen, such demeasuring inheres in the very nature of both the object and the mode of Wordsworth's critique, measure must be sought in the ordinary that remains, since language, again in the very terms of Wordsworth's endeavour, has no limits of art to fall back upon. An inquiry into a mode of writing which brings this to the fore reveals the conceptual basis of Wordsworth's theory of poetry: the written or engraved gestures with which Wordsworth's epitaphic inquiry is concerned leave temporal figures of the 'levelling muse' which had entangled poetry and prose in the same unbounded language.

Hazlitt's imagery of 'levelling', with which this essay began, can now be seen in the light of a new critical significance in which measure plays no small part. His conception of the 'levelling muse' is grounded in a description of Wordsworth's 'style':

> His style is vernacular: he delivers household truths. He sees nothing loftier than human hopes; nothing deeper than the human heart. This he probes, this he tampers with, this he poises, with all its incalculable weight of thought and feeling, in his hands; and at the same time calms the throbbing pulses of his own heart, by keeping his eye ever fixed on the face of nature. If he can make the life-blood flow from the wounded breast, this is the living colouring with which he paints his verse: if he can assuage the pain or close up the wound with the balm of solitary musing, or the healing power of plants and herbs and 'skyey influences', this is the sole triumph of his art.[13]

This quotation in itself contains quotation marks. That these should not be placed deliberately around 'skyey influences' by the critic of Shakespeare is difficult to conceive. 'Skyey influences' not only figure prominently in *Measure for Measure* in the Duke's 'Reason thus with life' speech, but they also give expression to life's contingency, the very opposite of its natural healing power which Hazlitt ostensibly invokes:

> Reason thus with life:
> If I do lose thee, I do lose a thing
> That none but fools would keep. A breath thou art,
> Servile to all the skyey influences,
> That dost this habitation, where thou keep'st
> Hourly afflict ...
> *(Measure for Measure,* III.1.6–11)[14]

Contextualized in this way, the language of 'skyey influences' betrays the 'healing power' Hazlitt ostensibly attributes to Wordsworth. As the Duke's speech draws out life in all its vitiating uncertainty, it points up precisely those things to which, according to Hazlitt's critical claim, Wordsworth establishes an antidote. Even in its very imagery, the language of 'hourly' affliction is opposed to 'healing'. Thus Hazlitt's Shakespearean gesture makes his language slip into the opposite of his critical assessment. This is significant for our context, as the contingencies of life and death are brought to bear upon Wordsworth's poetic project as a whole. Precisely these contingencies constitute a crucial precondition for Wordsworth's reflections upon epitaphs, ultimately triggering the deeply critical endeavour of judging language and its workings.

Wordsworth ostensibly opposes two models of language. On the one hand, there is the 'counter-spirit' with its potential 'to derange, to subvert, to lay waste, to vitiate, and to dissolve' (*PW*, 2:85). Not explicitly valorized, this model is presented with all the verbal force furnished by a list of infinitives, climactically arranged from derangement to complete dissolution. The opposite model comes in the form of a hypothetical negation in which it makes room for the 'laying waste' of the 'vitiating' counter-spirit: 'Language, if it do not uphold, and feed, and leave in quiet, like the power of gravitation or the air we breathe' (*PW*, 2:85). This first, 'non-counter-spirit' model of language is presented both as a hypothetical ('if ...') and as a negation ('if it do not ...'). Unlike the 'counter-spirit' model with its forceful enumeration of verbs, this first model of language almost appears as a mere speculative possibility through which to endow the 'counter-spirit' with its full resonance. Or is it the 'counter-spirit' itself which has turned traitor to any description of something not itself? In other words, does Wordsworth's language anticipate the subversive slippage of Hazlitt's critique?

Even the imagery of the 'positive' model of language which Wordsworth seems to valorize, i.e. the model which, as shown above, is presented negatively in Wordsworth's language, speaks of vitiation and entanglement. Does the 'power of gravitation' to which this first model of language is likened really 'leave in quiet'? Or is all the 'air we breathe' (the second part of the simile) a gentle blessing? We seem to be back with all the 'skyey' (or 'earthly') influences the contingency of which Hazlitt has marked in his quotation of Shakespeare. The language upheld as leaving 'in quiet' is unsettled by the figures of its description. Constructed, like Hazlitt's 'healing power', as an antidote to the vitiation of contingency, it is entangled in this very contingency by its own figurative manner of proceeding.

Wordsworth's language, in anticipating the entrapments of the figures and images of its critique, opens aesthetic judgement to the very risks which judgement had laid bare in poetry and prose. The 'levelling muse' does not stop short of its own position. As with measure – metrum – aesthetic judgement, too, is not elevated or fixed; for, in each sentence it pronounces, it too partakes of the ordinary figures and repetitions of language. Therefore, each epitaphic inscription projects a finality with which aesthetic judgement – figuratively inscribing its own 'levelling' and contingency – appears to be in fruitful tension.

On the other hand, as we have seen, the epitaph in its recourse to formal, even formulaic patterns clearly marks itself as a projection only. Its finality is an image that can recur with each new inscription. Judgement, falling from its own assertion by way of its linguistic and citational figures, keeps the finality of its predications as a mere gesture. This analogy to the epitaphic mode renders (Wordsworth's) aesthetic judgement like – and unlike – the object of its reflection in the *Essays upon Epitaphs*. As Wordsworth's critique points up the difficulties of adequation, showing how in the very recurrence of topoi and patterns epitaphs give an account of these difficulties, aesthetic judgement encounters its own problems of correspondence. Its figures do not correspond to the finality of predication it asserts *qua* judgement. At the same time, in projecting such finality, judgement succumbs – however momentarily – to the illusion of death. At each pronouncement, aesthetic judgement believes in the fixedness or at least the fixability of the art it critiques, while in Wordsworth's profoundly modern reflection it also marks the illusory nature of this belief. Aesthetic judgement puts its object in the past, as it were, thus asserting its own presence. At the same time, critical judgement implicitly articulates a commemorative future for which it predicates. The temporal gestures of the epitaph recur here; however, in aesthetic judgement they are merely figurative.

Epitaphs, on the other hand, deal with the reality of death. The illusion they project is therefore one of correspondence, of believing, at least for the moment of each inscription, that they can be adequate to this reality. In their ordinariness and recurrence, the formal patterns of epitaphic writing clearly reveal this illusion as such, and thus destroy it before it can become anything more than an abstract claim, decomposed in each epitaph that is being written. The great leveller in *Measure for Measure* 'makes these odds all even' (III.1.41). The ending of the Duke's speech in Shakespeare's play is ironized from the start, as it is addressed to Claudio, who hopes to live, and this irony is fully borne out as the scene progresses. Death's power, then, is highly uneven when viewed externally from life. In his critical complement to the ironization of Wordsworth's healing power, Hazlitt's invocation also points up the problematics of 'levelling', which cannot but be viewed perspectively from the outside.

In Wordsworth's theory of poetry, this unevenness recurs in the common (linguistic) grounds of aesthetic production and critical judgement as analysed above, with which, if it is to continue at all, each act of reading must come to terms while avoiding the completion of the equation or, metaphorically put, its own 'levelling'. Such avoidance, without evading the chasm of equivalencies Wordsworth's inquiry has opened up, is the challenge which his theorizations of poetic and epitaphic writing have posed for modern critique.

Notes

1. William Hazlitt, 'Mr. Wordsworth', in *The Spirit of the Age: Or Contemporary Portraits* (Oxford: Woodstock Books, 1989), p. 233.
2. Hazlitt, 'Mr. Wordsworth', p. 233.
3. 'Advertisement to *Lyrical Ballads*', in *The Prose Works*, ed. W. B. Owen and Jane Worthington Smyser, vol. 1 (Oxford: Clarendon Press, 1974), p. 116. The *Prose Works* are hereafter indicated as *PW* and cited by volume and page numbers in the text.
4. For a contextualization of Wordsworthian aesthetics in light of previous lines of thought, with some discussion of the restorative powers of the imagination generally attributed to Wordsworth, see Ronald Paulson, *Breaking and Remaking: Aesthetic Practice in England, 1700–1820* (New Brunswick: Rutgers University Press, 1989).
5. See Paul de Man, 'Time and History in Wordsworth', *Diacritics*, 17 (1987), 4–17. For an historical grounding of Wordsworth's epitaphic aesthetics as a chiasmic counter to neoclassicism, see Sanford Budick, 'Chiasmus and the Making of Literary Tradition: The Case of Wordsworth and "The Days of Dryden and Pope"', *ELH*, 60 (1993), 961–87. Budick's and de Man's accounts are complementary rather than mutually exclusive.
6. See Geoffrey H. Hartman, 'Wordsworth's Inscriptions and Romantic Nature Poetry', in *Beyond Formalism: Literary Essays, 1958–1970* (New Haven, CT: Yale University Press, 1970), pp. 206–30.
7. See Cynthia Chase, 'Monument and Inscription: Wordsworth's "Lines"', *Diacritics*, 17 (1987), 66–77.
8. For an interesting exploration of the epitaphic mode in its relation to poetic identity (including its positing of spontaneity and 'chance'), see Dewey W. Hall, 'Signs of the Dead: Epitaphs, Inscriptions, and the Discourse of the Self', *ELH*, 68 (2001), 655–77. For an analysis of poetic self-definition and its difficulties in terms of the language of epitaphs, see Frances Ferguson, *Wordsworth: Language as Counter-Spirit* (New Haven, CT: Yale University Press, 1977).
9. For an account – rather different from my own – of how epitaphs and monuments to the dead inscribe the building and changing of community under the duress of increasing industrialization, see Michele Turner Sharp, 'The Churchyard among the Wordsworthian Mountains: Mapping the Common Ground of Death and the Reconfiguration of Romantic Community', *ELH*, 62 (1995), 387–407.
10. This linkage occurs in the 1800 Preface to *Lyrical Ballads*, where the universalization of language away from 'poetic diction' is far more explicit as

a linguistic act than in the 1798 Advertisement. In her fascinating analysis, Theresa Kelley traces the role of the linguistic in Wordsworth's thought, as she uncovers the antitheticality of Wordsworth's aesthetics especially in so far as the workings of figures of speech are re-viewed between the 1800 and 1802 Prefaces. Kelley's example is that of personification, first admitted only in a few instances in 1800, and then transposed as a 'rare' figure attuned to exceptional instances of passions in 1802. Kelley's reading of the qualifier in the sub-clause in the first version, and the declaration of rarity in the main clause in the second one, perceptively reads the re-signification of figures for the 'business of poetry' and, we might add, of prose. See Theresa M. Kelley, *Wordsworth's Revisionary Aesthetics* (Cambridge: Cambridge University Press, 1988), esp. pp. 193–7.

11. G. W. F. Hegel, *Werke*, vol. 15, *Vorlesungen über die Ästhetik* (Frankfurt am Main: Suhrkamp, 1970), p. 282. Translation mine.

12. Aptly for the present context, Paul de Man's reading of Hegel's aesthetics links poetry to 'Gedächtnis' (the external term for 'memory') rather than 'Erinnerung' (memory which relies upon something internalized). See 'Sign and Symbol in Hegel's Aesthetics', in *Aesthetic Ideology*, ed. Andrzej Warminski (Minneapolis: University of Minnesota Press, 1996), pp. 91–104.

13. Hazlitt, 'Mr. Wordsworth', pp. 231–2.

14. See William Shakespeare, *Complete Works: The Riverside Shakespeare*, ed. G. Blakemore Evans (Boston: Houghton Mifflin, 1974).

7
Writing and Orality around 1800: 'Speakers', 'Readers', and Wordsworth's 'The Thorn'

Frances Ferguson

For all the prodigious scholarship of the past few decades on books and their readers, it remains notoriously difficult to write the history of reading. On the one hand, historians of the book are increasingly effective in identifying how many copies of various books were printed at various times, and historians of literacy can mount arguments about how pervasive the ability to read was in a given society at any given time. On the other, literary criticism urges us to consult letters, journals, and essays to see exactly what particular readers thought of particular poems. The approach of historians of the book and historians of literacy is aggregative; and statements made under its aegis have a conjectural force that may not directly correlate with the experience of any actual reader. The literary critical approach, by way of contrast, is, we might say, all too particular. It stresses what I. A. Richards would have seen as acts of communication by collecting testimony about exactly what one reader or another takes an individual poem to mean and exactly how much one reader or another values it.[1]

To some extent the division I have just characterized is merely an expression of the relatively social scientific cast of work on the history of the book and of the relatively philological, text-centred work in literary criticism. But much recent historicist work has proceeded to try to reconcile the two approaches by offering specific readings of individual texts that are authorized by the aggregate picture: since such and such a view would or would not have been available to persons living in such and such a time and situation, some historicist critics have suggested, this particular poem must have meant such and such to this particular poet or novelist and her readers. Such a procedure, much as Roland Barthes might criticize it for imagining that contextualism solves most of the problems of reading, has its plausibility, because historicism seems

119

to offer a way of avoiding the claim that literature is simply timeless – equally available to all readers at all times.[2] Yet historicist critics have all too often been led by their own methodologies to produce readings on behalf of spirits of an age rather than actual individual readers and to provide broad-brush accounts of what everyone must have thought at a given moment. They have, that is, treated the historical record as universally and uniformly known. And the perennial charge against literary criticism – that no one can ever confirm what a text really means – is not so much answered as compounded by the charge that no one can confirm the spirit of an age but can only assume its reach in advance.

I offer the discussion that follows as a kind of experiment in trying to think not merely about what a poem means or what contemporary references best explain it but also about the particular tension between writing (in the form of the published volume with its individual readers) and orality. Nicholas Hudson has shrewdly observed that 'European intellectuals achieved a clear perception of "orality" only after their own world had been engulfed in print.'[3] Late eighteenth-century ballad collections and contemporary literary work that took oral ballads as models suggest that orality became a topic of considerable interest not merely because it seemed unrecoverable but also because it raised questions about what literature is and what difference it might make for it to be transmitted in two different ways – either viva voce or through the sight of print.

Hudson points out that Protestants of the seventeenth century 'poured scorn on the belief that any substantial legacy of knowledge could be preserved orally' (163), and enables us to see the importance of the rise of print in promulgating the sense that binding opinions about religious and legal matters can be justified only by reference to written texts. The question of the standing of the oral changes rather dramatically, however, when we apply the Protestant view of oral and written tradition to literary fictions and have to confront the fact that a considerable number of sturdy Protestants were actively involved in the recovery and imitation of an oral literature of the folk. For while the emphasis on written texts increasingly funded the notion that national governments derived their legitimacy by appealing to constitutions and statutes that were there for anyone to see, a simultaneous counter-movement in literature transcribed, authenticated, and aped oral litera-ture. As various writers including Edward Said, Katie Trumpener, and Pascale Casanova have argued, literary nationalism – in the form of the recovery of languages and literatures that, in their oral transmission, are said to demonstrate the cohesiveness of various peoples became a leading edge for political nationalism.[4] Peoples claimed their right to self-determination, that is, less on the basis of their common interests in the present than of their ability to affirm that they had their own distinctive literatures. There had always been, they said, an England, a Germany, a Scotland, and one could see evidence of those nations' virtual existence in their native tales and ballads.

The significance of the orality of oral literature was that it was taken to be so nearly internal to the culture itself that it scarcely needed to be transmitted. Its every rehearsal was an endorsement, and an almost unnecessary one. As Propp would later observe about the Russian folk tale, literature that can become traditional is continually refined by the process of transmission, and something like the voice of a language itself stands in for the author function. Too many idiosyncrasies, and the tale is left stranded in a particular teller, and the tale disappears. Too many improbabilities, and the narrative loses its internal coherence. Susan Stewart has ably detailed the dilemmas that the collection and authentication of ballads entailed and has in the process suggested how the late eighteenth-century conception of oral tradition dramatized by way of contrast the situation of the contemporary author.[5] The 'location of voice within character in the ballad' involves 'the ballad singer' in taking 'the form of each of the "characters" in a ventriloquistic fashion', she writes; and 'the dissolution of the performing self in the performance style ... promises a total immersion of personality in context that is the antithesis of the literary author's separation from both the local and the living presence of audience' so that 'we have the appearance of tradition speaking through someone' (125). Orality does not merely involve voicing words before an audience; for a world 'engulfed in print' and different accounts of printed words, orality represents a consensus of past persons and opinions, the story that 'we' could all relate equally well of our collective past because it is a story generated by the sounds of our language and the logical operations of narrative.

The notion of an oral tradition is itself, as Stewart suggests, a tragic one. On the one hand, ballad collectors might fill out the transcriptions of certain ballads, almost as if they were able to participate in a collective voice that no longer existed. On the other, ballads provided a central occasion for the rise of historical scholarship, in which the scholar and collector exposed the forgery of a Macpherson or an Ossian by demonstrating how deluded they were to imagine that this collective voice might still speak. Every individual writer thinking in the terms of a full-blown oral tradition recognizes that she or he must speak as if she or he were a committee, must think of these words as theirs because they are everyone's, must see themselves uttering words that might as well be carried in someone else's mouth. The notion of the oral tradition, that is, creates an imagination of a prehistoric world in which all ballads and tales are essentially contemporaneous. The collection of ballads and tales and the attendant scholarly authentication are part and parcel of a fall into history, as literature comes to be treated as both assignable (to an individual author) and datable (the product of a particular time). Thus Propp expresses a fundamentally correct proposition about oral literature when he rejects the idea that it might be used for historical purposes (such as determining how land-measurement might have been done at some point in the historical past), because in doing so he rightly insists upon the fundamentally ahistorical character of the oral tale or ballad as an idea.[6] Oral tradition may not ever really have existed in the pure form of this conception, but only such an intensely formalist conception of oral tradition provides its genuine foundation, exposing it as the opposite of historical unfolding and creating the possibility of history when its fossilization subjects it to the trials of the written word.

The very title of the collection *Lyrical Ballads* in which 'The Thorn' appears suggests two different versions of literary orality – the lyric, which is said to have a speaker even when that speaker is only belatedly revealed to have an auditor (as in 'Tintern Abbey', with its sudden address to Wordsworth's sister Dorothy, or 'Nutting', with its concluding remarks to a 'dearest Maiden') and the ballad, always marked – actually or fictionally – as a form in which speaker and auditors are present to one another. 'The Thorn' gives many indications of being closer to a ballad than to a lyric, as generations of critics have acknowledged in stressing its balladic subject – infanticide. Indeed, when Stephen Parrish registers the dissenting view that the poem calls upon us to focus on the unreliability of the mariner (and thus describes it as a 'dramatic monologue', with the full range of implication that that term carries in the work of poets like Browning), he shifts his emphasis from message to messenger but in such a way as to assume the constant co-presence of speaker and audience.[7] The mariner who speaks the poem is precipitated out of the community that attends the tale he tells, but the storytelling community of the poem continues to resemble that of a ballad. In making the storyteller himself the real story, Parrish depicts the dramatic monologue as an implicit case study, in which the auditors are expected to affirm the assumptions of the community by recognizing how far the mariner departs from them.

'The Thorn' as dramatic monologue in this 'The Thorn' as scapegoat narrative. Attending to the tale itself identifies the community as everyone except Martha Ray, whose story the mariner attempts to imagine, while attending to the speaker along the lines that Parrish does defines the community as everyone except the mariner.

The suggestion that I want to press here is that previous discussions of the poem – and it has attracted an abundance of compelling accounts – have afforded scant attention to the audience that the poem projects. In analysing Wordsworth's 'The Thorn', I want to call attention to problems of interpretation that have perennially been seen to attach to it. Yet, rather than seeing the poem as a statement of either a determinate meaning or a transhistorical indeterminacy of the kind that deconstruction taught us to discern, I offer some conjectures about what the obliquity of the narrator's statements in 'The Thorn' might enable us to infer about reading situations in the late eighteenth and early nineteenth centuries. Without arguing that the poem was always read under the conditions that I shall detail below, I want to suggest that influential late eighteenth- and early nineteenth-century anthologies that collected literary excerpts for the purposes of public reading had an impact on the character of the poem that Wordsworth wrote. The hypothesis I shall develop is that literary anthologies like William Enfield's *The Speaker*, which first appeared in 1774, and Mary Wollstonecraft's *The Female Reader*, which appeared in 1789, exercised a significant influence on Wordsworth's thinking about questions that we usually characterize as those of authorial intention and audience reception. Enfield's *Speaker*, Wollstonecraft's *Reader*, and Anna Laetitia Barbauld's slightly later *The Female Speaker* (of 1811) all participate in the establishment of what William St Clair has taught us to think of as the 'old canon'.[8] Unlike the *Annual Anthology* or periodicals like the *Edinburgh Review* or *The Gentleman's Magazine*, the editors who compiled 'speakers' and 'readers' were not principally gathering their materials from contemporaries; they collected selections of literature from a variety of different periods. And while Dryden or Pope might have linked contemporary literary production with the classical past, the editors of the 'speakers' and 'readers' extended the reach of English literature from Chaucer through such contemporary productions as Wilberforce's parliamentary speeches. As the titles of the anthologies suggest, they aimed to provide selections for public and communal reading, of the kind that Dissenters – and Enfield, Wollstonecraft, and Barbauld were all Dissenters – practised. In contrast to the fictional situation of the ballad in which the singer was interchangeable with the auditors and in contrast to the Augustan affirmation of transhistorical community that Pope voiced in his happy affirmation of what 'oft was thought but ne'er so well expressed', the 'speakers' and 'readers' created readers and, I would argue, auditors who are markedly more individuated than we have acknowledged. My aim in this chapter is to suggest the heteroglossia of the poem and its imagined audience – even though the audience is never directly quoted or represented.

For the moment, let me suspend any direct attention to the anthologies known as 'speakers' and 'readers' and the ways in which they were used, so as first to explore the plausible line of analysis that has seen this poem as an example of the literary ballad. Scholars have for some time spoken of the poem in terms of the ballad revival of Germany, England, and Scotland of the late eighteenth century, and have identified an influential precedent in William Taylor's translation of Gottfried Bürger's new antique 'Des Pfarrers Tochter von Taubenheim' as 'The Lass of Fair Wone'.[9] They have recognized Wordsworth's use of ballad metre in 'The Thorn' and have taken its very indecisiveness about the content of its story as a mark of its continuity with the ballad tradition, which frequently represents its speaker as experiencing genuine wonderment about what he will say: 'What shall I tell?'

In Geoffrey Hartman's account of the poem, the indirection with which the mariner recounts the story of Martha Ray is one of the chief elements marking 'The Thorn' as a ballad. Although Hartman ultimately echoes Coleridge and the critics of 'the more experimental of Wordsworth's ballads' and suggests that Wordsworth's having felt a need to supply a note that distinguishes between himself and the narrator is a mark of the failure of the experiment, he speaks of the poem as 'courageously if not wisely' offering 'a caricature of Wordsworth's own imagination-in-process'.[10] With that summary judgement, Hartman both acknowledges Wordsworth's literary historical moment – one in which literature cannot speak in the language of the community as readily as it did in balladry – and insists upon the importance of the ballad for representing the motive forces of literature for Wordsworth. Although Hartman treats the speaker's strange way of talking around his subject as directly inspired by the ballad, now conceived as one literary genre among others, he also sees the narrator's inability to specify the story he recounts as ultimately betokening a recurrent Wordsworthian theme – that of the absorption of persons and their stories into nature, rather than into a human community.

Hartman has particularly commented on the speaker's fascination with a 'spot-syndrome', the continual return of the poem's main character, Martha Ray, to the place where the thorn grows. In describing the poem in that fashion, he uses the notion of Martha's fixation on

the place as a symptom of emotional imagination — and at justification
for the narrator's fixation on both the place and her story. The poem's
narrator, observing Martha come regularly to the same spot, offers a line
of connection between the character's recurrent plaint, 'Oh misery!
Oh misery! / Oh woe is me! oh misery' (ll. 65–6) and her frequenting
this particular spot.[11] Like a detective imagining that there must be
a connection between Martha's lament and the place at which she utters
it, the narrator details what he can observe and suggests conclusions.

Hartman's concern for literary psychology, then, lends support to the
account of poetry as a communicator and regulator of feelings, to his
description of poetry as 'the history or science of feelings' (*LB*, 351). For
'The Thorn', for all its awkwardness, operates for him as a series of analogies
generated by emotion rather than by direct statement. If a woman returns
to a thorn tree and utters a lament, her plaint establishes a connection
between the thorn and the tragic event that the poem's narrator responds
to even if he can only clumsily imagine a narrative; he has grasped what
T. S. Eliot would call an 'objective correlative' without knowing exactly
what it is correlative to. Moreover, the narrator's attachment to the emotion rather than to the story and his continual sense that the story he can
present is inadequate to the emotion appears to Hartman as something
like the deepest spirit of metaphor in Wordsworth (see 146–8). Indeed,
Wordsworth makes the mariner an epitome of a certain non-gentlemanly
version of the man of feeling. First, he distances himself, the poet, from
the mariner who speaks the poem in the Advertisement of 1798 by simply
saying that the poem, 'as the reader will soon discover, is not to be supposed
to be spoken in the author's own person: the character of the loquacious
narrator will sufficiently shew itself in the course of the story'.[12]

In 1800, however, Wordsworth offers his famous Note to 'The Thorn'.
On the one hand, the narrator occasions a kind of maxim. What had
been the personal 'loquacity' of the individual character in 1798 now
appears as a larger principle for the expression of emotion in language.
One man has become every man, not anomalous or eccentric but
universal, as Wordsworth writes that

> every man must know that an attempt is rarely made to communi-
> cate impassioned feelings without something of an accompanying
> consciousness of the inadequateness of our own powers, or the
> deficiencies of language. During such efforts there will be a craving
> in the mind, and as long as it is unsatisfied the Speaker will cling to
> the same words, or words of the same character.
>
> (*LB*, 351)

Coleridge had not yet published his criticism of the language of 'The Thorn' and the various other poems for which Wordsworth had adopted the language of rustic life, but his shift from the practice of this narrator to the practice of speakers generally suggests an anticipatory defence. For Wordsworth justifies his narrator in 'The Thorn' by making exactly the same sort of turn that Lévi-Strauss does in *The Savage Mind* when he insists that no society is symbolically deficient.[13] And his claim on behalf of narrative thus insists on according *a priori* standing to the tale. If we recognize a tale in everything, he suggests, we will also recognize that there are tellers and tellings for everything. The position is formalist in the full sense of the term, in that demands for the adequacy of a particular expression are subordinated to the larger conception; narrative has been defined in advance as successful, and approval for this particular performance follows from that (so that the tale is put outside the reach of the abstract formulation of conventions and values that Coleridge defends).

The Note to 'The Thorn' helps us to see exactly how Wordsworth's experimental poems of *Lyrical Ballads* really do differ from the magazine verse of the 1790s – however little their ostensible subjects would belie that difference. As Robert Mayo pointed out in a classic essay some time ago, beggars, mad mothers, and infanticides figure prominently in both Wordsworth's poems and what we might think of as the routinely published work of the day; thus the subjects – much as they represented a departure from Pope's satire, topicality, and commitment to precisely drawn 'characters' – were not wildly novel.[14] And although various commentators have thought that Wordsworth's poems were distinguished by their quality – their simply being better poems – that explanation is a bit hard to credit when the poem has invited a great deal of parody because it sounded as though it was parodic of itself. Rather, the sympathy that Wordsworth imagines the narrator generating – for himself and for the Martha Ray whose story he relates – takes precedence over the drama of the events. When Wordsworth says in the Preface to *Lyrical Ballads* in 1800 that the 'feeling ... developed [in his poems] gives importance to the action and situation and not the action and the situation to the feeling' he is not merely repudiating 'frantic' and 'sickly' (*PW*, 1:128) contemporary productions. He also distinguishes his poems from what we might think of as the forerunners of Hollywood action films – events that do not revolve around the aims of morality and acknowledgement that Wordsworth repeatedly mentions in his Preface.

Indeed, the conjectural, credulous, and superstitious character of Wordsworth's narrator and his report takes us so far beyond the facts of Martha Ray's case that these facts cease to seem particularly relevant to the workings of the poem. For the sentiment, the narrator's fierce commitment to the memory- and storm-tossed woman whose story he tells, occasions the narrative. That foundational sentimental gesture helps to suggest what I take to be the limitations of Stephen Parrish's brilliantly reductive reading of the poem, in which the mariner is judged by the facts of the case and found to be aberrant. The poem provides a tissue of reports that sort very uncomfortably with one another. The narrator first urges his auditor to go in search of the thorn he's describing when Martha Ray is in her hut ('You must take care and chuse your time ... / For oft there sits ..., / A woman in a scarlet cloak', [ll. 58–63]; and 'I never heard of such as dare / Approach the spot when she is there' [ll. 98–9]) and then suggests that she is always there, an unavoidable presence. Yet if we cannot quite make out exactly what the mariner thinks and cannot reconcile all the details of his account, the poem provides him with companionable thinking – rather than isolating him in the same way as characters in dramatic monologues are separated from their auditors by a conspicuous if implicit difference of view.

Parrish's case depends on our being able to pathologize the mariner, as if he were a near relation to a moral monster like Browning's Duke of Ferrara or one of Browning's casuistically adaptive monologists. Yet even if we discount a great deal of the mariner's testimony about what everyone in the neighbourhood says and believes, the narrator provides an especially telling detail in the penultimate stanza of the poem when he reports that the villagers who had determined to constitute themselves as a posse and search for a body that might enable them to bring murder charges against Martha Ray abandoned that plan when 'the beauteous hill of moss / Before their eyes began to stir; / And for full fifty yards around, / The grass it shook upon the ground' (ll. 236–9). While Parrish eloquently states his case that 'The Thorn' is nothing other than a story about a man and a tree (and thus assimilates it to *Peter Bell* and the questions of misplaced imagination), Josephine McDonagh draws a more plausible conclusion from the lines I quoted earlier:

Thus the attempt to bring Martha Ray 'to public justice' by disinterring the body of the child stimulates an uncannily protective response from the landscape. ... It is as though Nature itself is implicated in the concealment of Martha Ray's guilt, condoning her probable act in sympathetic identification with her plight. Martha Ray and her dead baby are absorbed into nature.[15]

While Parrish could plausibly claim that, in accepting the account of the protective action of the tree, the moss, and the surrounding ground, the mariner shows himself as a gull in his new community he is, Parrish might say, willing to believe anything, and the villagers might thus find amusement in trying out their tallest tales on him. Alternatively, Parrish could imagine that the mariner and the villagers are all equally benighted, that they all too easily accept the idea of hauntings.

McDonagh, in contrast, stresses the way in which the mariner and the villagers participate in 'the shared beliefs of the community'; and she thus appeals to the precedent of ballads, in which 'child murder is presented as the traditional response to unwanted pregnancy in rural communities' (79). Yet even though McDonagh makes a number of acute observations about the poem and about infanticide in the eighteenth and nineteenth centuries, she here relies excessively on an account of communal attitudes towards specific situations – such as unwanted pregnancy and acceptable responses to them – such as infanticide. For the poem does not merely detail 'the belief and landscape of traditional rural life' (80) in order to suggest that infanticide – if it had occurred – wouldn't have been particularly unusual in traditional rural communities. Rather, it depicts the villagers as holding two diametrically opposed views – first, that they should seek 'public justice' because they think that infanticide, an act that they view as a crime, has been committed and, second, that even if Martha Ray committed infanticide, it is no crime in their eyes, any more than in the eyes of the natural world that refuses to testify against her.

Thus, while I agree with McDonagh that the description of the chain of events 'is based not merely on the aberrations of an individual superstitious mind' (79), I think that the poem does not so much locate communal beliefs as insist, as I earlier suggested, that the point of a poetry in which 'feeling gives importance to the action and situation' is to try to imagine that everyone has a story that poetry might uncover in much the same way that psychoanalysis would do in the twentieth century – not so much to identify the pathological as to explain the logic of behaviours that are all too frequently dismissed and derogated. The mariner, however credulous and superstitious he may be, operates out of something other than superstition at the moments in which he explicitly sets a limit to the kinds of conjecture he is prepared to engage in. Although he arrived in the village well after the events recounted or conjectured in the poem (after Martha Ray's abandonment by Stephen Hill, after her discovery that she was pregnant, and after the infant died prematurely or at term, and of natural or unnatural causes), he repeatedly takes her side as vigorously as if he were

Anna Howe defending Clarissa Harlowe against the other members of her family. He introduces the information that he's heard that 'the moss is spotted red / With drops of that poor infant's blood' (ll. 221–2), only to deny the possibility that Martha might have murdered her child: 'But kill a new-born infant thus! / I do not think she could' (ll. 223–4).

The mariner here presents himself as a character witness for a woman he has never met (though he has, unless Parrish is correct, seen her); and he claims to know what she would and would not do. Moreover, he demonstrates his staunch confidence in this particular woman's behaviour, not in that of mothers or persons in general, and never resorts to the dismissive explanation that is readily available: 'A person would have to be crazy to kill her new-born child.' Although Martha has recurrently been described as having gone mad and as having 'a brain so wild' (l. 147), the speaker never treats her madness as evidence that Martha would have committed a crime. Indeed, he reserves his indignation for Stephen Hill: 'Oh me! ten thousand times I'd rather / That he had died, that cruel father!' (ll. 142–3).

What seems most striking about the mariner's position is that he makes no apologies for Martha Ray, saying neither that it would be understandable for a young woman who had been abandoned by her lover to kill her infant nor that madness would nullify our negative judgement against an infanticide. Instead, he simply states that there must not have been an infanticide because Martha could not have done such a thing and, further, wishes Stephen Hill dead (with the suggestion that he, rather than the infant, should have died). McDonagh has usefully called attention to the uncertainty that surrounds infanticide and to the difficulty of establishing whether an infant has 'been stillborn, [has] died of natural causes, or was the victim of a violent crime', and she has highlighted the way that the 1624 'Act to Prevent the Destroying and Murdering of Bastard Children' did not require positive proof of murder but took 'concealment of the death of an infant bastard' as presumptive legal proof that 'the mother was guilty of murder' (3). If she had tried to disguise her pregnancy, in other words, she would have been treated as if she had always planned to eliminate the child who would be conclusive evidence of a pregnancy.

The narrator of 'The Thorn', however, does not rehearse evidence about infanticide in terms that have any relevance to legal decisions. It is clear that Martha Ray's pregnancy was apparent for all to see, and it is equally clear that, had the villagers unearthed an infant's skeleton near the thorn, the discovery of the infant's body would still not have decisively answered the question of whether the infant had died of natural or unnatural causes. When, at the end of the poem, the mariner recounts how the hill of moss 'began to stir', not even that extraordinary occurrence (or the imagination of it) settles the question of Martha Ray's guilt or innocence. It is only suppressed, with the earth itself seeming to say, 'Don't ask'.

Were this poem the only poem we had of Wordsworth's, it would be easy to see it as a fairly typical ballad. Yet Wordsworth's insistence on an unusually intense conception of the relationship between humans and nature justifies the picture that Hartman has given and that McDonagh endorses in talking about how 'Martha Ray and her dead baby are absorbed into nature: literally buried in the landscape, but also in the community's experience of nature' (79). That convergence of the human and the natural world appears in the way the thorn and the infant come to be associated with one another, in a process that is only intensified by the peculiar effect of the narrator's recounting that he once mistook the mother for a crag. Yet what we can plausibly describe as Wordsworth's pantheism, his voicing of the spirit of the phenomena of the universe, takes the unusual form here of projecting a voice for the natural world as it appears in the thorn, the hill of moss, and the earth around them. As they alarmingly move or are imagined to move, they do not so much take the side of the infant or the mother as ward off anything that might lead to the uncovering of a body. In that, they speak the language of the censor and insist that the tale should proceed only along the oblique inferential path it has long traversed. Moreover, they share with the censor an inability to lay questions to rest. If the moving earth fails to aid in Martha Ray's condemnation, it also fails to dispel the questions that have arisen.

What I am here calling Wordsworth's pantheism obviously involves giving a speaking voice to earth, but we have only to think of such influential examples of an explicit pantheism as Anna Laetitia Barbauld's *Hymns for Children* to see that Wordsworth's poem is not here engaged in a positive pantheism like hers – a registration of the beauties of the earth as evidence of omnipresent divinity. For in such famous passages of *The Prelude* as the egg-stealing and boat-stealing episodes, Wordsworth presents an animated universe that does not so much offer constant recommendation of the world as introduce a new voice, which expresses a rebuke to the only character present who has a distinct human voice. Moreover, a poem like 'Nutting', published in *Lyrical Ballads* and intended for inclusion in *The Prelude*, may speak in the voice of the narrator when urging the 'dearest Maiden' (l. 52) to move delicately in the woods, but that voice has been radically altered during the course of the poem itself. This is poetry of dawning, specifically, poems in which the speaker continually says to himself, 'What have I done?' In the place of a pantheism that amounts to a universal embrace, Wordsworth offers up a pantheism in which the poetry narrates the advent of consciousness of other worlds and other minds. Indeed, I think that one could make a strong case that Wordsworth's apparently belated acknowledgement of his sister Dorothy at the end of 'Tintern Abbey' participates in this movement from an apparently all-inclusive pantheism into something that we might describe as a liberal pantheism, in that it imagines differences between the speaker and the universe and also acknowledges differences between the speaker and other persons.[16]

In describing Wordsworth's poetry in such terms as I have adopted, I am attributing to Wordsworth a different view from that which John Stuart Mill enunciated in his famous essay 'What Is Poetry?' when he distinguished between eloquence and poetry by saying that 'Eloquence supposes an audience; the peculiarity of poetry appears to us to lie in the poet's utter unconsciousness of a listener.'[17] For I have been concerned with the ways in which Wordsworth is not so much attempting to persuade an audience in the manner that Mill's eloquent speaker would as aiming to narrate the poet's own overcoming of his unconsciousness of a listener – be that listener natural or human. Wordsworth's narrator in 'The Thorn' addresses himself to an audience, but the obtuseness that numerous commentators have noted in him is principally a social insensitivity, an awkward relation to his auditors in which he talks at them rather than to them.

It is here that the speech situation of the poem comes into view. In *Lyrical Ballads*, as for a number of Wordsworth's contemporaries, one of the most experimental elements was an attempt to acknowledge the poetic audience. Under the influence of Rousseau's *Emile*, a number of writers had begun to think systematically about the question of age-appropriateness in writing addressed to children. Anna Laetitia Barbauld, perhaps the most famous and influential of the English Rousseauvians, had written *Lessons for Children of Two to Three Years Old* (1778), *Lessons for Children of Three Years Old* (1778), *Lessons for Children of Three to Four Years Old* (1779), with *Lessons for Children, Parts Three and Four* (1787, 1788) appearing along the way. While a writer like Hugh Blair had urged the auditors and readers of his *Lectures on Rhetoric and Belles Lettres* to make careful calculations about the various styles they should employ on different occasions, he was basically commending a modern version of the classical hierarchy of high, middle, and low styles for a conversation among adults that would be achieved by writing that might or might not be read aloud. A writer like Barbauld, however, had sifted her potential audience by age and explicitly attempted to write in a manner that would be comprehensible to children at various stages of development. Readers were, in the process, segregated by age.

Even if Mary Moorman had not provided the information that Wordsworth directed that a copy of *Lyrical Ballads* be sent to Barbauld, it is, I think, easy to make the case that at least some of the poems of the volume are thinking about 'the language really used by men' under the pressure of the consciousness of differences between the understandings of children and adults. For his effort was not simply to avoid the stilted poetic diction that Coleridge described the Reverend James Bowyer as having disciplined him out of. Instead, Wordsworth was as early as *Lyrical Ballads* addressing the ways in which different notions of direct and lucid speech obtain for children and for adults. In 1798, that is, he published 'Anecdote for Fathers' as the ninth poem in the volume, and followed it with 'We are seven', 'Lines written in early spring' and 'The Thorn' as the tenth, eleventh, and twelfth poems; and in 1800 he linked 'The Thorn', 'We are seven', and 'Anecdote for Fathers' even more tightly to present them as one continuous series. 'Anecdote for Fathers' presents a father who keeps trying to make his son say whether he prefers the farm or the seaside, and its subtitle is 'Shewing How the Art of Lying May Be Taught', to emphasize the strangeness of the adult's trying to make the child name his preference for one place over the other when the child has a hard time grasping the language of choice and the concomitant demand for reasons. 'We are seven' notoriously depicts a conversation between a little girl and a pedestrian tourist who quizzes her about her family and becomes increasingly exasperated as the girl repeatedly insists that she's one of seven children even as she reports that two of her siblings have died.

Seeing 'The Thorn' with the poems adjacent to it does not exactly do the work that Wordsworth imagined the prefatory poem he initially projected might have done.[18] But it does suggest that Wordsworth was thinking in this poem as in those others about the need for poetry to address questions of audience in a fashion that Popean urbanity would never have allowed for. Even as Rousseau and the English Rousseauvians had argued that adults and children thought very differently about the same words and attached very different meanings to them, and even as age-graded readers temporarily segregated children from adults, Wordsworth repeatedly depicted children as unwilling auditors to thoughtless adult speakers. And the popularity of Enfield's *Speaker*, Wollstonecraft's *Female Reader*, and, later, Barbauld's *Female Speaker* make it clear that the Wordsworth household was far from unique in its practice of reading aloud *en famille*. For the anthologies known as speakers and readers were designed to create occasions in which someone of virtually any age might read to an assembled company that included persons of all ages.

We might, from this distance in time, lump such anthologies together with the sort of aspirational anthologies that Hannah More denounces in her discussions of young women's education and that Jane Austen relied on in cementing her depiction of Augusta Hawkins Elton in *Emma* by having Mrs Elton offer up a few lines from Gay ('When there's a lady in the case ...') as a way of flaunting her insider knowledge of the nature of Jane Fairfax and Frank Churchill's relationship.[19] While Mrs Elton thinks she's paying tribute to the power of love, anyone familiar with the whole text would recognize that Gay describes a bull's interest in a cow, so that Austen can very efficiently locate her character's pretension. And anyone unfamiliar with the whole text (as Emma doubtless would be, since she always means to read more but does not) would participate in this game of leveraged knowledge under the banner of impotent protest.

The notion that literary knowledge might be harnessed for social display – that one might be concerned more with other people's reactions to one's apparent knowledge than with the literature itself – was scarcely new when Hannah More and Jane Austen outlined it. But the anthologies that were designed for public reading explicitly set out to offer an alternative to the aspirational anthologies that funded pretension – and in two ways, first, by making the text equally available to reader and hearer alike, and, second, by creating a situation in which the reader or speaker of a particular text needed to think about both her life situation and that of her auditors. She needed to consider whether she could utter this piece of writing in the presence of these particular individuals, who were nameable even when they were not named. The anthologies thus created a new form of orality for a written tradition. They consisted of excerpts from vernacular literature that were regularly identified (as they were in Wollstonecraft's descriptive title) as being – all of them – of high quality, the best. And their boast about excellence involved more than an empty sales pitch or appeal to snobbery. Rather, it was essential that the excerpts should all be 'excellent', because of the occasion for which they were destined: reading in public, certainly to one's family, most frequently to various family friends as well. These anthologies designed for public reading deliberately avoided excerpts that would betray their readers as Mrs Elton's purloined verses betrayed her. Moreover, they involved a heightened sense of the identities of the members of one's audience, and the acknowledgement that was due to them. One might well read portions of Enfield's *Speaker* to one's brother or sister, as Dorothy Wordsworth reports that she and William did; but one might also read to an entire family group consisting of persons of all ages and to an even more extended group as the members of the community around the Warrington Academy did. Peter de Bolla has written eloquently about the constraints imposed on individuals by public reading and has seen a repressive element in the requirement that novels be read aloud rather than silently and privately, but we might also think of the public reading of the Dissenters' anthologies as a forerunner of Brecht's attentiveness to the dramatic audience.[20] These anthologies heightened their readers' consciousness of whom they were reading to and created the conditions for an increased acknowledgement of those readers. Through their mediation, literature was always being addressed to a particular audience and tested by it; the public reader of literature was not merely trying to communicate information or argument to an imaginary or undifferentiated audience. She was trying to avoid what Wordsworth or Jane Austen would have seen as a failure of condescension – or, indeed, what might amount to inconsideration of the kind that would in the twentieth century come to be thought of as 'hate speech', speech that wilfully and insultingly ignores the nature of its audience.

Jane Austen would, within scarcely more than a decade of the publication of *Lyrical Ballads*, demonstrate the comic possibilities of a character's obliviousness to her associates by having Emma repeatedly say the right thing to the wrong person, as when Emma feelingly testifies to her own former governess about the horrors that await Jane Fairfax if she must become a governess. And Austen would also develop the courtship plot as a way of demonstrating the virtual omnipresence of misdirected statements; only romantic love, finally, suits speakers to understand one another's statements – and to see how little they once did. Wordsworth's experiment in having a speaker adjust himself to his audience in 'The Thorn' has less direction to it. There is no love plot to the mariner's story, and he seems, as a relative newcomer, to bring his audience into focus almost as little as if he were speaking to the invisible audience of writing. Only his desperate introduction and retraction of the question of infanticide suggests the possibility of his alertness to an audience that partially consists of children.

While 'Anecdote for Fathers' and 'We are seven' clearly introduce the notion of a dialogue between adult and child, 'The Thorn' introduces children into the audience for the mariner's tale only by having the mariner regularly mangle his own tale – as if suddenly conscious that he is speaking in the presence of at least one person, a child scarcely past infancy, who might be personally alarmed and not merely literarily shocked. I have been arguing that a chief feature of Wordsworth's practice in many of the *Lyrical Ballads* poems, including 'The Thorn', is his consciousness of the ways in which the public reading of written texts – an oral version of writing – precipitates out an awareness of the persons who make up the audience. And I have been suggesting that Wordsworth allows such reading practices to exert pressure on his writing – that just as he creates narratives of the growing awareness of pantheism in a poem like 'Nutting', so he develops a literary pantheism that involves dawning or sudden consciousness of his auditors as individuals, persons with lives, feelings, sensitivities.

One element of 'The Thorn' – the name of the young woman described in the poem – would, however, seem to present a significant challenge to the account I am offering: Martha Ray. On the March day when Wordsworth was struck by the appearance of a thorn and determined to write about it, he was in the company of his sister Dorothy and the seven-year-old Basil Montagu, who was living with William and Dorothy while his father, also Basil Montagu, was studying law in London.[21] Basil Montagu père, Wordsworth's friend from their Cambridge days, was himself the son of an actual person named Martha Ray who had been the mistress of John Montagu, Earl of Sandwich, and who had herself been murdered in 1779 by a disappointed lover, the Reverend James Hackman. Karen Swann and Josephine McDonagh have recently provided dazzling readings of the poem and have not stopped, as many scholars have, with expressing scholarly puzzlement at Wordsworth's having chosen the name Martha Ray for the mad mother of 'The Thorn' when the grandson of the actual Martha Ray was living in his household.[22] Both Swann and McDonagh examine the way in which the Hackman of real life and the Martha Ray of imagined life might be seen as suffering from what Erasmus Darwin termed 'erotomania', a love that misdirected itself as violence, and they are both alert to the public sensation that Martha Ray's murder caused and the scandalous publications that detailed it. In Swann's account, 'The Thorn' evidences Wordsworth's queasy inability to distance himself from lurid sensation and his sense that he too traffics in the suffering of women 'in a way that is advantageous to a literary career'.[23] Wordsworth in her view does not keep as much distance from the 'sickly and frantic' as he would like to think.

It would be a strong argument against the case for Wordsworth's heightened sensitivity to the members of his audience as individuals if he were merely using the name Martha Ray to remind young Basil Montagu of a family tragedy and scandal. But I suspect that Wordsworth saw himself as engaged in a different enterprise altogether – that of recognizing how little history children know and of turning that ignorance to good effect. For the Basil Montagu who had gone to Alfoxden in 1795 at the age of four to live with William and Dorothy and who was only seven at the time Wordsworth wrote 'The Thorn' might scarcely have registered the name of Martha Ray as having painful associations, or, for that matter, any associations. Indeed, I suspect that Wordsworth saw himself as reassigning the name Martha Ray and creating a virtual set of connections around the woman of 'The Thorn' that would act, by virtue of having been closer to young Basil's own experience, as a screen against the story of his actual grandmother by the time he would come to hear it. What I think Wordsworth aimed to achieve was a channelling and direction of Basil's own associations that would use the proximity of a fiction to shield him from the harshness of still-distant historical fact for Basil. The Wordsworth who can concern himself enough with his own future thoughts to say to himself that he will think about the leech-gatherer on the moor when next he is depressed is providing a counter-narrative for Basil's future.

'The Thorn' is a poem that not only shies away from talking directly and openly about possible infanticide to an audience including children scarcely past infancy. It also (and in a way that links it with 'Tintern Abbey') aims to provide a screen memory for its auditor – and its auditor's future thoughts. Poetry here speaks for the mind of man, but it sees itself as doing so most fully when it is proleptically responsive to and considerate of particular persons and kinds of persons. What I have been attending to here is the way in which individuals – and not just mountains and silent footsteps – suddenly loom up in Wordsworthian consciousness. Wordsworth's awareness of a distinctive reworking of the relationship between orality and writing enabled him to create poems that did not merely address an anonymous and distant community but figured an inconstant but real awareness of readers as listeners. These are poems that depict themselves as under the pressure of the sudden and looming consciousness of the individuality and sensitivities of their auditors.

Notes

1. I. A. Richards, *Principles of Literary Criticism* (New York: Harcourt, Brace & World, 1928), pp. 25–33. I would like to thank the organizers and

participants of a conference on ~~ịụḷiḷ(ḷ ịḷḷ(ḷ(ḷ(ḷ ̣iḷḷḷḷḷ~~ ~~éḷḷḷ ḷḷḷḷḷḷḷ ̣ṣḷ ṭḥ(~~ ~~P̣ḥḷḷḷḷ ṭḥ ̣ḥ ̣ḷ ̣ḷ ̣ḷḷ ̣ḷḷ ̣ḷ ̣ḥ ̣ṭḥḷ Ạṛṭṣ, Ṣḷḷḷ ̣ḷ Ṣḷḷḷḷḷḷ~~ and Humanities (CRASSH) at the University of Cambridge and of a lecture series at Princeton University for comments that helped me in the development of this chapter. Conversation with Susan Wolfson of Princeton University has been especially generative.

2. One of the most important of the moments in which Barthes advances this position is his claim that 'the reader is without history, biography, psychology: he is simply that someone who holds together in a single field all the traces by which the written text is constituted'. *Image, Music, Text*, trans. Stephen Heath (New York: Hill and Wang, 1977), p. 148.

3. Nicholas Hudson, '"Oral Tradition": The Evolution of an Eighteenth-Century Concept', in *Tradition in Transition: Women Writers, Marginal Texts, and the Eighteenth-Century Canon*, ed. Albert Ribeiro and James G. Basker (Oxford: Clarendon Press, 1996), p. 162.

4. See Edward Said, *Orientalism* (New York: Pantheon, 1978); Katie Trumpener, *Bardic Nationalism: The Romantic Novel and the British Empire* (Princeton, NJ: Princeton University Press, 1997); and Pascale Casanova, *The World Republic of Letters*, trans. M. B. DeBevoise (Cambridge, MA: Harvard University Press, 2004).

5. Susan Stewart, *Crimes of Writing* (New York: Oxford University Press, 1991), pp. 102–31. Hereafter cited by page numbers in the text.

6. Vladimir Propp, *Morphology of the Folktale*, trans. Laurence Scott, rev. Louis A. Wagner (Austin: University of Texas Press, 1968), pp. 13–14.

7. Stephen Maxfield Parrish, '"The Thorn": Wordsworth's Dramatic Monologue', *ELH*, 24 (1957), 153–63. See also Susan Wolfson's important essay 'Lyrical Ballads and the Language of (Men) Feeling: Wordsworth Writing Women's Voices', in *Men Writing the Feminine: Literature, Theory, and the Question of Genders*, ed. Thais E. Morgan (Buffalo: State University of New York Press, 1994), pp. 29–57. There Wolfson stresses the hysteria that unites Martha Ray and the mariner and their wandering words.

8. William St Clair, *The Reading Nation in the Romantic Period* (Cambridge: Cambridge University Press, 2004), especially pp. 66–83.

9. See Geoffrey H. Hartman, *Wordsworth's Poetry 1787–1814* (Cambridge, MA: Harvard University Press, 1987); Mary Jacobus, *Tradition and Experiment in Wordsworth's 'Lyrical Ballads' (1798)* (Oxford: Oxford University Press, 1976), pp. 219–20; Karen Swann, '"Martha's Name," or The Scandal of "The Thorn"', in *Dwelling in Possibility: Women Poets and Critics on Poetry*, ed. Yopie Prins and Maeera Shreiber (Ithaca, NY: Cornell University Press, 1997), pp. 60–79; and Josephine McDonagh, *Child Murder and British Culture 1720–1900* (Cambridge: Cambridge University Press, 2003).

10. Hartman, *Wordsworth's Poetry*, p. 148. Hereafter cited by page numbers in the text.

11. *'Lyrical Ballads' and Other Poems, 1797–1800*, ed. James Butler and Karen Green (Ithaca, NY: Cornell University Press, 1992), p. 79. Hereafter indicated as *LB* and cited by page numbers in the text. Poems in this volume are cited by line numbers in the text.

12. *The Prose Works*, ed. W. J. B. Owen and Jane Worthington Smyser, vol. 1 (Oxford: Clarendon Press, 1974), p. 117. This edition hereafter indicated as *PW* and cited by volume and page numbers in the text.

13. Claude Lévi-Strauss, *The Savage Mind* (Chicago: The University of Chicago Press, 1966), pp. 1–33.
14. See Robert Mayo, 'The Contemporaneity of the *Lyrical Ballads*', *PMLA*, 69 (1954), 486–522.
15. McDonagh, *Child Murder*, p. 79. Hereafter cited by page numbers in the text.
16. Margaret Homans has stressed Wordsworth's obliviousness to Dorothy's presence for most of the poem in her incisive reading of 'Tintern Abbey' and has seen it as a symptom of Wordsworth's exclusion of Dorothy from the symbolic and of his assigning her to a role as auditor and embodiment of his message. Although I think that Homans's case for her position is very strong, I myself emphasize the sudden turn to Dorothy as a genuine shift into acknowledgement rather than a sign of her exclusion. *Women Writers and Poetic Identity: Dorothy Wordsworth, Emily Brontë, and Emily Dickinson* (Princeton, NJ: Princeton University Press, 1980), pp. 26–7, 76–8.
17. *Autobiography and Literary Essays*, ed. John M. Robson and Jack Stillinger (Toronto: University of Toronto Press, 1981), p. 348.
18. In his Note to 'The Thorn' Wordsworth wrote, 'This Poem ought to have been preceded by an introductory poem, which I have been prevented from writing by never having felt myself in a mood when it was probable that I should write it well' (*LB*, 350).
19. Jane Austen, *Emma*, ed. Frances Ferguson (New York: Pearson Longman, 2006), p. 338.
20. Peter de Bolla, *The Discourse of the Sublime: History, Aesthetics, and the Subject* (Oxford: Blackwell, 1989), pp. 230–78. See also Lucy Newlyn, *Reading, Writing, and Romanticism: The Anxiety of Reception* (Oxford: Oxford University Press, 2000), esp. pp. 333–71.
21. Dorothy Wordsworth wrote, on 19 March 1798: 'Wm and Basil and I walked to the hill-tops, a very cold bleak day. We were met on our return by a severe hailstorm. William wrote some lines describing a stunted thorn.' *The Journals of Dorothy Wordsworth* (Oxford: Oxford University Press, 1978), p. 10.
22. See Swann, '"Martha's Name," or The Scandal of "The Thorn"', pp. 72–6; and McDonagh, *Child Murder* pp. 72–9. For a fuller account of Swann's view of Wordsworth's thinking about popular taste, see her 'Public Transport: English Romantic Experiments in Sensation', *ANQ*, 6 (1993), 136–42.
23. Swann, '"Martha's Name," or The Scandal of "The Thorn"', p. 76.

8
The Excursion and Wordsworth's Special Remainder

Paul Hamilton

Crimes against our 'species-being' (*Gattungswesen*) are the culminating charges Marx lays against capitalism in his early Paris manuscripts.[1] These writings were drafted in 1844, not published in full until 1927, and not Englished until 1961; they transformed Marxist thinking in the twentieth century; 'Marx before Marxism' inspired a humanistic Marxism as influential philosophically as the later science of *Das Kapital*. From Korsch and Lukács onwards, the Paris writings were understood as explaining the future for post-Kantian philosophy which Marx and Engels saw embodied in the German working class. For Engels, the 'outcome [*Ausgang*] of classical German philosophy' need not be exclusively the Catholic reaction Heine attributed to Schlegel and Novalis.[2] To redeploy philosophical insight in romantic fashion could also be to transform its speculative originality through practical collaborations heedless of disciplinary boundaries. From Lukács's praise of Novalis (one of his 'great thinkers of the art of living') to Benjamin's early inspiration in Friedrich Schlegel, new Marxists can be seen to go back to the future when they find precedents for the resuscitation in unlikely languages, sociological and technological, of a humanism whose conventional expression or German ideology had been discredited.[3]

Yet we still too often assume that to regard as a *species* the humanity whose despoliation through the commodification of labour Marx attacks would have appeared in the preceding period to concede the argument. Wordsworth's frequent invocation of the 'species' seems lodged within a discourse – at best anthropological, at worst Malthusian or proto-Darwinian – that has knocked off its perch Romantic talk of a uniquely human self-consciousness traditionally enlisting artistic support. Installed in its place is a scientific reduction treating human beings as a particular kind of animal and licensing a growing utilitarianism.

In Maureen McLane's recent fine study of the emergent languages of the human sciences in the Romantic period, Mary Shelley's novel, *Frankenstein*, is read as showing 'how biologization – the nominalization of a corporeal and social problem as a species *difference* – succeeds (that is, follows) and supports the failure both of humanism and the humanities'.[4] This is a succinct description of an anxiety undeniably typical of a culture nervous of a secular future it was beginning to acknowledge as inevitable. That Shelley's novel recognized its own fears and dramatized them critically is given little consideration. In this context, Wordsworth's trumping of Milton's epic machinery with his own anthropological idiom in the Prospectus to *The Excursion* is strikingly confident. The birth of anthropology, though, as John Zammito and others have argued, was a fraught affair engendered out of conflicts as complex as those between Kantian critique and Herderian hylozoism, in which judgements based on simple oppositions of humanists and scientists are unsafe.[5] Wordsworth's interest in the 'kind' is in keeping with contemporary literary–theoretical problematizings of generic notions, specifically Friedrich Schlegel's ingenious matching of a new scientific or philosophical sophistication to the freedoms of mythology and poetic self-surpassing. In Hamacher's formulation, Schlegel shows that 'by positing itself, genre poses for itself a limit and posits itself, as self-positing, beyond this limit'.[6] This is no prescriptive transgression of the kind Derrida attacks in his 'The Law of Genre', by which genre improperly steps outside itself to prescribe how we should read it.[7] That commentary or parabasis is, for Schlegel, already on the stage, part of the play, and so a non-coercive critical expansion of the original fiction. The 'belonging' Derrida denies its reflexivity is just that surrender to others in which Marx and Engels couch the philosophical afterlife. Habermas's later version of this concession is that '*The achievements of the transcendental subject have their basis in the natural history of the human species*'.[8] No master-discourse can presume over the practicalities of communication and must, to continue beyond its classical moment of mastery, submit to the material transformations Marx and Engels envisaged for philosophy. I want to argue that the human genre Wordsworth's *The Excursion* explores comparably outdistances its own definitions; or, as the Essay, Supplementary to the Preface to the *Poems* published a year later argues, poetic language solicits from the reader collaborative powers that weren't there before.[9] *The Excursion*'s official historicization of this insight is book nine's call to colonize. That 'imperial destiny', though, is only one possible outcome of a human self-surpassing whose ambition is to create a universal character. Following

ⵏⵏⴰⵔⵔ ⴰⵏⴷ ᴎⴰⵢⵡⵓⵉⵓ, ⵓⵓⵏ ⵡⵄ ⴰⵉⵄⵏⵍⵏⵏⵦⵀ ⵏⵉⵀ ⵙⵉⵏⴰⵍⵉⵍⴻ ⵍⵉⵓⵓⵓⴰⵓⵓⵦⵓⵓ ⵊⵔⵓⵓⵓ ⵜⵔⵓⵃ
undesirable politics?

Wordsworth's poetry is especially alive to the thought that in all things there is what Schelling called an 'indivisible remainder' (*der nie aufgehende Rest*), something unsusceptible of mediation altogether.[10] In *The Unmediated Vision*, Geoffrey Hartman quotes twice from Schelling's early treatise on 'The World-Soul', which anticipates his later formulation in his *Freiheitsschrift of der nie aufgehende Rest*, itself consistent with his much later description in his 1842 *Philosophy of Mythology* of Being's corresponding infinite lack (*der unendliche Mangel an Sein*).[11] This is the sphere, the socially impossible space of the ever 'casual passenger', which Wordsworth's narrators frequently inhabit and of which they speak. Hartman finds here as well the prototype for Rilke's *sein Aufgang ist Dasein*, where *Aufgang*, an 'explosive dilation' in Hartman's translation, is paradoxically measured by our human limitation to the here and now, to an unremarkable situatedness, a *da*.[12] In *Saving the Text*, Hartman epigraphs Adorno's severe insistence that *Geist* is no more an absolute than it is something that divides into an existing thing without remainder (*so wenig geht er auf im Seienden*). And in *The Unremarkable Wordsworth* he quotes Derrida's typical turning of the dialectical tables on Hegel, making him subject to *Geist*, his own means of surpassing others, but a *Geist* now shot with the indeterminacies of textuality: '*what has remained* [for us of Hegel] [is] infinitely calculable.'[13] Hartman draws the conclusion that 'there is always a remainder that cannot be purged, whatever violence of intellect we apply'.[14] Hegel's *Aufhebung*, the motor of his phenomenology, becomes for Hartman a kind of 'elation' when its overcoming of an explanation allows an excited glimpse of that inexhaustible reserve.

The resistance to interpretative violence, therefore, can come as much from simplicity as from complexity; and Wordsworth is unusual in being able to furnish both kinds of resistant text; in being able, in fact, to make them hard to tell apart. To that extent he addresses a problematic, largely created by Kant, stemming from the difficulty of defining our natural existence, our species, without appearing to capitulate to something hegemonic. Kant's somewhat baleful achievement was to make us question whether anything other than reason rightfully employed could be said to belong to us intrinsically. Natural feelings, desires, perceptual response, pragmatic concerns all could be cast as constraints upon a rational freedom which, by definition, was a freedom from everything except its own universal application. Nevertheless, following Kant's mentor, Rousseau (but the Rousseau of *Julie* and the *Rêveries* rather than the Rousseau of the *Discourses*), Schiller and the post-Kantians made man's own nature the target of their philosophical search. Was it possible to define us as belonging to a species without traducing our typical freedoms? As Kant had demonstrated, however, a nature free of the accidents of individual perceptions rapidly becomes an extremely rarefied business. The remainder left over after the subtraction of everything belonging to the unremarkable circumstances of time and place is elusive. The possessor of experience has to be what can remain after the division of that experience into all forms of conceptual return. For this exercise not to refine itself out of existence, we have to find a way of making perception its own thing, independently of its epistemological function, and so an *apperception*. We must relish aesthesis for its own felicities, its own workability, its own symmetries and coherence. But in his third *Critique* Kant made this investigation a matter of aesthetic *judgement*, or a feeling equivalent to judgement, by still following the model of establishing universals – this time through the medium of a *sensus communis*. Aesthetics is validated through its *logical* form, which shadows the form of cognitive judgements or conceptual knowledge, not as its *own* form of experiencing things.

Post-Kantian philosophy, enlisting the discursive help it can, tries to get aesthetics to acknowledge its dependence on *aisthesis*: to acknowledge, that is, what is special about precisely what it cannot elevate philosophically. There are things philosophy cannot do on its own, one of which is this discovery of, in effect, the special in the species. The extension of philosophy by other discursive means, though, in other genres, only makes sense as long as we remember their philosophical starting point. This is especially the case where apperception is concerned. What Ross Wilson has called 'the emptiness of the Kantian subject' for conceptual analysis is a void which all manner of expressions may rush to fill.[15] The philosophical insight these expressions should continue to elaborate remains that elusiveness to philosophical redaction possessed by sheer perception. The individual's resistance to being typecast by presumptive philosophical stand-ins keeps it on the move, in search of ever more adequate expression. As soon as archaeologists identify a human artifact, for example, they infer from it a certain view taken of the world which prompted an instrumental response. But the experience of having that response, the ability to relish its aisthesis, is a special human self-conscious character resulting from a further inference: one that recognizes the philosophically compensatory nature of expressiveness. (Computers and bats, we might say, lack this faculty, supremely competent aliens might not need it.[16]) Accordingly, no individual expression

used in these circumstances can be final or absolute, since its function
is always to offset the loss of just such authority. It is always a simile,
an excursus which is 'like' what it gets at philosophically; it is never
simply philosophical, but nevertheless figuratively successful only
because of its philosophical deputizing.[17] Kant's 'apperception' inau-
gurates this supplementary logic, and the necessary inconclusiveness
or unending expressiveness of the philosophical stand-ins it licenses
paves the way for the famous post-Kantian redefinition of the humanities as a 'progressive, universal poesie'.[18] Wordsworth is interested in
the 'species' or 'kind' around the same time that generic notions are
philosophically broken down in the manner of Friedrich Schlegel's
ingenious matching of a new scientific or philosophical sophistication
to the freedoms of mythology and poetic self-surpassing.

In his Paris Manuscripts of 1844, Marx can confidently assert that the
individual and species-life of human beings are indistinguishable; each
can particularize or generalize characteristics of the other.[19] The English
usage of 'special' confirms this by veering dizzily between meaning to
particularize a class or to classify a particular. Marx's account of the
'universal' character of our species-being boldly takes Kantian universality and makes of it a natural characteristic. Typically, we can reproduce
the world from different points of view, but in a manner detached from
the interests or purposes which have produced the objects we thus
reproduce. Our defining consciousness, that is, signifies the freedom
remaining to us that lets us take notice of, take pleasure in or simply gain
a sense of life from what we cognize; which affective supplement for cognition we choose to employ is never conclusive. Our experience of what
it is like for us to judge of things is possible for any judgement we make.
In reproducing in consciousness our environment 'to the standards of
every species and of applying to each object its inherent standard' we
can thus write our 'natural history'.[20] Our reproduction of the world to
its standards, natural history, can tell *our* natural history too.

Marx thinks that instead of exclusively reflecting *our* powers to conceive of them in this way, things simultaneously return to us a consciousness of the self-consciousness dictated by natural circumstances.
Every judgement we make about the world is also an experience *for
us*, proportionate to but not identical with the particular qualities of
what it is we judge. This apperception is not a perception but something aesthetic, functioning in accordance with what Marx, with some
abruptness, refers to as 'the laws of beauty'.[21] The laws of beauty apply
not to the felicities of the object judged, but to a pleasure in our own
judgement. This relish is scientifically disinterested or indifferent.

It enjoys the remainder which must be surplus to the objects judged for consciousness of them to be possible. If the remainder was explicable as just another object, then a further consciousness of it would be possible, itself generating another remainder to be explained, and so on *ad infinitum*. Marx's invocation of aesthetics cuts this regress short by calling an end to philosophical explanation in deference to what has to be expressed in other ways. What it feels like to be a human being is a quality of perception which cannot itself be perceived. We have to concede an intimacy with our natural humanity so close that we cannot slide any philosophical explanation between our existential condition and our awareness of it. As Marx puts it, the human being's 'own life is an object for him, only because he is a species-being'.[22]

The young Marx's next step is to argue that we act on the world because we change with it, changed by its changes. In a more familiar Marxist locution, we make our history, though not in ways of our own choosing. The Romantic remainder, the difference from nature, must be preserved in order for consciousness to be possible. Our species characteristic of being able to take our own life as an object for contemplation or feeling is a difference allowing for mutation; 'the *cultivation* [*Bildung*] of the five senses is the work of all previous history'.[23] Under capitalism, Marx argues, the industrial worker is deprived of this education. The remainder vanishes, and he or she becomes identified with the nature to which they have to conform. The power to reproduce becomes reduced to the power to produce. But the idea is then that to avoid this collapse into the natural world in which we nevertheless undeniably belong is not to identify ourselves with a homeless, content-less abstraction, but, just as any animal does, to occupy our natural state, our species-being. Being produced and consciously reproducing those conditions of production are reciprocal activities, and so we get the self-consciousness that our material circumstances permit. Marx's optimism is to believe in parallel development here. Increases in our powers of estimating nature will come with our development through its resources of our own. Ultimately, the young Marx seems to envisage a union of the two, where the Romantic remainder is assimilated without violence; where, in a just society, we encounter 'the realized naturalism of man and the realized humanism of nature'.[24]

1   Wordsworth's 'spousal verse'

Wordsworth, especially in his Prospectus to *The Excursion*, similarly fills out the aesthetic thought he has inherited and finds he can talk about

our species without doing violence to that irrationality which Kantianism
had rendered so abstract and which post-Kantianism's excursions from
philosophy typically tried to express. In the Prospectus, Wordsworth's
'spousal verse' celebrates an epistemological union in which Nature's
fostering of our self-consciousness achieves a natural status; or, it is
because of her fostering that we can look upon her as a natural mother
much less equivocally than in the 'Immortality Ode'.[25] On one side of
this marriage, the World is the World, without qualification. But the
identity of the other side is more mobile. Wordsworth moves from
extolling 'How exquisitely the individual Mind' is fitted to its significant other to the expansion, 'And the progressive powers perhaps no
less / Of the whole species' (*Excursion*, Prospectus: 63–5). It is perhaps
easy to overlook the transition from the 'individual' to 'the whole
species' and be more struck by 'the progressive powers'. Wordsworth
remained a Whig in many ways, and 'the mighty stream of tendency'
driving *The Excursion* is clearly meant to be going somewhere (*Excursion*,
9.88). While Blake believed that Wordsworth's trust in epistemological
fittingness betrayed an autocratic sense of propriety, Hazlitt suspected
a Whiggish gloss on true radicalism. In fact, he argued, 'the poem
stands stock-still'.[26] But what is the connection in Wordsworth's mind
between 'species' and 'progress'? Perhaps there is a thought here actually more radical than Hazlitt would like? Hazlitt might have expected
the link to be between 'progress' and 'individual' instead? But 'species', or our anthropological situation, how we fit in the world, is what
makes Wordsworth think of advancement. We move forward not in line
with a banal Whiggish interpretation of history, always for the better,
but, as a passage a little later suggests, through a more Marxian idea of
a natural history of self-transformation. This kind of creativity lets us
recover our natural selves and resume our place in their history. Nature
prescribes both our human power to take its current measure and our
power to figure our remaining experience, our feel, for seeing things in
this human way at this time. This, I think, helps explain Wordsworth's
invocation to the Muse in his Prospectus that inspires 'the human Soul
of universal earth' (*Excursion*, Prospectus: 84), akin, surely, to what we
have just heard Marx call 'the realised humanism of nature':

> —Come thou prophetic Spirit, that inspir'st
> The human Soul of universal earth,
> Dreaming on things to come; and dost possess
> A metropolitan Temple in the hearts
> Of mighty Poets; upon me bestow

> A gift of genuine insight; that my Song
> With star-like virtue in its place may shine.

> *(Excursion*, Prospectus: 83–9)

Already, you'll remember, the Prospectus has secularized the Miltonic theological apparatus that has become the staple of English vision. *Paradise Lost* made obligatory the subsequent adoption of a mock-heroic idiom which publicly accepted that, as it were, there was no alternative. The poise and authority of a Dryden and Pope surely rested on that acceptance, a resignation they turned into a neoclassical sense of proportion: only the immature and vapid could essay the visionary now, the Shadwells, the dunces. Wordsworth's trumping of Milton may seem hubristic but is also a way of acknowledging that, if the visionary project is to be recovered, if there is to be a future for Gray and Collins unclouded by personification and poetic diction, Milton needs to be displaced. Since Milton's authority is rhetorically tied to theology, secularization becomes the necessary angel of its visionary opposite and so doesn't mean 'secular' at all but can 'breathe in worlds / To which the heaven of heavens is but a veil' (*Excursion*, Prospectus: 29–30). Nothing, we are told,

> Not Chaos, not
> The darkest pit of lowest Erebus,
> Nor aught of blinder vacancy—scooped out
> By help of dreams, can breed such fear and awe
> As fall upon us when we look
> Into our Minds, into the Mind of Man,
> My haunt, and the main region of my Song.

> *(Excursion*, Prospectus: 35–41)

Now in its natural place, the mind of man bears witness to a species that takes the measure of all things, a cosmopolitan being who identifies 'The human Soul of universal Earth' (*Excursion*, Prospectus: 84). The qualifiers 'human' and 'universal' need each other here in the Marxian sense we construed earlier. There would be no universal were it not for the human power to reproduce all things to their own standards; but that human facility owes its universality – its characteristic expansion overcoming the confinement usually conferred by a species-being – to the variety of the world there to be thus reproduced, a world to which then universality is properly transferred. It all depends on the emphasis;

the proposition can be led either by human soul or by *universal earth*, in equal partnership. The mediations of mind and nature are so mutually implicating that they almost disappear. The spousal verse makes them virtually interchangeable. (Imagine the impropriety of introducing your spouse or significant other to someone as your 'mediator'.) Perhaps this espousal is as close as Wordsworth comes to an 'unmediated vision'?

As in the case of genre, so in the case of species we deduce the cause from the effect. From the generic variety of literary expression we grasp the being requiring such a range of expression; from the miscellany of the world, we infer the universal character of the species that can see reflected in such mundane multitudinousness its own ongoing power to reproduce the world to the world's standards – disinterestedly, and so in accordance with what Marx called the laws of beauty. The suggestion is that this activity is continuously progressive. Towards the end of the Prospectus, Wordsworth worries that he has slipped occasionally from such anthropological endeavour back into the autobiographical habit of *The Prelude*, contemplating 'the transitory Being that beheld / this Vision' (*Excursion*, Prospectus: 97–8). But then he recovers the overlap of *The Prelude* onto his current concerns, hoping that 'my Life / Express the image of a better time' (*Excursion*, Prospectus: 102–3). As we saw Marx argue, where our species-being is concerned there is no distinction to be made between individual and general. In *The Prelude*, the belief of poet and Coleridgean auditor that in the individual case 'what we have loved / Others will love' then releases the generalizations that follow, on the mind of man and its primacy over the earth.[27] In *The Excursion,* any individual colouring is quickly enlisted to 'Express the image of a better time'; the progressive powers, in this more reciprocal arrangement between mind and world, deliver a human experience increasingly observing natural proportions, 'More wise desires, and simpler manners' (*Excursion*, Prospectus: 104). Rousseauean rather than Nietzschean, this faith (that 'Nature never did betray the heart that loved her') assumes that the human subject remains inviolate, composed rather than dis-integrated by whatever it contemplates. The post-Kantian passage to Marx similarly argues that the subject's power to change and surpass its previous selves is continually progressive, not a recurrent Dionysian moment.

After such preparation, *The Excursion* repeatedly describes the tragedy of those who are forced to give up or be alienated from their species-being. This does not necessarily mean that they become debased or degenerate. The idea is that lives such as Margaret's in book one (and the class of dispossessed artisans her family represents) would have

been more naturally lived to another standard: to one of those standards which the human being can reproduce but by which, in typically
human fashion, it should remain undetained and from which it can
move on. But Margaret and her kind are

> ... shoals of Artisans [who]
> From ill requited labour turn'd adrift
> Sought daily bread from public charity,
> They, and their wives and children – happier far
> Could they have lived as do the little birds
> That peck along the hedge-rows, or the Kite
> That makes her dwelling on the mountain Rocks!
>
> (*Excursion* [1827], 1. 590–6)

The intelligence of this pathos (if one can put it that way) lies in giving them
the freedom of nature within the restricted terms – the determined existence of a kind of bird – precluding the consciousness or disinterested enjoyment of natural purposes allowing the birds to stand for freedom. Earlier,
the sensibility of the narrator (the Wanderer) had been commended for the
way it could hold love and faith in simple solution, without conceptual
addition or complication: 'in the mountains did he *feel* his faith; / ... nor
did he believe,—he *saw*' (*Excursion*, 1. 247, 253; my emphases). Similarly,
our power to imagine what it would be like to enjoy the existence of the
hedgerow birds or the kite estranges us from the birds as it increases our
intimacy with them. Really to be like the birds would be, like the 'Old Man
Travelling', not to be able to notice their otherness at all.

In book one of *The Excursion*, Margaret is increasingly denied self-
consciousness by her distraction from and forgetfulness of herself and
her kind. In decline she becomes like a natural creature we take the
standard of rather than someone who can do this for herself. The almost
unbearable quality of her tragedy lies here. For, as the Wanderer says,
her awful fate cannot but be reassuring to the human sympathizer; her
(literal) degeneration furnishes another moment in which the observer
is made aware of his or her generic universality. This seems an appall-
ingly instrumental or self-serving treatment of her, but the Wanderer
argues that it is 'a wantonness' not to take responsibility for the general
'thanksgiving', as he would call it, that lies dissolved in our perception
of anything (*Excursion*, 1.657, 238). The frequent assertions of 'faith'
and the doctrinal tone of *The Excursion* suggest that the Wanderer often
has in mind the consolations of the Christian afterlife more than did

the Pedlar narrator of the matrix poem, *The Ruined Cottage*. But the lines dissolving faith in perception are retained in the later work, and the Prospectus (again stemming from an earlier poem, 'Home at Grasmere' of 1800) works without orthodox theological support, leaving intact the poem's final juxtapositions of ruin and beauty, misery and happiness. Margaret's deterioration is one that allows the celebrations of a spousal verse. The crunch lines to make sense of are those when the Wanderer, responding to the beauty of the silvered spear-grass, tells us how

> Amid the uneasy thoughts which filled my mind,
> That what we feel of sorrow and despair
> From ruin and from change, and all the grief
> The passing shews of Being leave behind,
> Appeared an idle dream, that could maintain,
> Nowhere, dominion o'er the enlightened spirit
> Whose meditative sympathies repose
> Upon the breast of Faith. I turned away,
> And walked along my road in happiness.

(Excursion [1845], 1.978–86)

These lines, if they work, seem to transvalue mourning. Without need of elegy or monument, we mourn through the feeling that whatever dies is not the humanity of the person, because their natural dissolution reflects that shared category back to us. The union of mind and nature in Wordsworth's 'spousal verse' means that when mind is dissolved in nature – as in 'things silently gone out of mind, and things violently destroyed' (*PW*, 2:141) – nature redoubles its reminder to us of the indivisible remainder, the infinite lack, the significant other united in our perceptions of it. This produces a very simple pleasure, that 'sensation' which Wordsworth's poet, our representative, carries into all manner of abstruse knowledges and sciences. It cannot, though, be reduced to the functions that produce it, which must wither and die and, in their turn, remind us of an indivisible remainder. These functions are the 'idle dream' from which we can turn away in possessing again our conscious selves. We turn away from them in the act of seeing that their objects, that natural objects, are beautiful in Marx's sense: because they have returned us to our sense of what it is like to be a human being, a member of 'the vast empire of human society, as it is spread over the whole earth, and over all time' (*PW*, 2:141), a society of which, our mourning testifies, Margaret cannot lose her membership.

The rest of Wordsworth's *Excursion* triumphantly registers the human expansion that takes place when elegy is freed of monument and nature's very power to outlast us becomes poignant. The possibilities opened up for poetic remembrance are then inexhaustible. The narrator refers to epitaphs as 'notices', but the 'authentic epitaphs' (*Excursion*, 5.653) that the Pastor is asked to 'pronounce' on those buried in the graveyard where the little group of *The Excursion*'s protagonists gather are as 'uncertain' as were the natural semiotics of 'Tintern Abbey' or the little girl's assurances in 'We are Seven'. None of Wordsworth's characters is, as in Sir Thomas Browne's *The Urn-Burial*, 'a noble animal splendid in ashes and pompous in the grave', although they enter a sepulchral valley – 'Urn-like it was in shape, deep as an Urn' (*Excursion*, 2.353) – and search out its cemetery. Love of nature leads to love of mankind because of the indivisible remainder whereby nature *tout court*, without ornament, always reminds us of the peculiarly human feeling given in our perceptions of it. Attention to this, a growing aptitude for feeling or hearing our humanity, can be progress enough for Wordsworth. 'Science' can then become, we are told at the conclusion to book four of *The Excursion*,

> In furnishing clear guidance, a support
> Not treacherous, to the Mind's *excursive* Power.
> —So build we up the Being that we are.
>
> (*Excursion*, 4.1262–4)

Our species, our 'Being', improves rather than levels individual sensibility, so that

> Whate'er we see,
> Or feel, shall tend to quicken & refine
> The humblest functions of corporeal sense.
>
> (*Excursion* [1845], 4.1270–2)

This, at any rate, is one way of coping critically with the 'unremarkable' Wordsworth, a poet whose supposed humbleness actually surpasses his evident poetic gifts so as to appear, 'I don't know how else to put it', Geoffrey Hartman wrote recently, *'unemployed'*.[28] At the same time, bits of *The Excursion*'s narrative have always been difficult to stomach, such as its claim that 'the law, / By which Mankind now suffers, is most just' (*Excursion*, 4.304–5), which surely justifies the Solitary's 'faint sarcastic smile ' (Pinestan, 2.9111, all that the Wanderer's power of 'breathing in content / The keen, the wholesome air of poverty' (*Excursion*, 1.330–1). These seem more palatable if everything is a figure for the poem's turning of conventional impoverishment into a special endowment, of simple sensation into an expression of philosophical complexity. But even this expansion has its problems, when, in book nine, recalling the industrious bees of Virgil's fourth Georgic, it has us setting off with the burden of Wordsworth's enlightenment to found the British Empire: 'Even 'till the smallest habitable Rock, / Beaten by lonely billows, hear the songs / Of humanized Society' (*Excursion*, 9.389–91). The colonial imperative requires people already to be objects in order for them subsequently to be humanized. Wordsworth wants to see this as a delivery from existing slaveries, not least that of Napoleonic imperialism; but we are surely too wise about what colonialism really was like not to regret Wordsworth's new employment.

2 Dependencies and hopes

There is, however, another way of historicizing Wordsworth's 'employment' in *The Excursion*: to look at the discursive pressure that he would have put himself under at that time by trying poetically to describe his species. The poem has often been judged aesthetically inferior to *The Prelude* because the former tends to use religious expression to plug the gaps in experience that had excited the latter's aesthetic of the sublime. *The Excursion*'s prioritizing of religious apprehension is usually thought to work to the disadvantage of its artistic success. It is not immediately obvious why this should be so. The poem's openness to the incompleteness of human experience, the sense of a remainder never exhausted by retelling the facts of a life or by enumerating its memorabilia has, I have suggested, no need of conventional aesthetic monument. In fact this writing must be anti-aesthetic to the extent that it seeks human testimony undiscriminatingly in nature, as happy to 'stoop' with the Wanderer as to 'soar' in his celebration that 'Here are we, in a bright and breathing world' (*Excursion*, 3.236, 237, 242). In his review of *The Excursion* in the *Quarterly Review*, Charles Lamb stressed this universal franchise: 'in his poetry nothing in Nature is dead. Motion is synonymous with life.'[29] And certainly when scenes in *The Excursion*'s landscape become proverbial rather than apocryphal – 'The Ruined Cottage', 'The Path of perseverance', 'The Joyful tree' – nature is made to inhabit a common linguistic currency in which we can all find our own expression or idiom. What can appear to be an unfortunate sententiousness is actually another Wordsworthian pitch to describe 'the humanism of nature', or the making of motion 'synonymous with life'. Religion readily supplies a language for the inadequacy of any attempt to detain human significance in monumental fixture or icon and for the sense of the human arising from just that failure; it characteristically satisfies the need to honour our characteristic power of excursus from the most summative of descriptions. Hence 'the sublime attractions of the Grave' (*Excursion*, 4.239), that startling pronouncement with which the poem's main narrator, the Wanderer, leaves behind the aesthetic provenance of sublimity in his funereal but still poetic reworking of it. Coleridge, in *Biographia Literaria*, was surely right to query the aesthetic credentials of Wordsworth's poetry while remaining as confident as Lamb that it showed how much 'the man and the poet lose and find themselves in each other'.[30]

Nevertheless, religious language, while logically lending itself to this kind of anthropological sublimity, has its own defining doctrinal interests and ends. Does Wordsworth's other spokesman, the Pastor, not begin his peroration in the churchyard with 'those principles of faith / Announced, as a preparatory act / Of reverence to the spirit of the place' (*Excursion*, 6.89–91)? And does not such piety presume over the undifferentiated but supremely expressive human surplus dominant elsewhere in the poem? The poem criticizes those, especially its reclusive Solitary, who try 'to frame / Conceptions equal to the Soul's desires' (*Excursion*, 4.136–7).

> Oh! no, full oft the innocent Sufferer sees
> Too clearly; feels too vividly; and longs
> To realize the Vision with intense
> And overconstant yearning – there – there lies
> The excess, by which the balance is destroyed.
>
> (*Excursion*, 4.173–7)

But this 'excess' does have doctrinal religious content when Wordsworth writes 'Of our sublime dependencies, and hopes / For future states of Being' (*Excursion*, 5.240–1), in which the 'pale recluse' culpably loses faith. As the expression of sheer promise, or speculation about an eliminable logic of hope in human experience, the 'future states of being' could anticipate anything, including Marxian transformation. But in this poem, we are told, religion is 'a more vaunted name' than philosophy (*Excursion*, 5.327). The post-Kantian thought with which I have been contextualizing Wordsworth develops the indeterminacies

ration upon the quasi-spirituality of the sublime in order to cross disciplinary boundaries and license newly expressive discursive collaborations. Wordsworth, though, often appears to recover that spirituality in
fairly orthodox religious terms, achieving a closure on human indeterminacy as effective as his colonialist closure on ideas of excursion and
tendency.

I think these Wordsworthian terminuses undeniably monitor large
parts of *The Excursion*. They oppose his expansions of sublimity to
engineer a 'true equality' common to the species, an egalitarianism
that leaves the narrator 'for the injustice grieving, that hath made /
So wide a difference betwixt Man and Man' (*Excursion*, 9.247, 252–3).
No religious gloss adds anything to the species universal here, which
transcends social hierarchy although, by the same token, does not offer
a programme for social change. Nevertheless, the 'mighty stream of tendency' (*Excursion*, 9.88) resented by Hazlitt and others as a distraction
from desirable social reform, can also point to the fact that we can get at
the authentically human only through a discursive movement which,
for this purpose, renders any discursive establishment, any accredited
definition of us – political, religious, social – indeterminate. Our characteristic progress is rather excursive and, if so, the political dimension
Wordsworth is so often accused of effacing would be recovered at the
Marxian end of the post-Kantian road he has been treading. We have
seen how, for the young Marx, the aesthetically indeterminate was not
a Nietzschean recurrence of the same but led us through provisional
determinations to a complete political accommodation of our special
remainder – 'the realized [*durchgeführte*] naturalism of man and the realized humanism of nature.'[31]

I finish by suggesting that the logic of Wordsworth's oscillation
between religious and species explanations is also explicable in terms
of the Kantian ambiguities handed on for post-Kantian redevelopment.
Kant offers both religious and anthropological conclusions, although
outside the exposition of the sublime given in the *Critique of Judgement*,
when he reflects upon our natural history. On the one hand, in the 1788
Critique of Practical Reason, one postulate or precondition of the practical reason we undoubtedly possess is that for us to be completely rather
than intermittently moral in our actions we would have to progress
beyond what it is given us to be within our mortal dispensation. We
need, therefore, theoretically to assume a religious solution in order for
our sense of moral responsibility, our conviction that 'I ought' implies
'I can', to make sense. Dialectically, in other words, what appears to
us as an endless series through which we progress must, from another

point of view, be immortality. Kant, one always has to add, emphasizes strongly that we can't demonstrate the existence of that perfect point of view, but our commitment to the realization of our completely moral being requires us to presuppose it. Or, in other words, although the moral imperative is to do good for its own sake, the full realization of that good, since only achievable in eternity, leads to the recognition of a *divine* command (*zur Erkenntnis aller Pflichten als göttlicher Gebote*).[32] Kant has to make two discourses collaborate, moral and religious, to get his point across. The content of this presupposition of immortality, since it is denied scientific or experiential status, becomes that of 'hope' or 'grace' (*Seligkeit*). We are back with Wordsworth's 'sublime dependencies, and hopes / For future states of Being' (*Excursion*, 5.240).

On the other hand, Kant had already published in 1784 his short essay or series of propositions, *Idea for a Universal History with a Cosmopolitan Purpose*. There, the complete development of our reason – and, by implication, that moral existence in which we are entirely led by reason – is a possibility only for the species not the individual. And the species would be catered for only in a cosmopolitan not a national society; evolution and politics possess mutually explanatory teleologies. Immortality is therefore attributed not to the individual whose morality entitles her justifiably to hope for it, but to the species: a secular immortality in no need of the idea of an afterlife to make it thinkable. The failure of history so far to deliver the complete human being is also evidence of the 'unsocial sociability' (*ungesellige Geselligkeit*) necessary to keep us progressing towards that elusive remainder.[33] Here, the unattainable point of view from which this abrasiveness would be seen to have contrived an impregnable peace, a true cosmopolitanism, is the point of view of the species, a universal category taking up into itself all our individual differences. We, however, as individuals can only feel impulses to self-development which it would take the development of our entire species properly to realize. Unable individually to resume our species, we can only 'hope' that our human destiny will be fulfilled. Beings from other worlds can be thought of as individuals capable of full self-realization, but in our case it is different: only the species can hope for this (*nur die Gattung kann dieses hoffen*).[34]

Both explanations share the vocabulary of hope; only, in the case of the anthropological explanation, the hope is not dissolved in a postulate of immortality. Immortality is already a metaphor, a way of describing how our species can continue to develop our aims beyond our own individual lifespan. It is hoped that the series of such supersessions of individuals will eventually realize the ends for which

each strived. Kant commends the refusal to accept social norms in the
interests of a new sociability, a better kind of society. He sees problems
in how you go about describing a history based on such premises. For
such a purpose, it would seem to him, only a novel (*ein Roman*) would
be adequate. The attempt to get on terms with the human genus prob-
lematizes the genre with which one might be expected to do so. *Der
Roman* was the post-Kantian name for the discursive flexibility needed
to overcome the limitations of bare philosophy; and, I have argued,
the willingness to cross discursive boundaries in pursuit of an adequate
description of our species-being culminates in Marx's materialist transformation of his entire philosophical heritage. On the way, Wordsworth
gives us his excursus on or version of the naturalism of man and the
humanism of nature, 'this true equality' (*Excursion*, 9.247) and his
hopes for its realization. Seen in this light, his writing in *The Excursion*
tells us of much more than the locally historicized religious and colonialist aspirations he undoubtedly shared as well.

Notes

1. Karl Marx, *Early Writings*, trans. Rodney Livingstone and Gregory Benton
   (Harmondsworth: Penguin, 1975), esp. pp. 327–30. Also see Karl Marx,
   Frühe Schriften ed. H. J. Lieber and P. Furth, vol. 1 (Stuttgart: Cotta, 1962),
   esp. pp. 565–9. Also compare chapter seven of David McLellan, *Marx Before
   Marxism* (Harmondsworth: Penguin, 1972).
2. See Friedrich Engels, *Ludwig Feuerbach and the Outcome of German Classical
   Philosophy* (London: Martin Lawrence, 1934).
3. See George Lukács, *Soul and Form*, trans. Anna Bostock (London: Merlin
   Press, 1974), p. 51.
4. Maureen N. McLane, *Romanticism and the Human Sciences: Poetry, Population
   and the Discourse of the Species* (Cambridge: Cambridge University Press,
   2000), p. 108.
5. See John H. Zammito, *Kant, Herder, and the Birth of Anthropology* (Chicago:
   University of Chicago Press, 2002).
6. Werner Hamacher, *Premises: Essays on Philosophy and Literature from Kant to
   Celan*, trans. Peter Fenves (Cambridge, MA: Harvard University Press, 1996),
   p. 230.
7. Avital Ronell's influential translation of Derrida's 'The Law of Genre' originally appeared in *Glyph*, 7 (1980), and is reproduced in David Duff's excellent collection, *Modern Genre Theory* (Harlow: Longman, 2000), pp. 219–31.
8. Jürgen Habermas, *Knowledge and Human Interests*, trans. Jeremy J. Shapiro
   (London: Heinemann, 1978), p. 312.
9. See Wordsworth's statement, 'Therefore to create taste is to call forth and
   bestow power.' *The Prose Works*, ed. W. J. B. Owen and Jane Smyser, vol. 3
   (Oxford: Clarendon Press, 1974) p. 82. Hereafter indicated as *PW* and cited
   by volume and page numbers in the text.

10. F. W. J. Schelling, *Sämmtliche Werke*, ed. K. F. A. Schelling, part I, vol. 7 (Stuttgart: Cotta, 1856–61), pp. 359–60. Translation mine.

11. See Schelling, *Sämmtliche Werke*, II.2, p. 49.

12. Geoffrey H. Hartman, *The Unmediated Vision: An Interpretation of Wordsworth, Hopkins, Rilke, and Valéry* (New Haven, CT: Yale University Press), p. 167.

13. Geoffrey H. Hartman, *The Unremarkable Wordsworth* (London: Methuen, 1987), p. 192.

14. Hartman, *Unremarkable Wordsworth*, p. 192.

15. See chapter three of Ross Wilson, *Subjective Universality in Kant's Aesthetics* (Bern: Peter Lang, 2007).

16. I am obviously on Colin McGinn's rather than Daniel Dennett's side of the mind–body problem here. I am also thinking of David J. Chalmers's definition: 'We can say that a being is conscious if there *is something it is like* to be that being, to use a phrase made famous by Thomas Nagel. Similarly, a mental state is conscious if there is something it is like to be in that mental state. To put it another way, we can say that a mental state is conscious if it has a *qualitative feel* – an associated quality of experience.' *The Conscious Mind: In Search of a Fundamental Theory* (New York: Oxford University Press, 1996), p. 4.

17. This is my point of difference from Philippe Lacoue-Labarthe and Jean-Luc Nancy's *The Literary Absolute: The Theory of Literature in German Romanticism*, trans. Philip Barnard and Cheryl Lester (Albany: SUNY Press, 1988).

18. Friedrich Schlegel, *Lucinde and the Fragments*, trans. Peter Firchow (Minneapolis: University of Minnesota Press, 1971), p. 175 (*Athenaeum Fragment* no. 116).

19. 'Man's individual and species-life are not two *distinct things*, however much – and this is necessarily so – the mode of existence of individual life is a more *particular* or a more *general* mode of the species-life, or species-life a more *particular* or more *general* individual life.' Karl Marx, *Early Writings*, p. 350; also see *Frühe Schriften*, 1.597.

20. Marx, *Early Writings*, p. 329; also see *Frühe Schriften*, 1.568.

21. Marx, *Early Writings*, p. 329; also see *Frühe Schriften*, 1.568.

22. Marx, *Early Writings*, p. 328; also see *Frühe Schriften*, 1.567.

23. Marx, *Early Writings*, p. 353; also see *Frühe Schriften*, 1.601.

24. Marx, *Early Writings*, p. 350; also see *Frühe Schriften*, 1.596.

25. William Wordsworth, *The Excursion*, ed. Sally Bushell, James A. Butler, and Michael C. Jaye, with the assistance of David García (Ithaca, NY: Cornell University Press, 2007), p. 40 (Prospectus, l. 57). Hereafter indicated as *Excursion* and cited by book and line numbers in the text.

26. William Hazlitt, *Selected Writings*, ed. Duncan Wu, vol. 2 (London: Pickering and Chatto), p. 309.

27. *The Fourteen-Book 'Prelude'*, ed. W. J. B. Owen (Ithaca, NY: Cornell University Press, 1985), p. 271 (14.448–9).

28. Geoffrey H. Hartman, 'Reading: The Wordsworthian Enlightenment', in *The Wordsworthian Enlightenment: Romantic Poetry and the Ecology of Reading*, ed. Helen Regueiro Elam and Frances Ferguson (Baltimore: The Johns Hopkins University Press, 2005), p. 42.

29. Charles Lamb, review of *The Excursion*, *Quarterly Review*, 12 (1814), 102–3.

30. Samuel Taylor Coleridge, *Biographia Literaria*, ed. James Engell and W. J. Bate, vol. 2 (Routledge & Kegan Paul, 1983), p. 150.

31. Marx, *Early Writings*, p. 250, also see *Frühe Schriften*, 1. 594

32. Immanuel Kant, *Critique of Practical Reason*, ed. Mary Gregor (Cambridge: Cambridge University Press, 1997), pp. 102–3, 107–10. Also see Immanuel Kant, *Werkausgabe*, ed. Wilhelm Weischedel, vol. 7 (Frankfurt am Main: Suhrkamp, 1989), pp. 252–4 [A 220–3], 260–1 [A 232–3].

33. See Immanuel Kant, *Political Writings*, trans. H. B. Nisbet (Cambridge: Cambridge University Press, 1991), p. 44. Also see Kant, *Werkausgabe*, vol. 11, p. 37 [A 392].

34. My translation. See Kant, *Werkausgabe*, vol. 11, p. 41 n. [A 398].

9
Wordsworth's Late Melodics

Simon Jarvis

Wordsworth's Preface to the *Poems* of 1815, and the Essay, Supplementary to that Preface are recurrently concerned with two linked groups of questions about the relationship between verse and music: (1) Does verse require musical accompaniment, and, if so, do all kinds of verse require it equally? (2) What is the force of the music of verse itself, its metres and rhythms? How is this force best handled by the poet?

That music can have for Wordsworth an essential, rather than an accidental, relationship to verse, becomes clear at an early stage in the Preface. Wordsworth writes of his own poems that:

> Some of these pieces are essentially lyrical; and, therefore, cannot have their due force without a supposed musical accompaniment; but, in much the greatest part, as a substitute for the classic lyre or romantic harp, I require nothing more than an animated or impassioned recitation, adapted to the subject ... But, though the accompaniment of a musical instrument be frequently dispensed with, the true Poet does not therefore abandon his privilege distinct from that of the mere Proseman;

> 'He murmurs near the running brooks
> A music sweeter than their own.'[1]

These comments are not wholly clear. They appear to imply that in some cases, those which are 'essentially' lyrical, Wordsworth does indeed require more than an impassioned recitation: that he requires music. They therefore also imply that those compositions which require 'nothing more than an animated or impassioned recitation', while they are indeed 'lyrical', are not in the same way 'essentially' lyrical. In these cases, the right kind of recitation will carry out those lyric functions which, elsewhere, have to be performed by music proper. Nor does it ever become quite clear why the loss of music in most cases should be so readily conceded. In relation to epic poetry, indeed, Wordsworth thinks that to insist on any connection with music is now affected:

> Epic Poets, in order that their mode of composition may accord with the elevation of their subject, represent themselves as *singing* from the inspiration of the Muse, "Arma virumque *cano;*" but this is a fiction, in modern times, of slight value: the Iliad or the Paradise Lost would gain little in our estimation by being chanted. The other poets who belong to this class are commonly content to *tell* their tale; – so that of the whole it may be affirmed that they neither require nor reject the accompaniment of music.
>
> (PW, 3:27)

The view that the 'singing' of epic poetry is now a fiction chimes with the opinion approvingly attributed by Coleridge to Bowyer, his schoolmaster: '"*Harp? Harp? Lyre? Pen and ink, boy, you mean!*"'[2] Yet even here the possibility of music is not wholly ruled out. Wordsworth concludes that it is neither required nor rejected.

Just what kind of recitation Wordsworth has in mind as an impassioned or animated one is, in any case, itself a complex matter. One might expect this to be a recitation which would emphasize an underlying metrical set over the local expressivities of rhythm. This, certainly, would fit with what little we know of Wordsworth's own manner of reciting poetry. David Perkins has drawn attention to the significance of Hazlitt's remarks on the contrasting delivery styles adopted by Wordsworth and Coleridge respectively.[3] And Brennan O'Donnell has linked this to a powerfully convincing interpretation of Wordsworth's strong interest in 'the passion of meter': in the requirement which verse imposes for metrical expectations to temper or modify requirements introduced by prose rhythm or by rhetorical or other expressive purposes.[4] In particular, this emphasis on the metrical set would make sense as an interpretation of what is meant here by 'animated' or 'impassioned' recitation precisely because musical or melodious intonational patterns, the sense of 'chanting', have usually been associated with strongly metricalist delivery styles.

What Wordsworth says at this particular point, though, emphasizes the other side of this equation, the need for verse to allow enough flexibility for expressive variation:

> Poems, however humble in their kind, if they be good in that kind, cannot read themselves; the law of long syllable and short must not

be so inflexible, – the letter of metre must not be so impassive to the spirit of versification, – as to deprive the Reader of all voluntary power to modulate, in subordination to the sense, the music of the poem; – in the same manner as his mind is left at liberty, and even summoned, to act upon its thoughts and images.

(PW, 3:29–30)

It becomes clear here that the passion in the recommended 'impassioned reading' is the 'passion of the sense', not the 'passion of the metre'. What makes the difference between a flat delivery style and an animated one, here, is the freedom to vary the music according to the requirements of the sense. And this voluntary power is associated with the need for the reader, literally, to 'animate' the poem. To place the remark that 'poems ... cannot read themselves' as an introduction to this particular argument about versification is to suggest that, if the letter of metre were completely to bind down the spirit of versification, if a reading were given in which only the requirements of the metrical set were met, and not those of 'sense', then it would be as though the reader were saying that the poem could read itself. The perfectly metrical recitation, were it imaginable, would convert the poem into a kind of verbal automaton, a sounding idol.

That last note, of course, is added by me. Wordsworth does not mention automatism, except negatively and by implication, in this passage, nor idolatry. But elsewhere in these critical documents the potential connection, for Wordsworth's critical instincts, between verse melody and superstition, becomes powerfully evident. In this essay I want to follow through this aspect of Wordsworth's later poetics – his interest in the power of melody in general and verse melody in particular – and to do so with reference to two separate kinds of writing: the explicit criticism of the 1815 documents and of some of Wordsworth's recorded remarks about his own poetry, on the one hand, and, on the other, a group of later lyrics whose chief, if often implicit, subject is, I shall suggest, the poetics of verse. Wordsworth's accommodation with the irrational rationality of verse melodics, I shall suggest, is an especially inwardly felt instance of his broader ambivalence about the relationship between superstition and enlightenment, idolatry and idol-breaking. It enriches our sense of Wordsworth's broader understanding of 'philosophic song', that such poetry cannot be a neat fit between pre-concerted content and later verse ornamentation, but is rather a continually transformative, antagonistic co-operation among two rivalrous and well-matched powers.

1

One important task which Wordsworth assigned his Essay, Supplementary to the Preface was to show that genius had not always been recognized in its own time, and so to provide support for his concluding distinction between the 'public', that temporary, and the 'people', as permanent, arbiter of taste. In this history Alexander Pope occupies an especially important place, not as an instance of unrecognized genius, but as an instance of admitted genius diminishing itself from too much regard to the public, to immediate rather than to lasting popularity:

> The arts by which Pope … contrived to procure to himself a more general and a higher reputation than perhaps any English Poet ever attained during his life-time, are known to the judicious. And as well known is it to them, that the undue exertion of those arts is the cause why Pope has for some time held a rank in literature, to which, if he had not been seduced by an over-love of immediate popularity, and had confided more in his native genius, he never could have descended. He bewitched the nation by his melody, and dazzled it by his polished style, and was himself blinded by his own success.
>
> (*PW*, 3:72)

Pope's brilliance as a versifier is treated here as something separate from his 'native genius'. It is the exercise of 'arts' which are not merely meretricious but, it is implied, morally improper. Pope himself is seduced by his excessive love of immediate popularity, and then he does his best to seduce his readers through the 'undue exertion' of these arts. These arts, in fact, are dark ones: 'He bewitched the nation by his melody.' The remark can instructively be compared with later, less acutely attentive, rejections of Pope. Matthew Arnold's way of downgrading Pope is diametrically opposed to Wordsworth's. For Arnold, Pope is not too melodious, but so bereft of melody that he can count only as a classic 'of our prose'.[5] Wordsworth is not indifferent to Pope's powers, but all too vividly susceptible to them. If, for Arnold, Pope is a proseman, for Wordsworth he is, on the contrary, a kind of siren: the witch and seducer through melody.

The connection between witchcraft and melody occurred once more to Wordsworth a few years later. One of the sites which Wordsworth visited during his 1820 tour of the continent was the Staub-Bach at Lauterbrunnen. The rock formations here allowed for hauntingly powerful vocal performances, which made a deep impression

on Wordsworth, as they were also to do on Southey, whose remarks
Wordsworth appended to printings of the poem after 1827:

> While we were at the Waterfall, some half-score peasants, chiefly
> women and girls, assembled just out of reach of the Spring, and set
> up, – surely, the wildest chorus that ever was heard by human ears, –
> a song not of articulate sounds, but in which the voice was used as
> a mere instrument of music, more flexible than any which art could
> produce, – sweet, powerful, and thrilling beyond description.[6]

Wordsworth's own note, which initially appeared without the quotation from Southey, adds a number of features not present in the latter's
account:

> The vocal powers of these musical Beggars may seem to be exagger-
> ated; but this wild and savage air was utterly unlike any sounds I had
> ever heard: the notes reached me from a distance, and on what occa-
> sion they were sung I could not guess, only they seemed to belong,
> in some way or other, to the Waterfall – and reminded me of religious
> servives chaunted to Streams and Fountains in Pagan times.
>
> (*SS*, 414)

Southey mentions peasants; in Dorothy's journals we hear simply 'two
women' (*SS*, 425). Here the performers are mendicants. The note already
introduces, in fact, much of Wordsworth's ambivalence about the performance: the voices merge with a natural water-feature, the waterfall, in a way
which very often provides a figure for the beneficent powers of metre
elsewhere in Wordsworth's verse. They also remind Wordsworth of pagan
river-worship, even though there is nothing in the context to suggest that
the singers are worshipping anything; that Wordsworth voluntarily introduces this assertion indicates the power of this idea of water-worship for
him (we recall that Nab Well prompted him to think of the 'Millions of
Kneeling Hindoos' who 'at this day / Bow to the watery Element').[7] This
ambivalence emerges still more markedly in the poem itself:

> Tracks let me follow far from human-kind
> Which these illusive greetings may not reach;
> Where only Nature tunes her voice to teach
> Careless pursuits, and raptures unconfined.
> No Mermaid warbles (to allay the wind
> That drives some vessel tow'rds a dangerous beach)

More thrilling melodies! no caverned Witch

Chaunting a love-spell, ever intertwined
Notes shrill and wild with art more musical!
Alas! that from the lips of abject Want
And Idleness in tatters mendicant
They should proceed – enjoyment to enthral,
And with regret and useless pity haunt
This bold, this pure, this sky-born WATERFALL!

(*SS*, 369)

Any association between such chanting and Pope's versification seems improbable, and yet the lexical proximity establishes its possibility, if only at an unconscious level. 'Melodies' are swiftly followed by 'Witch', although here, of course, this bewitching tune is just what the wordless vocal music surpasses. Just as the power of Pope's versification is an improper coercion or seduction of his public, so these melodies, too, coerce admiration: they 'enthral' enjoyment. At the same time, Wordsworth's attitude to the singing is almost even-handedly ambivalent. It surpasses not only the power of dark magic, but also that of good magic: the mermaid benevolently and apotropaically singing to avert a shipwreck. The sonnet, in fact, closes by separating just those elements which Wordsworth puts together in his note. There the singing seemed to belong to the waterfall. Here, however, it is as though the fact that it is produced by beggars were to make any such belonging impossible: 'regret and useless pity haunt' that waterfall which, left to itself, is 'bold', 'pure', and 'sky-born'. And at this point, ambivalence crystallizes in an ambiguity. The syntax tells us that it is the melodies that enthral or compel enjoyment. The melodies are the 'they' immediately preceding the infinitive 'to enthral'. But the penultimate line suggests another reading. Whose are the 'regret and useless pity'? Not the singers', so they must be the listener's. As soon as the listener realizes that the sounds are made by beggars, regret and useless pity come to haunt melodies which would otherwise have been pure and sky-born. The listener cannot feel what he would like to because he is too aware of the suffering of those who have made the sounds. So that this suggests a directly opposed reading. Enjoyment, in this reading, is 'enthralled' precisely in so far as it cannot be felt. Enjoyment is locked up by the fact of the beggars' situation, which occasions regret and useless pity. Enjoyment, therefore, is hampered.

Not only the direct verbal echo of the Essay, Supplementary to the Preface, but also the association of wordless melody with superstition, with pagan magical power in general, leads us to add this sonnet to that group of poems and passages in which Wordsworth is, consciously or not, working through problems associated with those of verse melody and its powers. The ambivalence which is so exacerbated in this poem is also present in the critical writing. Pope used melody to bewitch; but other poets may offer us melodies more like the mermaid's. There is 'a pure and refined scheme of harmony', as well as the 'glaring hues of diction' (*PW*, 3:64) of Pope's work, a colouring by which we are 'dazzled'. The taste for this chaste music is driven out by the appetite for that bewitching one. But poetry written according to this purer melody may itself be a kind of efficacious magic: a magic put to purer purposes. This much emerges when Wordsworth considers the fatal passivity of the kind of reader which he thinks Pope's kind of poetry produces, an account which joins others in Wordsworth's work in associating the passive consumption of an overbearing or enthralling art with political despotism:

> Is it to be supposed that the reader can make progress of this kind, like an Indian Prince or general – stretched on his palanquin, and borne by his slaves? No; he is invigorated and inspirited by his Leader, in order that he may exert himself; for he cannot proceed in quiescence, he cannot be carried like a dead weight. Therefore to create taste is to call forth and bestow power, of which knowledge is the effect; and *there* lies the true difficulty.
>
> (*PW*, 3:82)

Poetry which creates the taste by which it is to be enjoyed is not poetry which ascetically dispenses with all irrational powers. Instead, its force is itself a kind of summoning. It does not renounce power but is 'to call forth and bestow power'.

Wordsworth's figure for these good powers, of course, is not witchcraft but prophecy. The witch is associated with anthromorphitism, fancy and enthralment; the prophet, with the invisible, with imagination and with power. But, as I have demonstrated elsewhere in the case of other oppositions arranged along this axis in Wordsworth's poetry, prophet and witch, the pure and refined scheme of harmony and the bewitching and dazzling one, are sometimes separated not by a gulf but by a nuance. Telling them apart is not usually as conveniently performed as separating sheep from goats, but requires subtle attention and steady discrimination.

2

This is especially true of Wordsworth's poetry after 1815. An ambivalence towards pagan religion is present from quite early on in

Wordsworth's writing "The world is too much with us; late and soon" offers a rhetorical protestation that even outright superstition would be preferable to the theodicy of enlightened self-interest. Yet the fact that the protestation is offered with a great shout to a monotheistic 'Great God!' itself performs the other side of Wordsworth's ambivalence.[8] In the 1815 preface this question of pagan religion and its anthromor-phitism is brought directly to bear on poetry through Wordsworth's celebrated praise of Hebrew prophecy and lyric, Milton and Spenser:

> The grand store-house of enthusiastic and meditative Imagination, of poetical, as contradistinguished from human and dramatic Imagination, are the prophetic and lyrical parts of the Holy Scriptures, and the works of Milton; to which I cannot forbear to add those of Spenser. I select these writers in preference to those of ancient Greece and Rome because the anthropomorphitism of the Pagan religion subjected the minds of the greatest poets in those countries too much to the bondage of definite form; from which the Hebrews were preserved by their abhorrence of idolatry. This abhorrence was almost as strong in our great epic Poet, both from circumstances of his life, and from the constitution of his mind. However imbued the surface might be with classical literature, he was a Hebrew in soul; and all things tended in him towards the sublime.
>
> (*PW*, 3:34–5)

Even this praise, of course, does not leave everything completely clear, because of the admission that the 'surface' of Milton's verse – a category whose precise extent remains unclear but which might perhaps include diction, rhetoric, and versification – may be to a presumptively consid-erable extent 'imbued ... with classical literature'. Milton's Hebrew soul, as it were, Hebraicizes, sanctifies, and renders sublime this pagan sur-face. That surface is not represented as a flaw in Milton's verse (we can compare Blake, who regarded it as a militaristic and idolatrous remnant which had to be removed). It is implied, instead, that the Hebrewness of Milton's soul renders the pagan surface harmless or perhaps even imbues it with further powers of his own. Nevertheless, the possibility is at once presented that this 'surface' might be a pagan seduction. To pay too much attention to it might indeed be to become bewitched by melody, to relapse to 'old idolatry'.[9]

In this context it is especially interesting that Wordsworth himself, in the years after the 1815 critical writings, shows every sign of wanting to relax the severities of this Miltonic regime. The bondage of definite form, in the shape of allusions to, or outright descriptions of, or stories about, the pagan gods, is returned to ever more frequently, and the tone of those passages in which Wordsworth legitimates this return is especially interesting, because it indicates a desire to be let off, a weariness of the long labour of renunciation. The remarks which Wordsworth made late in his life to Isabella Fenwick about his 'Ode to Lycoris' are especially instructive in this respect:

> [T]his poem originated in the four last lines of the first stanza. These specks of snow reflected in the lake, & so transferred, as it were, to the subaqueous sky, reminded me of the Swans which the fancy of the ancient classic poets yoked to the car of Venus. Hence the tenor of the whole first stanza, & the name of Lycoris, which with some readers who think mythology & classical allusion too far-fetched and therefore more or less unnatural and affected, will tend to unrealise the sentiment that pervades these verses. But surely one who has written so much in verse as I have done may be allowed to retrace his steps into the regions of fancy which delighted him in his boyhood, when he first became acquainted with the Greek & Roman Poets ... Classical literature affected me by its own beauty [but as it is obvious from the mould in which Milton's Lycidas is cast, that the dead languages being the *del*]. But the truths of scripture having been entrusted to the dead languages, and these fountains having been recently laid open at the Reformation, an importance & a sanctity were at that period attached to classical literature that extended, as is obvious in Milton's Lycidas, for example, both [in *del*] to its spirit & its form in a degree that can never be revived. No doubt the hackneyed & lifeless use into which mythology fell towards the close of the 17th century, and which continued through the 18th, disgusted the general reader with all allusion to it in modern verse. [In deference *del*] And though, in deference to this disgust, & also in a measure participating in it, I abstained in my earlier writings from all introduction of pagan fable, – surely, even in its humble form, it may ally itself with real sentiment – as I can truly affirm it did in the present case.[10]

The Fenwick note is worth quoting and examining at length because, in its nearly dialectical twists and turns, it is one of Wordsworth's deepest pieces of literary–critical thought: it indicates both how thoroughly Wordsworth had thought about this issue, and how intense were his investments in it. It is rare to find Wordsworth addressing heartfelt and ᴀᴄᴛᴉᴏᴎꜱ ⱼᴅ ᴀꜱ ꜰᴏʀ ᴉᴎᴅᴜⱦᶢᴇᴎᴄᴇ ᴉᴎ ꜰᴇꜱᴘᴇᴄᴛ ᴏᴉ ᴁᴉꜱ ⱼᴏᴇᴛᴉꜱ 'ꜱᴜᴉᴇʟᴠ', ᴛᴁᴇ ᴘᴏᴇᴛ pleads twice, this may be permitted. The poet appears almost to appeal to our pity: he has written a good deal of verse now, after all, and so it is surely reasonable to allow some relaxation of the rules so that he may revisit those childish pleasures which he has previously so determinedly put away. There is an undertone of uneasiness, because the poet is not only coming back to enjoy later those joys which he has earlier set aside, but offering us the steadfastness of his own previous good conduct in palliation of this relapse. It is this structure of relapse – gorging later on something you 'abstained from' earlier and offering the extent of that very abstention as the excuse for the relapse – which recalls Wordsworth's own contemptuous expression for Napoleon's eventual resort to imperial trappings: the dog returning to its vomit. Here, it is as though Wordsworth's apologetic tone is sheltering from some bitter self-accusations which he has ready prepared in another part of his psyche.

It is this unease, perhaps, which produces here a rather different account of Milton's relation to classical religion and culture than that offered in the 1815 Essay. There the classical surface was made safe by Milton's Hebrew soul. Here the classical languages are made safe by their association with sacred scripture. In an ingenious turn, in fact, the classical languages and the poetry written in them are temporarily made *Protestant*: the superstitions of classical poetry are reformed, not Papist, because their diffusion is associated with the laying open of the fountains of scripture at the Reformation, after a period in which those fountains had been improperly sealed up. This sanctity by association is allowed to excuse Milton his *Lycidas*, both in spirit and form. And yet Wordsworth does not relent on his self-examination: this may have excused Milton, but cannot excuse Wordsworth himself, because this association is now far in the past, and 'can never be revived'. Mythology has become disgusting. Wordsworth himself admits to having shared this disgust. He has stripped himself bare all over again and must now – 'surely' – throw himself on our mercies with a bare affirmation that the 'sentiment' in *this* poem was 'real'.

The Fenwick note, in fact, is the continuation in critical talk of a series of twists and turns first developed in the 'Ode to Lycoris' itself, which is among Wordsworth's more impressive later achievements. The poem's argument is that whereas when we are young, and happy in a way we take for granted, our pleasures are those of sublime melancholy – 'the darksome lawn / Brush'd by the owlet's wing' (ll. 19–20) – in age we should, alerted by our proximity to death and the dwindling of our powers, instead prefer 'hopeful Spring' (l. 51) to autumn. The poem's pathos descends directly from those tremendously sad passages of the great Ode ('There was a time') in which Wordsworth is attempting to cheer himself up. The course of later life is not doubted to be 'downward'. So that the poem's final affirmation of the love of Spring is confessedly willed, rather than spontaneous. Indeed, that willedness is the whole point of it. As we decay, 'life requires an *art*' (l. 39), which means that even if Spring isn't our favourite, our own diminishment requires that we make it so:

> While blossoms and the budding spray
> Inspire us in our own decay;
> Still, as we nearer draw to life's dark goal,
> Be hopeful Spring the favourite of the Soul!
>
> (ll. 51–4)

Despite what has earlier been said about that 'vernal Deity / Whose home is in the breast' (ll. 47–8), the inspiration brought here by spring is not owed to any happy coincidence with our mood, but rather to the striking contrast between its blossoming and budding and our 'decay'. Especially striking here is the phrase 'dark goal'. Life is claimed to have a *telos* rather than just a cut-off point, and yet this goal is 'dark', either in the sense that it is mournable or in the sense that it is uncertain.

But why should any of this have required the elaborate justifications in the Fenwick note? All the classical mythology is in fact concentrated in the first of the poem's three eighteen-line stanzas. And this stanza's relevance to the poem's argument about spring and autumn, youth and old age, is an extremely indirect one, in the sense that the poem would make perfect, and more straightforward, sense if the first stanza were omitted:

> An age hath been when Earth was proud
> Of lustre too intense
> To be sustain'd; and Mortals bowed
> The front in self-defence.
> Who *then*, if Dian's crescent gleamed,
> Or Cupid's sparkling arrow streamed
> While on the wing the Urchin play'd,
> Could fearlessly approach the shade?
> – Enough for one soft vernal day,
> If I, a Bard of ebbing time
> And nurtur'd in a fickle clime,

May haunt this horrid bay;
Whose amorous water multiplies
The flitting halcyon's vivid dyes;
And smoothes its liquid breast – to show
These swan-like specks of mountain snow,
White, as the pair that slid along the plains
Of Heaven, when Venus held the reins!

(ll. 1–18)

The cell of the poem as identified by the Fenwick note – the last four lines of the stanza – are a creation of pure fancy, the pleasure of comparing specks of snow with Venus's swans. This moment of fancy, Wordsworth tells us, came first, and, in a way, it is what all the rest of the poem is apologizing for and trying to overcome. In this stanza it is lengthily prepared for by a penetrating historical retrospective. Wordsworth shows his painful awareness that what is 'enough' for him, the bard of 'ebbing time', is already far *too much* for those eras in which these deities were in all seriousness believed. The treatment of classical mythology in the stanza as a whole is in fact not especially fanciful, but, rather, enlightened and austere. The poet's pleasurable play with this apparatus of long-disbelieved gods is set in chastening contrast to how people felt about them when they thought them to be real. Now, we can play around with them. Then, people were too terrified to go near them.

And so, because of this first stanza, we are when we read the last two consciously or unconsciously working out, beneath the direct argument about spring and autumn, an implicit argument about the spring and autumn of humanity. In humanity's youth the lustre is 'too intense / To be sustain'd', just as in an individual's youth he or she may turn away from light to dark:

Sad fancies do we then affect,
In luxury of disrespect
To our own prodigal excess
Of too familiar happiness.

(ll. 23–6)

The extraordinary compression and momentum of thinking here is one of the characteristic excellences of Wordsworth's later verse. There is a clottedness that is usually absent from his earlier writing, a loss of lightness, but, if anything, a still more tenacious adherence to precision of thinking. The retrospective implication is that *humanity*'s youth, too, has its 'prodigal excess'. In the youth of civilization, the gods are too bright to be enjoyed: they are feared. In its decay, its old age, the implication is, we should make sure we enjoy them. Hopeful spring should be our favourite. So the modern poet, just in so far as modernity is the time of decay, the ebbing time, should not hesitate to sport with the sweets of antique myth.

The poem thus brings off a peculiar sleight of thinking. It effects a purely implicit apologia for the use of disbelieved classical mythology in poetry. It legitimates the poetical, the as-if, use of pagan myth, tacitly – without ever having to admit that that is what it is doing. And, of course, at the same time, it overcomes it. The untrue gods appear only in this first stanza and are in practice renounced in the last two, even as their implicit apologia is being developed. The poem is truly a sublation of the pleasures of the poetical possibilities of pagan mythology, which are first enjoyed, then overcome but also preserved.

3

The tour de force performed by the 'Ode to Lycoris' and its later Fenwick note, then, indicates the strength of feeling attaching to this question of a prohibited and then recuperated pagan mythology in Wordsworth's verse. I want now to return to that connection between pagan deities and vocal and verse melody established in the first section of my essay.

Melody had, at various times from at least 1815 onward, been associated by Wordsworth with magical powers, beneficent like the mermaid's or manipulative like the witch's, or like the witch Alexander Pope's. The poem which began developing in 1828 on the power of sound, therefore, was the culmination of a long series of negotiations in poetic thinking. What began to emerge was a poem which Wordsworth consciously thought of as written in his highest style, the 'loftier' strain which the first epigraph to the great Ode ('There was a time') had mentioned. A. D. Dyce had written to Wordsworth offering the opinion that the poem was as fine as anything Wordsworth had done, an opinion with which the poet, rather unsurprisingly, concurred.[11] The poem goes through a number of stages, of which the most distinct are a six-stanza version probably complete by 15 December 1828, and a fourteen-stanza version on which work took place at various times between then and the poem's publication in 1835. The poem's first stanza, in this fuller version, recalls in a singular way the sonnet on the Staub-Bach. Those peculiar rock formations which to allow a haunting music in the mountains becoming, in this stanza, the nooks and crannies of the inner ear itself:

> ... a Spirit aerial
> Informs the cell of hearing, dark and blind;
> Intricate labyrinth, more dread for thought
> To enter than oracular cave;
> Strict passage, through which sighs are brought,
> And whispers, for the heart, their slave;
> And shrieks, that revel in abuse
> Of shivering flesh; and warbled air,
> Whose piercing sweetness can unloose
> The chains of frenzy, or entice a smile
> Into the ambush of despair;
> Hosannas pealing down the long-drawn aisle,
> And requiems answered by the pulse that beats
> Devoutly, in life's last retreats!

> (ll. 3–16)[12]

Why is 'the cell of hearing' 'more dread for thought / To enter than oracular cave'? Not simply because it is 'dark and blind', but because of the powers which shelter there – oracles, for one, but also a whole series of other efficacious noises. The whispers, shrieks, warbled air, hosannas and requiems are chiefly distinguished for their powerful effects upon the listener. The catalogue ascends in a kind of scale of merit from shrieks to requiems, but also at the same time descends in a scale of vivaciousness, from what is sharply alive to death. The power of sound, it is at once clear, need in no way be a wholly auspicious power. It can enslave its listeners, has involuntary and even unwished effects upon them. So Wordsworth's decision to write a lyric poem to it is already generically ambiguous. The poem, it seems, is itself at once conjuration and periapt. It wants to call forth the good magic of sound while driving away the bad one.

This double approach is developed throughout the poem. Wordsworth frames celebrated myths about the pagan magic of music – Orpheus (stanza eight); Amphion, Arion (stanza nine); Pan (stanza ten) – within two other kinds of musical power: the sounds of nature, above all, of ocean, air, mountain, birdsong, and so on; but also a Christian music – not only the requiems and hosannas of the first stanza, but also the *'measured* glee' (l. 38) (Wordsworth's emphasis) of the church bells (stanza three), and, at last, the voice of God which creates light (stanza fourteen). The three stanzas evoking the efficacious musics of antiquity are thus brought to an abrupt close with a *memento mori*: 'Ye who are longing to be rid / Of Fable, though to truth subservient, hear / The little sprinkling of cold earth that fell / Echoed from the coffin lid' (ll. 154–7). The 'magic verse' (l. 127) associated with pagan antiquity is absorbed and framed within sacramentally Christian sounds. The poem, in fact, appears to be offering not only an exhaustive inventory of the various kinds of powerful sound – the 'Argument' prefixed to the printed text encourages that impression – but also a hierarchical ordering of them.

Throughout, Wordsworth's interest is distinguished from aesthetics precisely because it concerns not only pleasure, but also pain. Aesthetics, in fact, could begin only at the moment at which we were to take for granted that sound has no power of its own, no real efficacity, but only that with which human consciousness endows it. Sound's powers are not only for delight, but also for mortification. The moments of greatest tension in the poem come, perhaps, when Wordsworth imagines the total overcoming of the moral complexity of the power of sound: as he puts it in stanza eleven, 'O for some soul-affecting scheme / Of *moral* music …' (ll. 169–70); the poet's emphasis joins that on the '*measured*' glee of the church bells, while the idea of a 'scheme' of moral music immediately recalls the 'pure and refined scheme of harmony' which was to provide a preferable alternative to Pope's bewitching melodies in the Essay, Supplementary to the Preface. Especially striking among the poem's efforts to imagine a '*moral* music' is the disconcerting account in stanza seven of the effect of music upon idiots:

> As Conscience, to the centre
> Of Being, smites with irresistible pain,
> So shall a solemn cadence, if it enter
> The mouldy vaults of the dull Idiot's brain,
> Transmute him to a wretch from quiet hurled –
> Convulsed as by a jarring din;
> And then aghast, as at the world
> Of reason partially let in
> By concords winding with a sway
> Terrible for sense and soul!

> (ll. 97–106)

In the final lines of this passage we recognize again, as in that passage of the 'Ode to Lycoris', what we might call the cognitive virtuosity of

Wordsworth's late lyric manner, in which compu sw il thinking purlluk paut
line endings, yet with no sense of strain other than the difficulty of the
thought itself. What service is music going to render the idiot? To calm or
cheer him, perhaps? Hardly: music transforms him to a wretch, precisely
because music is not merely aesthetic, a pleasing pattern of sounds, but
performatively rational, an efficacious mode of knowledge. It is 'reason'
which is partially let in to the idiot's mind by music, with painful results.

Any poem explicitly about sound, of course, immediately opens the
possibility of a reflexive echo in its own sonic structure. Wordsworth
seems to have been largely uninterested in the idea of representative versification; and although some such technique could no doubt
be squeezed out of this poem with sufficient ingenuity, there is a more
persuasive way to think about this question here.

The poem belongs to that genre of compositional feats, the regularized
irregular ode. This genre has its origins in Congreve's protests against excessive Pindaric licence.[13] Congreve's Pindarics produce individual rhyme-
schemes and line-length patterns which yield little in complexity to those
of the irregular Pindaric. Yet they mark, in fact, an entirely distinct mode of
verse composition, rather than one which would be essentially like the
Pindaric but a little more regular. In a poem like Dryden's on the death of
Anne Killigrew, very large degrees of variation can be achieved on the basis
of what is essentially quite a familiar prosodic repertoire: the heroic line
and the heroic couplet. These shapes form a kind of home base to which
the poem keeps returning. Composition of irregular odes need not present
greater difficulties, then, than that in the repertoire with which Dryden is
most intimately familiar. But in Congreve's Pindaric, everything is altered,
because once the complex strophe has been devised, it must then, in every
detail, be *repeated* in every strophe and antistrophe that follows. The epode
may present a new combination of rhymes and metres, but then that combination itself must be identically repeated in every epode that follows.
This change changes everything about the Pindaric. It makes it a mould
instead of a repertoire. Thinking must be poured into the stanza, once
elaborated. The degree of compositional difficulty is greatly increased.

The Ode ('There was a time') belongs to the irregular genre. None of its
stanzas or verse paragraphs has the same shape as another. It is from time
to time an extremely metrically unstable poem. The underlying metre is
predominantly rising or iambic, but there are suggestions of a wavering
between falling and rising rhythms throughout the poem, and in one
extended passage towards its end, a whole series of trochaic lines suddenly bursts into the poem.[14] 'On the Power of Sound', by way of contrast,
reproduces fourteen times precisely the same rhyme and metrical scheme,

right down to the reproduction of a 'feminine' ending for the first and third lines of each stanza. The metre is entirely a rising one, with a single recurrent exception: the fourth last line in every stanza is trochaic. Here the single falling line in each stanza is like a trace element of the chanting trochaic passages of Gray's *The Bard* or of Wordsworth's own earlier Ode.

It is as though the poem wants to take a grip of the wayward powers of sound in Wordsworth's own earlier lyric: to detain them and master them, but at the same time also to thematize them, to write explicitly about them. If in the earlier great Ode, as I have suggested elsewhere, the poem's melodics ring out *against* the tendency reductively to organize the poem as a narrative, the melodics have here been organized into a mould both recurring and internally quite complex.[15] The poem's thinking drives on through these ample stanzas. Present is the 'loftier strain' mentioned in the early epigraph to the great Ode; absent, though, are the 'fluctuations of generous feeling' which are allowed to make their marks in the earlier poem.[16] 'On the Power of Sound' does indeed move on, as the earlier poem does not, through a series of powerful sublations, in which, as in the 'Ode to Lycoris', the 'dangerous passions' aroused by a magically efficacious pagan music are at once superseded and exploited to power Wordsworth's own writing. Pagan music is *consumed* within the sounding fabric of Wordsworth's own late high style.

The complex engagement with efficacious music and with the melody of verse in 'On the Power of Sound' comes at a point in the history of verse melody and relations with poetic thinking which could be thought of as significant. Two poets who were to prove perhaps even more influential than Wordsworth for the remainder of the century's verse – Keats and Shelley – had surrendered themselves much more fully than Wordsworth could ever do to verse melody as an engine of poetic invention. Both Keats and Shelley, in various ways, are often prepared to accept a rich inexactness of thinking as compensation for the rich variety of melody which their verse practice allows them. For Wordsworth verse melody always figures as a deep and, potentially, an extremely troubling, kind of power. Its collisions and collusions with 'sense' would, therefore, always be figured in terms carrying moral, philosophical, and even religious freight. Hence the relevance of Wordsworth's ambivalent relation to idolatry, superstition and paganism. It provides an idiom through which to work these difficulties out. The tenacity and intelligence of the way in which Wordsworth's later critical writings and his later lyric mode conduct this working out leave us with work of lasting importance, work which would be much better known were it not for the effulgence of Wordsworth's own earlier achievements.

Notes

1. *The Prose Works*, ed. W. J. B. Owen and Jane Worthington Smyser, vol. 3 (Oxford: Oxford University Press, 1974), pp. 29–30. Hereafter indicated as *PW* and cited by volume and page numbers in the text.
2. Samuel Taylor Coleridge, *Biographia Literaria*, ed. James Engell and W. Jackson Bate, vol. 1 (London: Routledge & Kegan Paul, 1983), p. 10.
3. David Perkins, 'How the Romantics Recited Poetry', *Studies in English Literature, 1500–1900*, 31 (1991), pp. 655–71.
4. Brennan O'Donnell, *The Passion of Meter: A Study of Wordsworth's Metrical Art* (Kent: Ohio State University Press, 1995).
5. Matthew Arnold, 'The Study of Poetry', in *English Literature and Irish Politics*, ed. R. H. Super (Ann Arbor: University of Michigan Press, 1973), p. 181.
6. *Sonnet Series and Itinerary Poems, 1820–1845*, ed. Geoffrey Jackson (Ithaca, NY: Cornell University Press, 2004), p. 414. Hereafter indicated as *SS* and cited by page numbers in the text. Jackson points out that Wordsworth has substituted 'Spring' for the 'spray' which appeared in Southey's text (*SS*, 425).
7. 'Composed when a probability existed of our being obliged to quit Rydal Mount as a residence' (late version), in *'The Tuft of Primroses', with Other Late Poems for 'The Recluse'*, ed. Joseph F. Kishel (Ithaca, NY: Cornell University Press, 1986), p. 89 (ll. 118–19).
8. *'Poems, in Two Volumes' and Other Poems, 1800–1807*, ed. Jared Curtis (Ithaca, NY: Cornell University Press, 1983), p. 150.
9. Compare Simon Jarvis, *Wordsworth's Philosophic Song* (Cambridge: Cambridge University Press, 2007), pp. 35–55.
10. *Shorter Poems, 1807–1820*, ed. Carl H. Ketcham (Ithaca, NY: Cornell University Press, 1989), p. 544. The 'Ode to Lycoris' is cited by line numbers in the text.
11. Wordsworth to Alexander Dyce, 23 December 1837, in *The Letters of William and Dorothy Wordsworth: The Later Years. Part III, 1835–1839*, ed. Ernest de Selincourt, rev. Alan G. Hill (Oxford: Clarendon Press, 1982), p. 502 and n.
12. *Last Poems, 1821–1850*, ed. Jared Curtis with Apryl Lea Denny-Ferris and Jillian Heydt-Stevenson (Ithaca, NY: Cornell University Press, 1999), p. 117. The 'Stanzas On The Power of Sound' (1835 text) are cited by line numbers in the text.
13. William Congreve, 'A Discourse on the Pindarique Ode', in *A Pindarique Ode, Humbly Offer'd to the Queen, on the Victorious Progress of Her Majesty's Arms, under the Conduct of the Duke of Marlborough* (London: Tonson, 1706).
14. *Poems, in Two Volumes*, ed. Jared Curtis (Ithaca, NY: Cornell University Press, 1983), p. 276 (ll. 174–7).
15. See Jarvis, *Wordsworth's Philosophic Song*, pp. 195–213.
16. *Wordsworth's Convention of Cintra: A Facsimile of the 1809 Tract*, ed. Gordon Kent Thomas (Provo, UT: Brigham Young University Press, 1983), p. 9.

10
Composing Sound: The Deaf Dalesman, 'The Brothers', and Epitaphic Signs

Mary Jacobus

> And yon tall Pine-tree, whose composing sound
> Was wasted on the good Man's living ear,
> Hath now its own peculiar sanctity;
> And at the touch of every wandering breeze
> Murmurs not idly o'er his peaceful grave.
> —Wordsworth, *Essays upon*
> *Epitaphs, III,* (ll. 583–7)

> Oh silence, independent of a stopped ear,
> You observe birds, flying, sing with wings instead.
> —David Wright, 'Monologue
> of a Deaf Man', (ll. 4–5)

The pine tree's 'composing sound' in Wordsworth's epitaph for the deaf Dalesman, at the end of the third and last of the *Essays upon Epitaphs*, has been read as the defining instance of his epitaphic mode.[1] For Paul de Man, 'the sad privation' (l. 582) stoically endured by the Dalesman – 'the story of a deaf man who compensates for his infirmity by substituting the reading of books for the sounds of nature' – is the condition imposed by writing as it silences voice.[2] Using the deaf Dalesman as his exemplary autobiographical text, de Man interprets the privation of deafness, along with disabilities and accidents that include muteness, mutilation, blindness, and drowning, as a figure for the dangerous autobiographical enterprise glimpsed in *The Prelude* at moments when 'a sudden shock ... interrupts a state of affairs that was relatively stable' (73). I want to suggest a different approach to the auditory effects that murmur 'not idly' in Wordsworth's poetry, situating them within late eighteenth-century debates about the education of the deaf. These debates coincided with Enlightenment redefinitions of the

human, ıı ı ıılı ,ı ıı y ı ı |ıaııı.Jeıl ıı ı uıııuıuuıı ıııı ̈ ıııııt ı — pıı ̈ vıı ıııslyı ıı ̈ ı,ıaıı.lıwll ̈ ı ̈ ı
lıIeducabİe automata — along with the mad, the disabled, the primitive,
and the child. During the same period, Enlightenment philosophers and
educators also came to view deaf signing as a human system of communication that did not conform to graphic conventions such as writing.
What is at stake is not just the opposition between speech and writing,
but a visual sign-system specific to the deaf, yet imagined as universally
accessible. In addition, the phenomenology of reading as experienced by
the deaf serves to break down distinctions between deafness and hearing,
making that hearing itself an ambiguous category. The Dalesman's epitaph
goes to the heart of this double and enlarged understanding of deafness as
both silence and hearing, muteness and communicative signing.

1   Eye-music

Wordsworth's verses on Thomas Holme (d. 1773), the original for
the deaf Dalesman, were inspired by 'a concise epitaph which [he]
met with some time ago in one of the most retired vales among the
Mountains of Westmoreland' (*PW*, 2:93) (Mardale churchyard, at the
head of Hawesdale): 'HE WAS DEPRIVED OF THE SENSE OF HEARING / IN HIS
YOUTH AND LIVED ABOUT 50 YEARS / WITHOUT THE COMFORT OF HEARING
ONE WORD / HE RECONCILED HIMSELF TO HIS MISFORTUNE / BY READING AND
USEFUL EMPLOYMENT / WAS VERY TEMPERATE HONEST AND PEACEABLE / HE
WAS WELL RESPECTED BY HIS NEIGHBOURS AND / RELATIONS AND DEPARTED
THIS LIFE AFTER A SHORT / SICKNESS ON THE 22D OF MARCH 1773 AGED 67
YEARS' (*PW*, 2:118–19).[3] In book seven of *The Excursion* ('The Churchyard among the Mountains, *continued*'), the story of the deaf Dalesman
is paired with that of a blind man. Wordsworth represents deafness as
a condition of sight absolutely deprived of sound (a condition that does
not necessarily tally with the experience of the post-lingually deaf, as
we shall see). In book eight of *The Prelude*, he writes of places marked
by what had been done or suffered there as 'thronged with impregna-
tions', like the wild places of his childhood whose 'audible seclusions ...
into music touch the passing wind' (*1805 Prelude*, 8.794–6).[4] The world
of the deaf Dalesman, in contrast, lacks the 'touch' of natural music:
'this deep mountain valley was to him / Soundless, with all its streams'
(ll. 510–11). Unable to hear rousing cocks, shouting cuckoos, murmuring bees, or stormy winds, he inhabits a mute pictorial world: 'The agitated scene before his eye / Was silent as a picture' (ll. 520–1).

Silent, but not motionless. A revealing parallel can be found in the
testimony of the twentieth-century poet and translator, David Wright.

Like the Dalesman, Wright became deaf during childhood. But for him 'the world a deaf man inhabits is not one of complete silence' – or, at any rate, 'the world in which I live seldom *appears* silent … In my case, silence is not absence of sound but of movement'.[5] As he goes on to explain, citing Wordsworth:

> Suppose it is a calm day, absolutely still, not a twig or leaf stirring. To me it will seem quiet as a tomb though hedgerows are full of noisy but invisible birds. Then comes a breath of air, enough to unsettle a leaf; I will see and hear that movement like an exclamation. The illusory soundlessness has been interrupted. I see, as if I heard, a visionary noise of wind in a disturbance of foliage. Wordsworth in a late poem exactly caught the phenomenon in a remarkable line:
>
> *A soft eye-music of slow-waving boughs*
>
> … The 'sound' seen by me is not necessarily equivalent to the real one. It must often be close enough, in my case helped by a subliminal memory of things once heard. I cannot watch a gale without 'hearing' an uproar of violent movement: trees thrashing, grassblades battling and flattened; or, at sea, waves locked and staggering like all-in wrestlers – this kind of thing comes through as hubbub enough. On the other hand I also live in a world of sounds which are, as I know quite well, imaginary because non-existent. Yet for me they are part of reality. I have sometimes to make a deliberate effort to remember I am not 'hearing' anything, because there is nothing to hear.[6]

Wright continues: 'Such non-sounds include the flight and movement of birds' which '*appears* audible, each species creating a different "eye-music"'.[7] To regain his hearing would resemble a second disability: like a hermit-crab in its shell, he has learned to be at home with his deafness.

Wright's testimony is at odds with Wordsworth's representation of the deaf Dalesman's deafness. Despite the silencing of birdsong, a visual form of 'sound' creates an exclamatory moving world. His quotation comes from Wordsworth's 'Airey-Force Valley', a late blank verse fragment of 1835 that describes suspended animation, 'Where all things else are still and motionless' except for the stream and the slightest breeze:

> … to its gentle touch how sensitive
> Is the light ash! that, pendent from the brow
> Of yon dim cave, in seeming silence makes

A soft eye-music of slow-waving boughs,
Powerful almost as vocal harmony
To stay the wanderer's steps and soothe his thoughts.

(ll. 7, 11–16)[8]

The 'seeming silence' and 'soft eye-music of slow-waving boughs' is perceived both alliteratively and visually: 'Powerful almost as vocal harmony.' The stilled landscape is *'almost'* vocal, since movement is rendered as a concert of semi-audible eye-music – or as poetry itself: audible eye-music to an internal ear.[9]

In the deaf Dalesman's epitaph, however, the agitated movement of waves, trees, and clouds – worked, rocked, or driven by stormy winds – remains as stilled and silent as if he had been born congenitally deaf. The soundless nature inhabited by the Dalesman becomes a metaphor for the isolation often associated with pre-lingual deafness: 'He grew up / From year to year in loneliness of soul' (ll. 508–9). Until the mid-eighteenth century, congenital or pre-lingual deafness consigned the individual to muteness. In his soundless world, the Dalesman is 'upheld' by 'the solace of his own calm thoughts' (ll. 523–4). Thus upheld, he labours for its own sake, without desire for ownership or accumulation: 'neither field nor flock he owned, / No wish for wealth had place within his mind' (ll. 531–2). Lacking a family of his own ('Nor husband's love, nor father's hope or care', l. 533), he lives with his parents and later with his older brother ('An inmate of a second family', l. 541). Home (Holme) is somewhere he never leaves. He inhabits this preternatural familiar calm as Wright inhabits the carapace of deafness. Un-roused by cockcrow, un-delighted by cuckoos, unmoved by storms or desires, he is guided by duty and sustained by the seasonal activities of Lake District farming. But the deaf Dalesman is also a reader. Reading, like extended childhood – or premature death – compensates his 'introverted spirit' for loss of hearing. Predicated on visual signs and rapid eye-movement, reading constitutes a form of eye-music (almost) as powerful as vocal harmony; the look of poetry on the page is an aspect of its unheard music.

For the lonely Dalesman, 'From whom in early childhood was with-drawn / The precious gift of hearing' (ll. 507–8), books are a substitute community. De Man remarks that the reason the deaf Dalesman takes to books so readily is that 'for him the outside world has in fact always been a book' – not so much a picture-book as 'a succession of voice-less tropes' (80). As we have seen, this is not strictly accurate (the deaf Dalesman has not always been deaf). But deaf literacy was unusual at least until mid-century, so the Dalesman's reading implies a tribute to the literacy of his Lake District community. Books hold the promise of an idealized sociality:

> ... books
> Were ready comrades whom he could not tire,—
> Of whose society the blameless Man
> Was never satiate. Their familiar voice,
> Even to old age, with unabated charm
> Beguiled his leisure hours; refreshed his thoughts;
> Beyond its natural elevation raised
> His introverted spirit; and bestowed
> Upon his life an outward dignity
> Which all acknowledged.
>
> (ll. 545–54)

The Dalesman's library – 'Song of the muses, sage historic tale, / Science severe, or work of holy writ' (ll. 556-7) – conforms to the outlines of Wordsworth's own in *The Prelude*. Books promise 'immortality and joy ... From imperfection and decay secure' (ll. 558, 560). The Dalesman is redeemed even before his death, pre-assured of the tranquility and equanimity of literary afterlife; hence 'his peaceful smiles, / The gleams of his slow-varying countenance' (ll. 566–7). The unobtrusive manner of his dying – the powers of nature 'insensibly consumed' (l. 570) – marks a change of degree rather than kind; 'the profounder stillness of the grave' (l. 574) is continuous with his stilled life. The composing sound that 'Murmurs not idly o'er the peaceful grave' (l. 587) accompanies this insensible merging of life and death.

The Dalesman's literacy restores 'The precious gift of hearing', but at a cost. Books converse with the introverted spirit like an un-dead family. Redemption by reading pre-assures an afterlife; yet the ear of the deaf is imagined as that of the dead-already. In a sonnet sequence of 1804, 'I am not One who much or oft delight' ('Personal Talk'), Wordsworth declares that he much prefers reading to fireside gossip: 'Dreams, books, are each a world; and books, we know, / Are a substantial world, both pure and good' (ll. 33–4).[10] Offering a Holme-like glimpse of his own domestic hearth – 'There do I find a never-failing store / Of personal themes' (ll. 37–8) – Wordsworth attributes his best sources not to fireside gossip, but to books. Solitary reading defends against a hostile or persecutory world, ensuring 'Smooth passions, smooth discourse, and joyous thought' (l. 48). Blessing 'The Poets, who on earth have made us

Heirs / Of truth and pure delight' (ll. 50–1), Wordsworth writes himself
optimistically into the dead poets' society: 'Oh! Might my name be
numbered among theirs, / Then gladly would I end my mortal days'
(ll. 55–6). His inclusion in the community of dead poets links him to
the salvation of the deaf Dalesman, who joins 'the assembled spirits of
the just' (l. 559) even before his death.

Reading involves a kind of deaf-muteness. Historians of literacy argue that
silent reading became increasingly common during the eighteenth century,
accompanying the expansion of print-culture.[11] Reciting his own 'poetic
numbers' at the start of *The Prelude*, Wordsworth is cheered when he hears
both his own voice and 'the mind's / Internal echo of the imperfect sound'
(*1805 Prelude*, 1.64–5). Deciphering epitaphs during a visit to the church in
The Excursion, the Poet whispers them out loud: 'to the silent language giving
voice, / I read ... With whisper soft' (*Excursion*, 5.187–8, 206).[12] This auditory doubling also forms part of the experience of the post-lingual deaf.[13]
Whether or not Wordsworth sounded his poetry as he composed, the evidence of the murmuring pine tree and the whispers of *The Excursion* suggest
that he may have sounded poetry, internally and 'with whisper soft', as he
read by graveside or hearth.[14] What are the implications of this auditory doubling for the realm of silent signing? I want to explore this question by way
of Enlightenment writers on deaf education who pose issues about literacy
and signing that speak more generally to Wordsworth's poetry.

2   A second horn-book

Wordsworth calls the epitaph 'a second horn-book' (*PW*, 2:59) where
learning to read begins again. Eighteenth-century debates about educating
the deaf – no longer considered incurable imbeciles – are bound up with
Enlightenment philosophies of language.[15] The late eighteenth-century
movement for deaf education involved a tug-of-war between those who
advocated teaching the deaf by using their own gestural sign system and
those who believed that the deaf should be 'given' a voice and taught to
speak. On the one hand, deaf educators championed autonomous signing
practices that had grown up among deaf communities themselves. On the
other, their opponents believed that deaf-mutes should be brought within
the oral sphere of the dominant hearing majority. The Enlightenment debate
over deaf education involves the politics of integration: should the deaf be
allowed to live and learn in their own world, or should they be integrated
as far as possible into the oral mainstream, and taught to speak? Or, a third
possibility, should the deaf be considered bilingual, fluent in two languages,
both signing and spoken? Among the most effective (and vocal) proponents

of deaf education were two French Enlightenment near-contemporaries of the deaf Dalesman.[16] Both had been helped to overcome their deafness by pioneering educators, at least one of whom – the Abbé de l'Epée – would have been well known in late eighteenth-century Britain.

Saboureux de Fontenay was presented to the Royal Academy of Sciences in Paris in 1751 as a deaf mute who had successfully learned to speak. His teacher was Jacob Péreire, who developed a system for countering the mutism that accompanies congenital deafness, adapting a seventeenth-century Spanish manual alphabet for use in French as a form of finger spelling (also used for communicating with the blind by touch). Under his tuition, Saboureux became not only literate, but the first person born deaf who went on to publish a book. His *Lettre de M. Saboureux de Fontenay, sourd et muet de naissance, à Mademoiselle* *** (1764) insists on the unimpeded communicativeness of pictures:

> at the sight of a picture, the eyes, rightly called the mirror of the soul, communicate to the deaf person the whole thought of the person who painted it (by writing or fingerspelling or signs or whatever means), much as his mind imagined it ... the thought goes from the person imagining it to the person receiving it.[17]

Picture-writing mediates between mind and mind.

Saboureux installs the deaf squarely within eighteenth-century print-culture and the conversational public sphere:

> you should recognize that print, signs, words, phrases, conversation, and the reading of books give deaf persons as much pleasure as hearing people get from the sounds of speech and conversation.
>
> (*DE*, 23)[18]

Alongside his laborious acquisition of speech, Saboureux had learned the writing-based system that Péreire called 'dactylology':

> The hand is used like a pen for making drawings in the air of the periods and accent marks and to indicate the capitals and small letters and abbreviations. The finger movements mark the long, medium, and very short pauses observed in speech. Dactylology ... is as rapid and convenient as speech itself, and as expressive as good writing. Other signs can be added freely to accommodate the rules of prosody, music, poetry, and the like.
>
> (*DE*, 26)

Dactylology implies literacy in the most literal sense, promising access to music, prosody, and poetry. Saboureux's advocacy of a graphic system derived from both writing and speech aligns him with the oralist camp that rejected the use of deaf sign language altogether. Rival proponents of deaf education, by contrast, supported manualism, a self-sufficient sign-system independent of fingerspelling or 'dactylology'.

Pierre Desloges, for instance, defends the autonomous signing world of the deaf in his *Observations d'un sourd et muet* (1779), responding to a publication denigrating sign language by another of Péreire's supporters. L'Abbé Deschamps's *Cours élémentaire d'éducation des sourds et muets* (1779) required the deaf mute to use their mouths to imitate the mechanics of speech and to learn to lipread the mouths of the hearing. Desloges (like the deaf Dalesman) became deaf in childhood, but only after he had learned to read and write. His knowledge of sign language initially came through contact with an illiterate under-class; prior to that, his only form of self-expression had been writing. As an adult, he discovered the signing language used by the deaf community of urban Paris and adopted for teaching by the saintly Abbé de l'Epée, the most famous of all Enlightenment pioneers of deaf education. De l'Epée's support of signing reflected his belief that deaf language was an autonomous system resembling the 'native' or 'natural' language of another nation – a potentially universal language intelligible to all peoples who constituted a living dictionary of signs.[19] His fantasy of a universal sign language was unfounded; deaf language systems are as culturally and nationally varied as oral languages. But signing proved invaluable for teaching the deaf, and remains linked to high levels of literacy and educational achievement today.[20]

Desloges argues that the deaf inhabit a compensatory world whose privations enhance attentiveness and encourage reflection. He represents deaf signing as a means of communication that

> being a faithful image of the object expressed, is singularly appropriate for making our ideas accurate and for extending our comprehension ... This language is lively; it portrays sentiment, and develops the imagination. No other language is more appropriate for conveying great and strong emotions.
>
> (*DE*, 36)

Citing Condillac's linguistic theories, Desloges posits the existence of a language that 'represents or recalls the idea of things by signs that are not arbitrary, but natural' (*DE*, 47). Deaf signing was at once more faithful to nature and more passionate than arbitrary signs. The Abbé de l'Epée's public demonstrations at his Paris school during the 1770s, along with his *Véritable manière d'instruire les sourds et muets, confirmée par une longue expérience* (1784), helped to disseminate the international use of deaf signing.[21] De l'Epée's successor, the Abbé Roch-Ambroise Sicard, pleads in his *Cours d'instruction d'un sourd-muet de naissance* (1803) for the inclusion of the congenitally deaf in the category of the human: 'Why is the uneducated deaf person isolated in nature and unable to communicate with other men? Why is he reduced to this state of imbecility?' (*DE*, 84–5). The solution lay in the pictorial dimensions of deaf sign language.

Sicard – the enlightened overseer of the National Institute for Deaf-Mutes to which Victor, the Wild Boy of Aveyron, was brought in 1800 – planned a dictionary of deaf language. Published as *Théorie des signes* (1808), it envisaged a gestural or 'natural' sign language that was predicated on non-arbitrary signs 'taken from the nature of the objects they represent' (*DE*, 97). Its figurative (i.e. pictorial) basis was capable of overcoming the muteness of nations, enabling them to converse with one another across national boundaries:

> This figurative language even has a definite advantage over spoken language, for it is not restricted to any one dialect. It is a kind of universal language that, if well articulated, is understandable to people of every nationality ... Beyond its own territorial limits, every nation is mute, but the nation using gesture is nowhere mute. For this language is the language of nature and is to some degree spoken everywhere.
>
> (*DE*, 97–8)

Whereas sounds largely derive their meaning from convention, the deaf person mimes objects 'with a probably clearer and less ambiguous pantomime'; as in spoken language, analogies 'enrich the mimic vocabulary of the deaf' (*DE*, 99). Thus imagined, mimetic sign language promised a universally intelligible language of analogy.

Wordsworth's *Essays upon Epitaphs* champion the epitaph for its universality: 'not a proud writing shut up for the studious: it is exposed to all – to the wise and the most ignorant' (*PW*, 2:59). The epitaph is a democratic form of reading matter, 'concerning all, and for all', that returns the old to childhood and lets the child take pride in reading. Even the sun gets a look-in:

> [I]ts story and admonitions are brief, that the thoughtless, the busy, and indolent, may not be deterred, nor the impatient tired: the stooping old man cons the engraven record like a second horn-book; – the

child is proud that he can read it, and the stranger is introduced
through its mediation to the company of a friend: it is concerning all,
and for all: – in the church-yard it is open to the day; the sun looks
down upon the stone, and the rains of heaven beat against it.

(*PW* 2:59)

In this environmentally friendly form of literacy, the sun is the universal reader that looks down on the weathered stone – in de Man's terms
'the large, overarching metaphor for this entire system' (74);[22] the rain
performs its tribute to a naturalized text. Commenting on the affecting
figures and analogies of epitaphs, Wordsworth lists natural processes: life
as a journey, death as a sleep, misfortune as a storm, beauty as a flower,
virtue as a rock, hope undermined like a poplar by the river that feeds
it, or blasted like a pine tree by lightning (*PW*, 2:54). One might add to
this list the sun, the trope that de Man calls 'more than a mere natural
object ... a figure of knowledge as well as of nature'. This is 'the eye that
reads the text of the epitaph' (75). Mute nation becomes reading nation.

Such graveyard analogies, Wordsworth speculates, must have given
'to the language of the senseless stone a voice enforced and endeared
by the benignity of that nature with which it was in unison' (*PW*, 2:54).
Nature's universally 'figurative' language both gives a voice to the senseless stone and is united with it. As de Man puts it, 'the *speaking* stone
counterbalanc[es] the *seeing* sun' (75). Hence the rhetorical figure, prosopopoeia, that confers the power of speech, and whose phenomenological
effects include 'hearing' the voice of the epitaphic text. This figure allows
the mute stone to speak while making every reader a natural reader. For
de Man, the threat of a deeper logical disturbance emerges at this point:
the trope that gives voice also signals its symmetrical opposite, dumb-
ness. I want, however, to take a different path. What are the implications
of this mimetic theory of signs as natural analogy – figures 'taken from
the nature of the objects they represent' – for 'The Brothers'?

3   A pair of diaries

The deaf Daleman's story belongs with other pastorals by Wordsworth that
mourn the passing of the Lake District Statesmen ('men of respectable education who daily labour on their own little properties'). Anchoring them
by domestic affections and inheritance, 'Their little tract of land serves as
a kind of permanent rallying point for their domestic feelings, as a tablet
upon which they are written.'[23] Wordsworth's 1801 letter to Charles James
Fox singles out 'Michael' and 'The Brothers' – the poem he intended to

open the second 1800 volume of *Lyrical Ballads*.[24] His letter merges pastoral, inscription, and epitaph; landscape becomes the memorial 'tablet' on which the Statesman's feelings are written. Geoffrey Hartman observes of this generic convergence, 'Nature is herself a larger graveyard inscribed deeply with evidences of past life.'[25] For the Priest of Ennerdale in 'The Brothers' nature is also God's 'great book of the world' (l. 262).[26] Defending *The Excursion* in 1815, Wordsworth refers to 'the innumerable analogies ... transfused into that Poem from the Bible of the Universe'. He ends: 'Do not you perceive that my conversations almost all take place out of Doors, and all with grand objects of nature surrounding the speakers for the express purpose of their being alluded to in illustration of the subjects treated of.'[27] Underpinned by religion, his illustrative mode treats landscape as a biblically authorized sign language.

'The Brothers' was originally known as 'the pastoral of *Bowman*'. It commemorates a tragedy that Wordsworth had learned about during his Lake District walking tour with Coleridge in the autumn of 1799.[28] The opening lines of 'The Brothers' contains an early usage of the word 'tourist' when the Priest of Ennerdale mistakes Leonard Ewbank for a sentimental traveller: 'These Tourists, Heaven preserve us! needs must live / A profitable life ...' (ll. 1–2). The Priest is puzzled, since there are no epitaphs or markers to detain him:

> —In our church-yard
> Is neither epitaph nor monument,
> Tomb-stone nor name, only the turf we tread,
> And a few natural graves.

> (ll. 12–15)

The *Essays upon Epitaphs* recall the halting of the passer-by at 'the invitation, "Pause, Traveller!" so often found upon [classical] monuments' (*PW*, 2:54). Leonard – not the idle tourist the Priest mistakes him for – is a halted traveller indeed, lingering beside an unmarked grave.[29] Wordsworth's own Lake tour had involved stories gleaned not only from grave-stones, but from the Dalesmen who taught him to read the landscape: 'The poem arose out of the fact mentioned to me at Ennerdale that a shepherd had fallen asleep upon the top of the rock called The Pillar, and perished as here described, his staff being left midway on the rock' (*LB*, 380).[30]

'The Brothers' twins epitaphic landscape and communal memory. In the poem's opening lines, the Priest describes how tourists, recording the

landscape in sketchbooks in journals, 'He pored, with book and pencil
on their knee, / And look and scribble, scribble on and look' (ll. 6–7). 'The
Brothers' employs a similar technique of comparison between landscape and
sign. When Leonard comments on the absence of grave-monuments, the
Priest replies: 'We have no need of names and epitaphs, / We talk about the
dead by our fire-sides' (ll. 176–7). Leonard's leading question – 'Your dalesmen, then, do in each other's thoughts / Possess a kind of second life ...?'
(ll. 181–2) – echoes the Priest's explanation that the landscape provides its
own chronicle of events: 'we all have here / A pair of diaries, one serving,
Sir, / For the whole dale, and one for each fire-side' (ll. 160–2). Everything
in 'The Brothers' comes in twos: two books, two bells, two hours – even
'the twin cards tooth'd with glittering wire' which the Priest uses to feed his
child's spindle (laid aside – like the brothers themselves – 'each in the other
lock'd' [ll. 22, 33]).[31] This insistent doubling makes landscape a figurative
record not only of local history, but of the separation of the two intertwined
brothers, Leonard and James. The language of second life hangs on the analogy between natural and human change.

The first of the *Essays upon Epitaphs* refers to 'the thoughtless, the
busy, and the indolent' (*PW*, 2:59) whose reading habits suit the brevity
of the epitaph. The Priest, in contrast, reads the record with exasperating
thoroughness while Leonard, 'the Stranger', finds it confusing and illeg-
ible: is this a new grave or an old one? Such moments of unreadability
alternate with excessive legibility. Returning from the sea after a twenty-
year absence, Leonard loses his way up the familiar valley, and, in a moment of over-reading, fancies that he sees 'Strange alteration wrought
on every side / Among the woods and fields, and that the rocks, / And
the eternal hills, themselves were chang'd' (ll. 94–6). Elsewhere, however, the Priest points to real changes in the landscape: a lightening-rent
pike and a single spring bubbling where before there had been two,
'Companions for each other' – 'brother fountains' as Leonard and James
were 'brother Shepherds on their native hills' (ll. 140, 141, 72). Through
this insistent visual doubling, Wordsworth signposts landscape as one
of the 'pair of diaries' that chronicle pastoral life:

—On that tall pike,
(It is the loneliest place of all these hills)
There were two Springs which bubbled side by side,
As if they had been made that they might be
Companions for each other: ten years back,
Close to these brother fountains, the huge crag

Was rent with lightning—one is dead and gone,
The other, left behind, is flowing still.

(ll. 136–43)[32]

The rent crag and the lone spring provide figurative analogies for the brothers' separation. Landscape functions in 'The Brothers' as if Wordsworth – like the Priest – is already anticipating the out-of-doors illustrative mode of *The Excursion*.

When their grandfather dies, the Ewbank land consumed by debts and mortgages, the two brothers are left destitute. Leonard, the older, goes to sea to support them both, leaving James to be cared for by the community: 'If he had one, the Lad had twenty homes' (l. 383). James's underlying disturbance shows itself in the sleepwalking that is blamed for his death. Anxious to play down the possibility of suicide, the Priest conjectures that he tumbled from the crag ('the Pillar') after falling asleep as he waited for his companions to return: 'They found him at the foot of that same Rock / Dead, and with mangled limbs' (ll. 377–8). His traumatic fall puts a human mark on the landscape, 'His shepherd's staff; for midway in the cliff / It had been caught, and there for many years / It hung—and moulder'd there' (ll. 400–2). The same overdetermined verb, 'to hang', links Leonard's vision of the calenture to James's fatal fall. Leonard (hearing the noise of waterfalls, caverns, and trees in the sound of the rigging) 'would often hang / Over the vessel's side, and gaze and gaze' at 'images and hues, that wrought / In union with the employment of his heart' (ll. 51–2, 54–5). The illusory landscape of the calenture was thought to tempt delirious sailors to leap to their deaths:

He, thus by feverish passion overcome,
Even with the organs of his bodily eye,
Below him, in the bosom of the deep,
Saw mountains, saw the forms of sheep that graz'd
On verdant hills, with dwellings among trees,
And Shepherds clad in the same country grey
Which he himself had worn.

(ll. 56–62)[33]

Dreaming himself at home, Leonard anticipates James's sleepwalking plunge. Their parallel home-sicknesses – James's unquiet sleep, Leonard's feverish passion – threaten to confuse mental and visible worlds.

In 'The Brothers', the intervention of imagination leads to prolonged uncertainty and unbalance. The effects of separation divide landscape from itself, mis-remembered or dreamed as unstable, even treacherous. Landscape's double inscription of trauma – the crag riven by lightning or the spring stopped at its source – is left hanging like the shepherd's mouldering staff. A form of undecidability, this suspension complicates the pairing of diaries whereby landscape supposedly underwrites communal memory. Either landscape is as mutable as the sea, or the sea is as fickle as the once-familiar fields where Leonard misses his homeward path (l. 90). This uncertainty overcomes Leonard himself as he lingers in the graveyard: 'as he gaz'd, there grew / Such a confusion in his memory, / That he began to doubt' (ll. 83–5). The chiasmus or crossing marks the onset of doubt; he (and we) lose our footing in a landscape that proves as precarious as James's sleeping place. Landscape and memory are liable to the same slippage.

The precariousness (even danger) attributed to figuration emerges in a prominent passage from the *Essays upon Epitaphs*:

> Language, if it do not uphold, and feed, and leave in quiet, like the power of gravitation or the air we breathe, is a counter-spirit, unremittingly and noiselessly at work to derange, to subvert, to lay waste, to vitiate, and to dissolve.
>
> (*PW*, 2:85)

Underlining the violence of Wordsworth's fantasy, de Man observes that 'The most violent language of all is saved ... for language itself' (79). Wordsworth's language is symptomatic in other ways. In 'The Brothers', James is not upheld and left in quiet by the air he breathes, nor does the power of gravitation work for him when he falls to his death. Like the sea, or like landscape, all language (not just language that 'incarnates' thought), to the extent that is inherently figurative, acts to dissolve as well as uphold. This is true whether or not it is founded on the visible world or natural analogies, as some Enlightenment theorists had claimed for universal sign language. A derangement-effect accompanies both separation and signs, cleaving the bond of brotherhood in the place where it is supposed to be most firmly grounded. This is not to suggest that Wordsworth had 'The Brothers' in mind when he wrote the *Essays upon Epitaphs*. But the fault lines are already visible in the instability of the trope of natural analogy that permeates 'The Brothers'.

Wordsworth had personal reasons for fearing separation and death and associating them with the sea. His brother John, whose arrival was eagerly awaited when he and Coleridge returned from their walking tour at the end of 1799, had made his career as the captain of an East Indiaman; like Leonard, John hoped to support his brother's less lucrative career at home in Grasmere.[34] Wordsworth called his brother 'a Poet in every thing but words'.[35] The reticent Leonard is thought to have traits borrowed from John (see *LB*, 380). Wordsworth reacted to his brother's death at sea in February 1805 with intense grief: 'there is something cut out of my life which cannot be restored'.[36] Recollections of his drowning surface at the start of the second *Essay upon Epitaphs*, where the confused depths of the sea image the perturbations that underlie the apparent calm of a country graveyard: 'my fancy has penetrated into the depths of the Sea – with accompanying thoughts of Shipwreck, or the destruction of the Mariner's hopes' (*PW*, 2:64–5). Wordsworth recalled that 'The Brothers' was 'composed in a grove at the north-eastern end of Grasmere Lake' (*LB*, 379). He also records that during John's protracted Grasmere visit of 1800, when he was working on 'The Brothers', his brother had been fond of pacing in a nearby grove, 'With that habitual restlessness of foot / Wherewith the sailor measures o'er and o'er / His short domain upon the Vessel's deck'.[37] Composing poet and restless sailor converge at the site of 'The Brothers'.

The most poignant of all epitaphs in the *Essays upon Epitaphs* is that of a new-born infant in an overgrown corner of a country churchyard. The grave bears only a name and two dates:

> In an obscure corner of a Country Church-yard I once espied, half-overgrown with Hemlock and Nettles, a very small Stone laid upon the ground, bearing nothing more than the name of the Deceased with the date of birth and death, importing that it was an Infant which had been born one day and died the following. I know not how far the Reader may be in sympathy with me, but more awful thoughts of rights conferred, of hopes awakened, of remembrances stealing away or vanishing were imparted to my mind by that Inscription there before my eyes than by any other that it has ever been my lot to meet with upon a Tomb-stone.
>
> (*PW*, 2:93)

The absence of words becomes the most legible of epitaphs. In lines that Coleridge categorized as '*mental* bombast' ('thoughts and images too great for the subject'),[38] the Immortality Ode refers to the infant as a deaf mute who penetrates the depths of the sea: 'thou Eye among the blind, / That, deaf and silent, read'st the eternal deep'.[39] The eye of a deaf mute *infans* stands in for the poet's compensatory over-reading of epitaphic signs as he stands, like Leonard, puzzling over a minimally marked grave.

Notes

1. *The Prose Works*, ed. W. J. B. Owen and Jane Worthington Smyser, vol. 2 (Oxford: Clarendon Press, 1974), p. 96. Hereafter indicated as *PW* and cited by volume and page numbers in the text. Wordsworth's epitaph for the deaf Dalesman is cited by line numbers in the text. Written in 1810 for *The Friend*, only the first of the three *Essays upon Epitaphs* appeared; in 1814 the deaf Dalesman's epitaph formed *The Excursion*, 7.395–481.

2. 'Autobiography as De-Facement', in *The Rhetoric of Romanticism* (New York: Columbia University Press, 1984), p. 72. Hereafter cited by page numbers in the text. De Man's singling out of prosopopoeia ('to compose by means of faces') as the defining trope of autobiography has received extensive commentary; see, for instance, Lorna Clymer, 'Graved in Tropes: The Figural Logic of Epitaphs and Elegies in Blair, Gray, Cowper, and Wordsworth', *ELH*, 62 (1995), 347–86, which briefly criticizes the reading of the deaf Dalesman in my earlier 1985 essay, reprinted as '"Dithyrambic Fervour": The Lyric Voice of *The Prelude*', in *Romanticism, Writing, and Sexual Difference: Essays on The Prelude* (Oxford: Oxford University Press, 1989), pp. 159–83.

3. Wordsworth notes that the deaf Dalesman's epitaph is founded on the original Mardale epitaph, and on 'enquiries concerning the Deceased made in the neighbourhood' (*PW*, 2:94).

4. *The Thirteen-Book 'Prelude'*, ed. Mark L. Reed, vol. 1 (Ithaca, NY: Cornell University Press, 1991), p. 230. Cited as *1805 Prelude* by book and line numbers in the text.

5. *Deafness* (New York: Stein and Day, 1969), p. 11. The lines which form my second epigraph appear on p. 3. Wright's autobiographical account provides an exceptional insight into the auditory experience and 1930s education, as well as the war-time Oxford years, of a post-lingually deaf poet. Cf. Wright's admiration of Wordsworth's lines on the pine tree 'whose composing sound / Was wasted' on the deaf man's ear, otherwise 'a portrait of a deaf man [that] carries no particular insights' (p. 201).

6. Ibid., pp. 11–12. See also Oliver Sacks, *Seeing Voices: A Journey into the World of the Deaf* (Berkeley: University of California Press, 1989), pp. 2–13; Sacks was given Wright's book by a fellow-poet, W. H. Auden.

7. Ibid., p. 12.

8. *Last Poems, 1821–1850*, ed. Jared Curtis, A. L. Denny Ferris, and J. Heydt-Stevenson (Ithaca, NY: Cornell University Press, 1999), p. 285.

9. See Wright, *Deafness*, pp. 73–4, for his recitation of poetry after lights-out as a form of 'concert': 'probably the best training I could have given myself in metric and the handling of vowels and consonants, in the relations of sense and sound, in the orchestration of a poem' (p. 75).

10. *'Poems, in Two Volumes', and Other Poems 1800–1807*, ed. Jared Curtis (Ithaca, NY: Cornell University Press, 1983), pp. 253–5. Richard Cronin notes the link with Holme, arguing that the collapse of the Lake District community forced Wordsworth to transfer his faith to the society of letters. See 'Wordsworth's Poems of 1807 and the War against Napoleon', *RES*, 48 (1997), pp. 33–50.

11. For the cumulative impact of print culture on orality, and for the development of the modern sense of private reading see, for instance, Walter Ong, *Orality*

and Literacy: The Technologizing of the Word (New York: Routledge, 1988), pp. 117–22, 130–2.

12. *The Excursion*, ed. Sally Bushell, James A. Butler, and Michael C. Jaye, with the assistance of David García (Ithaca, NY: Cornell University Press, 2007), p. 173. Cited as *Excursion* by book and line numbers in the text.

13. Dorothy Miles, a Welsh-born deaf poet who also makes use of sign language in her poems, writes that they 'are written from the words and music that still sing in my mind'. *Gestures* (1976), quoted from Brian Grant, *Deafness in Literature*, intr. Margaret Drabble (London: Faber and Faber, 1987), p. 51. Cf. Robert Panara, who also lost his hearing as a child: 'My ears are deaf, and yet I seem to hear / Sweet Nature's music and the songs of Man' (ibid., p. 227).

14. Cf., however, Andrew Bennett, *Wordsworth Writing* (Cambridge: Cambridge University Press, 2007), pp. 58–77 for 'the denial of writing' in Wordsworth's compositional and poetic practice; and, for a provocative reading of sound in the deaf Dalesman's epitaph (pp. 73–6). The term 'composing' (referring to typesetting) offers an alternative gloss on the pine tree's 'composing sound' (see Ong, *Orality*, pp. 121–2).

15. See Jonathan Rée, *I See a Voice: A Philosophical History of Language, Deafness, and the Senses* (London: Flamingo, 1999), esp. chapters 15–17, for an informative account of Enlightenment debates over deaf education, signs, and natural language up to and during the period of the French Revolution; I am indebted to Rée's imaginative history of Enlightenment and post-Enlightenment attitudes to deafness. See also Harlan Lane (ed.), *The Deaf Experience: Classics in Language and Education*, trans. Franklin Philip (Cambridge, MA: Harvard University Press, 1984), and Harlan Lane, *When the Mind Hears: A History of the Deaf* (New York: Random House, 1984).

16. In Britain, deaf education was pioneered during the 1760s by Thomas Braidwood at the Edinburgh Academy for the Deaf and Dumb, visited by Dr Johnson in 1773, the year of Thomas Holmes's death. In 1783 the Academy moved to Hackney, and in 1792 another academy opened in Bermondsey; see Rée, *I See a Voice*, pp, 137–40, 154, 196–7. Braidwood taught the deaf successively to read, write, and speak, using a method he refused to share.

17. Quoted from Lane, *The Deaf Experience*, pp. 22–3. Hereafter indicated as *DE* and cited by page numbers in the text.

18. For the association of the deaf with printing and print-culture during the French Enlightenment period, see Nicholas Mirzoeff, *Silent Poetry: Deafness, Sign, and Visual Culture in Modern France* (Princeton, NJ: Princeton University Press, 1995), p. 33.

19. For de l'Epée's gestural methods and their relation to signs, see Renate Fischer, 'Abbé de l'Epée and the Living Dictionary', in *Deaf History Unveiled*, ed. John Vickry Van Cleve (Washington, DC: Gallaudet University Press, 1993), pp. 13–26. For philosophical claims about universal language, see Mirzoeff, *Silent Poetry*, p. 33, and Rée, *I See a Voice*, pp. 166–76. In his *Essai sur l'origine des langues* (1781), written during the 1750s, Rousseau had speculated that gestural language preceded speech.

20. The defeat of manualism by oralism at the end of the nineteenth century, when medical science reclassified deafness as an abnormality, forced both signing and deaf teachers out of the classroom. For an impassioned defense of autonomous deaf sign language (as well as its regional and national

variations) and the prohibition of signing in favour of oralism, see Sacks, *Seeing Voices*, pp. 21–36; and, for a vivid account of the Gallaudet College student strike that led to the appointment of the first deaf President in 1988, pp. 125–9. See also Rée, *I See a Voice*, chapters 20 and 21, and, for the association of sign language with primitive man, Douglas C. Baynton, '"Savages and Deaf-Mutes": Evolutionary Theory and the Campaign against Sign Language in the Nineteenth Century', in Van Cleve, *Deaf History*, pp. 92–112.

21. De l'Epée's sentimental standing at the end of the eighteenth century can be gauged from the successful London production of Thomas Holcroft's play *Deaf and Dumb, or the Orphan Protected* (1801). Holcroft's play, a translation of Jean-Nicolas Bouilly's equally successful *Abbé de l'Epée* (performed in Paris in 1799), was first performed in London at the Drury Lane Theatre in February 1801 with the future Mrs Charles Kemble as the orphaned deaf mute. Bouilly's play was also translated by Kotzebue, then retranslated into English by Benjamin Thompson as *Deaf and Dumb; or the Orphan* (1805). See Mirzoeff, *Silent Poetry*, pp. 74–5, 79–80, 281–2 nn. 121–2.

22. 'At this point it can be said of "the language of the senseless stone" that it acquires a "voice," the *speaking* stone counterbalancing the *seeing* sun' (75). For an interesting account of what we 'see' in (de Man's) reading, see Rei Terada, 'Seeing is Reading', in *Legacies of Paul de Man*, ed. Marc Redfield (New York: Fordham University Press, 2007), pp. 162–77.

23. To Charles James Fox, 14 January 1801, in *The Letters of William and Dorothy Wordsworth: The Early Years 1787–1805*, ed. Ernest de Selincourt, rev. Chester L. Shaver (Oxford: Clarendon Press, 1967), pp. 314–15. Hereafter cited as *EY*.

24. Wordsworth to Messrs. Biggs and Cottle, 1 August 1800, in *EY*, p. 290.

25. 'Inscriptions and Romantic Nature Poetry', in *The Unremarkable Wordsworth*, intr. Donald G. Marshall (Minneapolis: University of Minnesota Press, 1987), p. 34. Hartman's concern with the unstable generic form of the nature-inscription leads him to *Lyrical Ballads*, particularly 'Michael'. For a perceptive discussion of 'The Brothers' in relation to epitaph, see Frances Ferguson, *Wordsworth: Language as Counter-Spirit* (New Haven, CT: Yale University Press, 1977), pp. 42–53.

26. *'Lyrical Ballads' and Other Poems, 1797–1800*, ed. James Butler and Karen Green (Ithaca, NY: Cornell University Press, 1992), p. 151. Hereafter indicated as *LB* and cited by page numbers in the text. Poems from this volume are cited by line numbers in the text. See pp. 379–80 for an account of the composition of 'The Brothers' between December 1799 and April 1800.

27. To Catherine Clarkson, January 1815, in *The Letters of William and Dorothy Wordsworth: The Middle Years. Part II, 1812–1820*, ed. Ernest de Selincourt, rev. Mary Moorman and Alan G. Hill (Oxford: Clarendon Press, 1970), pp. 188, 191.

28. Wordsworth to S. T. Coleridge, 24 and 27 December 1799, in *EY*, p. 277 and n. 3: 'I have begun the pastoral of Bowman: in my next letter I shall probably be able to send it to you.' By 1800, the literary tour of the Lakes was well-established.

29. Wordsworth notes: 'Some of the country church-yards, as here described, do not contain a single tombstone, and most of them have a very small number' (*LB*, 382).

30. Coleridge's notes of the walking-tour record how Bowman 'broke his neck ... by falling off a Crag ... – supposed to have layed down & slept – but walked in his sleep, & so came to this crag, & fell off ... – his Pike staff stuck midway & stayed there till it rotted away' (*LB*, 380).
31. The two books are the brothers' school books 'lying both on a dry stone' (l. 258); the two hours are the time it takes James's companions to return to their meeting place (l. 368); 'those two bells of ours, which there you see / Hanging in the open air' (ll. 309–10) would have sounded for Leonard's safe return from the sea.
32. Introducing the record formed by change and accidents to the landscape itself may have been the awkward passage on which Wordsworth found himself stuck in late December. See *LB*, 380, and 568, 570–1 for a draft of the relevant passage (ll. 136–43).
33. Wordsworth footnotes: 'This description of the Calenture is sketch'd from an imperfect recollection of an admirable one in prose, by Mr. Gilbert, author of the Hurricane' (*LB*, 144). The reference is to Willliam Gilbert's *The Hurricane; a Theosophical and Western Eclogue* (1796).
34. Wordsworth writes to James Losh, 16 March 1805: 'we had at that time little to live upon and he went to sea high in hope and heart that he should soon be able to make his Sister independent and contribute to any wants which I might have' (*EY*, p. 563).
35. To Sir George Beaumont, 11 February 1805, in *EY*, p. 541.
36. To James Losh, 16 March 1805, in *EY*, p. 565.
37. *Poems, in Two Volumes*, ed. Curtis, p. 565, ll. 71–3.
38. *The Collected Works of Samuel Taylor Coleridge: Biographia Literaria*, ed. James Engell and W. Jackson Bate, vol. 2 (London: Routledge & Kegan Paul, 1983), pp. 136, 138.
39. *Poems, in Two Volumes*, ed. Curtis, p. 274, ll. 111–12.

11
Wordsworth and Metapsychology

Geoffrey Hartman

> On Poetry, and geometric truth,
> And their high privilege of lasting life,
> From all internal injury exempt,
> I mused ...
> —Wordsworth, *1850 Prelude* (5.65–8)[1]

1

Wordsworth's vivid picture of his early development, and its abiding and remedial influence, suggests imagination's primordial link to a 'zone of material reveries', that is, to dream-like states about the material universe of nature.[2] These reveries put him in touch not only with childhood memories but also with an elemental, ageless, immemorial residue: the impact or subterranean action of 'mute insensate things'.[3] Primal matter, for the poet, has a sort of consciousness and influence. The non-human world in its vast passivity, its mute, inertial force, weighs on mind and sense.[4]

Wordsworth even attributes a 'passion' to the 'forms / Of Nature' (*1850 Prelude*, 13.289–90), as if the 'insensate' were itself not devoid of feeling but exhibited an inarticulate appeal. This should not be dismissed as a moody projection or conventional rhetorical animism. Rather, I suggest, it brings the poet into the haunt of Freud's metapsychology – or the most disputed part of it. The impact of matter on the imagination begins to matter.

Now this region of metapsychology is a murky one, even if it prompts Freud's startling aphorism: '*The aim of all life is death.*'[5] Freud's unusual overstatement serves the purpose of viewing life as a detour between its inorganic origin and inorganic finale. A 'long way round to Nirvana', Santayana remarked.[6] The metapsychological thesis that human beings, like all organisms, manifest a conservative compulsion to repeat, and seek to return to an inertial state, allows Freud to link, by his version of *Naturphilosophie*, psychological processes to the cosmic realm in *Beyond the Pleasure Principle* (1920). He argues that 'everything living dies for *internal* reasons' (*BPP*, 38; also see 36–7), as if psychological processes too were governed by something like consent to a cosmic law. Human life and consciousness, in any case, are not supra-natural developments guided by a mysterious 'instinct toward perfection' (*BPP*, 42) that culminates in a higher destiny. Such a belief would have been hard to sustain with European 'civilization' sorely tested by the First World War.

2

I focus on two related questions. First, does Freud's *metapsychological* speculation on how conscious life emerged, yet provokes a reactive, iner-tial, even death-tending instinct, have a bearing on poetry's *psychological* function? Stated somewhat differently: is also our coming (in)to speech accompanied by an antithetical tendency, by instinctive elements like the subverbal tow of sound and rhythm, difficult to place totally on the side of meaning? One might also mention surprising formations (idioms and images) that make poetry less transparent for conventional communicative discourse. Correlatively, could Wordsworth's view of early development, reflecting his intense childhood awareness of Nature, his relationship with 'the kinematics of surrounding nature', throw a light on poetry as further-ing a remedial anti-self-conscious, even anti-traumatic effect?[7]

Freud summarized in a well-known paragraph his thoughts on the natural workings of death in life as well as the generation of life from death:

> The attributes of life were at some time evoked in inanimate matter by the action of a force of whose nature we can form no conception. It may perhaps have been a process similar in type to that which later caused the development of consciousness in a particular stratum of living mat-ter. The tension which then arose in what had hitherto been an inani-mate substance endeavoured to cancel itself out. In this way the first instinct came into being: the instinct to return to the inanimate state.
>
> (*BPP*, 38)

I propose that poetry imaginatively supports both phases: that which 'evokes' the presence of life, and often conscious life, even in what is apparently inanimate, and that which inhibits this process that I add the idea (or to the idea) that the inhibiting phase may have a remedial and creative component, rather than working for the 'aim' of death. This 'cure of the ground' (to adapt a phrase from Wallace Stevens's 'The Rock'), as long as it is also 'a cure beyond forgetfulness', would favour the widening detours Freud called life and take us into an uncharted region of the aesthetic that fosters reverie, daydream, or something akin to a trance state, though stopping short of delusion.[8] But how effective this 'cure' is, whether it reaches into the depth of depth-psychology, rather than remaining wishful and analgesic, is something I cannot answer.[9]

3

Poetry's nature-animations are so ubiquitous that they are taken for granted and rarely considered a subject for theoretical exploration. Yet why is poetic fiction so commonly marked by the use of images, pro-sopopoeias, and other figures attributing awareness and utterance to matter, and in particular to cliff, field, wood, stream, sky, those nature elements generally? An orphism endemic to poetical thought addresses this wordless, non-human universe as if it could be responsive ('O earth, cover not thou my blood' [Job, 16: 18]).[10] An initiative also seems to come from strong landscape impressions. 'I deem that there are powers, / Which of themselves our minds impress' (ll. 21–2), Wordsworth avers in 'Expostulation and Reply'.[11] That the non-human creation not only has feelings but transmits them is reinforced, as I have mentioned, by Wordsworth's use of 'passion'. It suggests nature often has an appeal (passively or actively exerted) as strong as speech, without being speech.[12]

In various autobiographical passages the poet describes his overflow-ing verbal emotion in response to rural nature's subverbal influence. So, by his seventeenth year, 'Coercing all things into sympathy, / To unorganic Natures were transferred / My own enjoyments'. But he goes further and adds, 'or the power of truth / Coming in revelation, did con-verse / With things that really are' (*1850 Prelude*, 2.391–5).[13] His sensitiv-ity to rural phenomena also brings, during childhood, intense moments of dread ascribed to Nature's 'severer interventions' (*1850 Prelude*, 1.355). And while the images haunting the poet-to-be do not habitually feature nightmarish hulks or bulks, semi- or superhuman shapes rising up to stride after him like the cliff in *The Prelude*'s boat-stealing episode (*1850 Prelude*, 1.357–400), they do evoke the latent power of the elements. The poetic imagination grounds mythology in the earth, or, according to Bachelard, also in air, water, fire, and their oneiric combinations. It senses a cosmic navel, a phylogenetic link. It overhears the 'ghostly language of the ancient earth' (*1850 Prelude*, 2.310). It is this intuitive connection with what is usually considered inanimate, or animate yet non-human, that gives rise to thoughts of preter- or supernatural presences, 'unknown modes of being' (*1850 Prelude*, 1.393).

4

My remarks, having linked matter and the imaginative consciousness, should now also cover the reverse dynamic of a return to the inanimate, or, borrowing Wordsworth's term, the 'unorganic'.[14] Poetry's impact does tend in that direction as well. But what Freud views as an instinctive 'return to the inanimate state', to a degree zero of excitability, enters Wordsworth's poetry not as an unconsciously willed reflex, a drive, or *'urge inherent in organic life'* (*BPP*, 36). Rather, the poetic mind shelters a memory of mute nature's communicativeness. It cultivates a refusal to leave behind something deeply relational, something fundamental to the imaginative life rather than its negation – even when the muteness in question is associated with suffering rather than tranquillity or happiness.[15]

If there is, then, an instinctive return to the inanimate, it does not ease or erase the memory of the poet's early relationship to Nature (especially a near-traumatic 'ministry' of fear). In fact, it heightens his recall of episodes he names 'spots of time'. 'Spots' refers not only to specific places in nature imbued for the boy with a sublime and often frightening affect, but also to flashbacks that condense time. They punctuate the routine temporal flow; they radiate from specific place-experience with a 'renovating virtue', that is, a capacity to maintain their original lineaments and affect while accruing new associations. This allows them to remain in memory and even to be claimed as experience that eventually overcomes the ravage of adult traumatic shock – in particular that of the revolutionary turmoil which in the poet's crisis years tempted him to make a total break with the remembrance of time past.[16] Once alienated by such a break from everything he valued under the name of Nature, his poetic mission would have been in jeopardy.

The return to nature, then, has nothing weakly primitivistic or regressive about it. It is a totally attentive if, at times, involuntary return to childhood experiences, to that 'heroic' age fostering the poet's consciousness of having been strong enough already then to endure – 'survive' is also appropriate – his own imagination, its unmediated contacts with Nature's powers and presences.[17]

Freud's 'we can form no conception' of 'the action of a force' by which the 'attributes of life were at some time evoked in inanimate matter' (*BPP*, 38) neglects, then, not only poetry's nature ventriloquism (or Nature speaking through the poet), but more crucially its amplification of the aphasia in a sub-articulate stratum of life. That type of active mute-ness could be linked, moreover, to Freud's understanding of mental illness as 'the way a patient speaks even when he is mute' – the mute speech, in this case, leading to Wordsworth's representations of non-human nature's appeal.[18] One could also cite a famous pronouncement of Saint Paul, in his *Letter to the Romans*. He declares that 'the whole [non-human] crea-tion groaneth and travaileth in pain together until now [because desiring, like human kind, to be delivered]' (Romans, 8: 19–23).[19]

Freud's discretion, when it comes to the metapsychological aspect of art, is all the more intriguing since no thinker in the human sciences respected poetry more. Perhaps that very respect made him cautious, made him hesitate on the threshold of theorizing poetry's biofunc-tion. He may have suspected, moreover, that the hypothesis of a death instinct, of a biological *vis inertiae* that seeks to cancel the tension pro-duced by the evolution of life and consciousness in matter, and is later mythically enlarged as Thanatos in combat with Eros – that this could itself be a species of imaginative rather than scientific truth.[20]

5

A return of the organism to the unorganic may imply that consciousness is a problematic evolutionary advance insofar as it increases the sensitiv-ity to, or fails to adequately defend against, trauma – trauma defined as a psychic injury caused by too great an internal or external excitation. Quantitatively so great, in fact, that the traumatic cause cannot be inte-grated except as a phantasm; it is dissociated or falls outside (beyond?) natural experience. Wordsworth's own claim for poetry pits the latter against trauma or what he named 'internal injury'. Poetry is surprisingly paired with 'geometric truth' because of its 'high privilege of lasting life, / From all internal injury exempt' (*1850 Prelude*, 5.65–7). In its immediate context that claim compensates the poet for the thought that books are subject to *external* forces of destruction.[21] But it also suggests a counter-force abetted by Nature's 'dark / Inscrutable workmanship' that 'recon-ciles' (*1850 Prelude*, 1.341–2) discordant elements, so that poetry's truth, like that of geometry, reflects, in its own way, a harmonious internal development, a mature consciousness ideally free of contradiction. As a counter-force, then, the poetic imagination could be described as an anti-self-consciousness principle, a balm or homeopathic antidote similar to what is symbolized by Spenser's 'Mirrhe sweete bleeding in the bitter wound'.[22]

The metapsychological analysis of a well-known lyric from the Lucy cycle in the 1800 *Lyrical Ballads* shows the barely scrutable working of this reconciling process, of a healing or consoling that relies on the material reverie of a nature-oriented imagination. The lyric consists of two quatrains juxtaposing a past and a present state of mind, separated by a death, real or imagined:

> A slumber did my spirit seal,
> I had no human fears:
> She seem'd a thing that could not feel
> The touch of earthly years.
>
> No motion has she now, no force;
> She neither hears nor sees;
> Roll'd round in earth's diurnal course,
> With rocks and stones and trees!

The tone of these lines is hard to determine. The question posed by that atonality concerns the speaker's relation to a death inscribed, as it were, in the mute space between the stanzas. The stanzas themselves are characterized by a strange symmetry that modifies the antithesis of life and death.

In the poem's first half, the cherished person seems immune to the touch of time, and in that respect is already beyond life. In the second half, obversely, a negative immortality is implied: though dead, the girl retains a kind of presence. She is with Nature; she has migrated to a larger mode of being.

It is as if life and death were seeking an interchange or equipoise. At first the poet escapes the consciousness of *his* mortality ('I had no human fears') by denying the mortality of the *girl*. Then, as mourner, accepting her passing, he still virtually denies, or 'sees *through*', death.[23] The sempiternity of the cosmic substratum with which the girl has merged in the second stanza's material reverie brings to mind a consolatory myth that in its more exalted form views the deceased as a star. So Shelley ends his elegy for Keats: 'The soul of Adonais, like a star, / Beacons from the abode where the Eternal are' (ll. 494–5).[24]

In another Lucy lyric ('Three years she grew in sun and shower'), the poet transforms a related theme of consolatory rhetoric. That Lucy dies now infers that Nature decided not only to bring up the child but also to take her fully to herself at the point of maturity. (That the aim of Lucy's life, guided solely by Nature, should be her early death, is left unexplained;[25] the conventional implication would be that the girl was too good for this world.) Moreover, though the brevity of Lucy's life tilts these lyrics towards disillusion, there are traces of a vacillating perspective on whether her death is as absolute as it seems. Lucy approaches the status of a *genius loci*, a guardian nature-spirit whose habitat could have expanded from her rural English home to the entire earth. Or ... was she indeed mortal all along, and so is now but a passive particle of the revolving planet?[26] Called by prolepsis 'a thing' in the first stanza of 'A slumber', she is endowed in the second with an *élan immortelle*.

Lucy's duality (dead thing/departed elemental spirit) is not resolved; and this may intimate a doubt about poetry's capacity to renew, within a realistic frame, the consoling mythic or spiritualizing option I have mentioned.[27] That Wordsworth entertained such an option is evident from 'Home at Grasmere', a long rhapsodic poem which remained unpublished but was probably begun the very year the Lucy lyrics appeared. In 'Home at Grasmere' the poet exalts his native region by addressing his Muse expansively as 'Thou human Soul of the wide earth'.[28] He summons us, in his most bardic mode, to recognize a soul in non-human nature. Without that recognition, the earth would seem dead, and the image of gravitation, which subsumes that of the grave in the second stanza of 'A slumber', confirms a mechanistic universe.

The emerging myth, therefore, is that Lucy, passing into the landscape, adds her soul to its soul. In the context of the Enlightenment, the French and Industrial Revolutions, the Continental war, indeed in the context of their combined fallout, only the memory of Lucy's closeness to nature keeps the poet's imagination linked to the pastoral English countryside.

The simplicity of this nature-girl (modelled, if there is a living model, on Dorothy, the poet's sister) makes her a surprising avatar of a major Romantic theme: the passing or twilight of the gods. Here, especially, Wordsworth's originality shines forth. Without breaching the convention of realism he endows Lucy with the essential features of a 'middle spirit'. In Classical mythology such 'middle spirits' are divine or daemonic, yet less than gods: most are immortal only within the limits of the particular cosmic element they guard and inhabit. (So the hamadryad, guardian spirit of its tree, lives as long, but only as long, as that tree itself.) Wordsworth resumes this tradition without adopting – in the manner of Coleridge's 'The Ancient Mariner' – an explicit supernaturalism. He avoids the gothic mode, or any mock-traumatic, ghosting artifice.

Thus the unresolved status of Lucy is also tied to the necessity of consolation. The lover as mourner is faced with an instinctive inclination to join the dead person, to become inanimate himself; or, what can amount to the same impulse, with a refusal to acknowledge the deadness of the dead, even the deadness of anything; and so he thinks of the dead as still alive, as having become one with nature. A present day sci-fi fantasy could certainly invent a cryonic preservative; but the second stanza of 'A slumber', which does not offer an explicit spiritual or mythic option, achieves something else, more like a resolution of the life/death antithesis.

But we do enter, with Lucy's death, the twilight zone of premonition. Given the girl's closeness to nature, Lucy's death, however personal, has a larger resonance. Nature herself could pass away: Nature as the jeopardized pastoral and imaginative aspect of England's agrarian spirit. Is the link between spirit (*genius*) and place (*locus*), between the human imagination and the land, in danger of breaking down? If so, would this not leave imagination without its natural sustenance, and so incite apocalyptic fantasies? A foreboding insight of this kind might well have led the poet to his *in memoriam* mood and the imaginary epitaph – a subgenre of the Greek Anthology's elegiac epigrams, especially its short lyrics on the death of virgins.[29] In terms of historical poetics we glimpse a remarkable romantic transformation of neoclassical topoi.

6

The moral implications of the above reading remain akin to what is always found in Freud: the difficult tempering of an imperious wish, of a transgressive thought or desire (residue of 'the omnipotence of thoughts'[30]) that coerces natural fact. Confronted by death, especially the premature death of a loved child or person, the imagination takes what comfort it can. Its conceptions keep that being immortal in or beyond nature. While Wordsworth acknowledges a need of this kind, he refuses to liberate his imagination in that direction. Instead, he creates a mode of expression out of the intensity of his restraint. Lucy remains a borderline being, between maiden and myth. She does not become an Astraea, a cosmic figure, or a hyperbole like Elizabeth Drury in Donne's 'Anatomy of the World'. The sorrow following her death is totally unlike what traditionally and vociferously accompanies explicit cosmic bereavements. Contrast the 'voice of weeping ... and loud lament' accompanying the 'parting Genius' (ll. 183–6), namely Pan and his retinue of nature spirits, as they are displaced at Christ's birth, according to a traditional theme taken up in Milton's 'On the Morning of Christ's Nativity'.[31]

Indeed, the grieving in the Lucy poems is so quiet that a more radical metapsychological interpretation must be considered. While 'Lucy' yields the pattern for a post-Enlightenment myth that would keep English nature 'green to the very door' ('Tintern Abbey', l. 18), I sense that, in the act of creating this new mythic template and its sophisticated (in)animism, a mind-shift occurs. *Does Thanatos, does the death instinct show its seductive force? Is the poet's imagination attracted to the girl's deathly sleep; do his thoughts 'too deep for tears' (see the ending of 'Ode: Intimations of Immortality') lie beside her?*[32]

Why else does 'A slumber' contain no direct cry of sorrow? Even the 'She died' is elided and replaced by a periphrasis that takes up the entire second stanza. There isn't even a soft complaint like 'And O, the difference to me!' ('She dwelt among th'untrodden ways', l. 12). An emotional anaesthesia has muted shock and allowed the incipience of a consolation even from within the negatives of the second stanza ('no/no/neither/nor'). The 'still, sad music of humanity' ('Tintern Abbey', l. 92) merges with what G. Wilson Knight called 'the hidden eternity-music in the inanimate'.[33]

So, at last, we gain a distinct view of poetry's anti-traumatic effect. A becalming (partly rhythmic), a renewed slumber or sealing of the spirit, hints at the appeal of an inert state of being. Organic and inorganic even out. A deep continuity between life and death is intimated. The poet diverts us from thoughts of an abrupt, untimely, absolute death to the image of a timeless fading, an entropic, 'unimaginable touch' that perpetually carries things along and away.[34]

The relation between poetry and the slumber referred to in the poem's opening line – more precisely, between poetry, material reverie, and death – is not uncommon in Romantic poetry. It is rarely as literal, though, as in an episode reported by Wordsworth's sister, covering in her Grasmere Journal the early years of the poet's return to his birthplace region. She describes his fantasy of lying in the grave, listening to the sounds of nature all around.[35] Peculiar as this is, and suggestive of what the Wanderer in *The Excursion* calls 'the sublime attractions of the Grave' (*Excursion*, 4.239), it is less a morbid anticipation than the wish to be, even in death, a permeable consciousness, a super-aeolian instrument submitted to the immensity of nature's influences. Is there a healing element in this evocation of a mode of being at once conscious and 'far more deeply interfused' ('Tintern Abbey', l. 97)? Keats too, who wrote an early 'Sleep and Poetry', was 'half in love with easeful Death' ('Ode to a Nightingale', l. 52).[36]

7

My aim has been to align Freud's thoughts on the death instinct with an untheorized aspect of poetry's anti-traumatic role. Also to suggest the support Wordsworth might have given a thinker who made such powerful conceptual use of Greek tragedy and Shakespeare. There could have been a Lucy complex, enriched by 'local romance', by a culturally specific locus.

I doubt, however, that poetry's function can be theorized across the board. More examples other than from Wordsworth would obviously be called for. The distance between tragic drama and lyric poetry, moreover, can be great; while the historical uses to which poetry has been put, or that grow from within basic needs, are various. It is more reasonable to consider only the function of poetry in its pastoral, memorial, and elegiac modes, especially when these are part of a strongly personal lyricism that strives to respect a world not primarily created by mankind. The lyricism of the Lucy poems conveys a *speaking muteness* influenced by that of non-human nature, including the inscriptive pathos of a landscape's mortuary stones.

In historiographical terms I have emphasized the Romantic Enlightenment and its need to compensate for demythologizing tendencies. A deep loss was felt or feared, a loss not of the gods as such, nor of a godly religion as such, but – certainly in Wordsworth – of the bond between imagination and Nature, between the mind of man and the goodly earth, an archaic bond that had to be strengthened by means of science as well as poetry. I am tempted to think that Wordsworth's unusual juxtaposition of poetry and geometry in the epigraph from book five of *The Prelude* comes from his hearing 'geo-matry' (earth-mother-matrix) in 'geometric'.[37]

It may be confusing to view poetry as active on both sides of the metapsychological tension. Nature consciousness brings often a disturbing awareness (close to dread) of non-human life – in gothic fantasies this spreads potentially to any inanimate object. But there are also chthonic glimpses with a tranquillizing effect. Insofar, moreover, as poetry evokes a natural balm, a renovating freshness deep down things, or releases the seductive image of an 'easeful death', it seems to have only a doubtful relevance to the ideological and suicidal violence all around us. Wordsworth, for many readers, remains a reactionary rather than revolutionary poet, a pastoralist in an era that began to add industrial forms of misery to rural poverty, and foreshadows the horror of large-scale wars.

But my aim does not include a judgement on the limits of Wordsworth's achievement. I wish to gain a clearer picture of poetry's role in the development of a humane imagination. Wordsworth is exemplary in that he focuses so clearly on the need to humanize the human by recalling the crucial importance of an imaginative and sympathetic relation to the non-human (albeit pastoral and, in that sense, man-made) countryside. It is also important to emphasize that his understanding of the developmental process informing the poetic imagination does not lead to an elision or transfiguration of the non-human. The poet's nature visionariness remains linked to a non-anthropomorphic material reverie, including its aversive (obscure, frightening) elements.

Individuals and collectives vary hugely in what they mean to protect, keep alive, nurture, seek to understand, allow into the permanent memory of family, tribe, nation. Conventions and codes arise to direct and control the flow of thoughts, emotions, sympathies. A subliminal sense, often becoming a conscious guilt – that we live at the expense of other creatures – directs us to the relational reality that beyond the human there is a non-human world, call it Nature or the cosmos, something given absolutely, in the midst of which persons grow up, and with which they have an unmediated as well as mediated relationship. The nature of this Nature becomes part of the poetic subject in Wordsworth; and his vividly rendered convictions about it (parallel to yet quite distinct from Winnicott's) focus on a living, guiding, at once intimate and independent environment that plays a crucial role in the child's psychic development.[38] If the human needs humanizing, this cannot happen without a strong empathic relationship to a world we have not created, even though we have the power to exploit and even destroy what exists by turning the laws of nature against Nature.

8

Finally, characterizing the Lucy complex in a more definitive way will highlight the most troubling aspect, psychologically, of the cycle. In 'Three years she grew', Nature herself speaks; and her prosopopoeia anticipating Lucy's growth into womanhood seems to bring it about. 'Thus Nature spake – The work was done' (l. 37). This 'done' includes Nature taking Lucy back (Lucy's death at puberty), and so seems to mimic with irony the biblical fiat. The girl is withdrawn from the sexual consummation of human love. Shrouded in virginity at death, she indeed will never feel the touch of earthly years.

An unexplained and even earlier death befalls the Boy of Winander. 'There was a Boy', clearly autobiographical in its initial, manuscript version, was composed about a year prior to the Lucy poems, but like them is first published in the second volume of the 1800 *Lyrical Ballads*.

Freud's turn from psychology to metapsychology in *Beyond the Pleasure Principle* coincides with a new and stronger dualism. The conflict in the psyche is now said to take place 'not between ego-instincts and sexual instincts but between life instincts and death instincts' (*BPP*, 53). In Wordsworth that opposition of life and death resolves itself by images of a seductive continuity and a *mytho-logic* of growth. A claim is proffered that poets (and who is not potentially a poet?) can mature without 'internal injury' despite their consciousness of loss and mortality.

However, as autobiography turns into thanatography, these deaths (of Lucy, the Girl from the Springs of Dove, and of the Boy from the Lake Winander region, both reared by the direct agency of Nature) signal an impasse in human development. It is not at all certain, despite the poet's insistence, that love of Nature can dress, rather than address, the wound of consciousness, exempt us developmentally from 'internal injury', and lead to love of human kind. Indeed, a growing up is depicted that is *not* exempt from internal injury, even if remedied by an integrative force, a 'dark, inscrutable workmanship' that resembles Freud's death instinct yet grows the mind 'like harmony in music' (*1850 Prelude*, 1.341–2).[39] The Boy of Winander experiences a discordant or deeply surprising access of consciousness early on, tutelary shocks apparently administered by Nature herself: they teach him the natural world's independence, as well as his own. His premature death is then portrayed as a return to nature, as if that were a comfort. Winander merges the Boy's birth-place and death-place.[40]

The Lucy lyrics are brief, like the precarious ego-emergence of these barely more than children. Yet the lurking developmental impasse fails to cancel the poet's faith in an ideal pattern of mental and emotional growth. He refuses to give up the thought that persistent memories of childhood ecstasies, testifying to an imaginative strength of response – the virtual poetry in us – may carry over into maturity and counter later shocks from the social and political sphere.

There are those, however, as Wordsworth recognizes, who *will* to not grow up, haunted as they are by memories of an early splendour and its correspondingly youthful response. For them death is preferable to having that early light fade into common day. Then Thanatos, in the form of imagination's deathwardness, defeats Eros, or becomes a love-death accomplice.

9

I concede that the relation between poetic affect (a complex pleasure) and metapsychological processes is as speculative as metaphysics itself, and introduces via the death instinct a disconcerting factor. But it does make place for an imagination in touch with sensory and material agency – even the agency of the apparently inanimate. My specula-tion, moreover, includes science (its *geo-metric-matric* truth) and recalls tendencies in Bachelard, Whitehead, and Goethe, perhaps Spinoza. As philosophers or artists these do not stint the scientific imagination. Non-human nature enters as alive, nurturing, ominous, even partaking of the divine. In that respect, humanism is not enough. The transhu-man or non-finite, whether described in material or spiritual terms, adds a special poignancy to Goethe's post-Kantian aphorism that Nature and Art are too great to aim at ends. If my remarks bring a fuller understanding of psyche's relation to matter by linking poetry and material reverie as an interactive binary, it may be possible to revise not only a narrow historical materialism but also adversarial and coercive doctrines of transcendence.

Notes

1. *The Fourteen-Book 'Prelude'*, ed. W. J. B. Owen (Ithaca, NY: Cornell University Press, 1985), p. 95. Indicated as *1850 Prelude* and cited by book and line numbers in the text.
2. The phrase comes from Gaston Bachelard, the French philosopher of science, and refers to poetic reverie in general. See Mary McAllester Jones, *Gaston Bachelard, Subversive Humanist: Texts and Readings* (Madison: The University of Wisconsin Press, 1991), p. 95. Bachelard's relation to Freudian psychoanalysis was highly nuanced: he wished to liberate symbols and images from being pinned down by a reductive psychological meaning. His method respected such symbols' 'somnology' and 'polylogism' as they connected with elemental nature (air, fire, water, earth). This materiality, he claimed, was voluntarily dreamed, or else performed through writing, not passively perceived and then conceptualized. So far as I know, Bachelard did not explore the relevance of this kind of material imagination to either prac-tical or visionary socio-economics. For a consideration of the 'materialism of the beautiful', see Simon Jarvis, *Wordsworth's Philosophic Song* (Cambridge: Cambridge University Press, 2006), especially chapter three.
3. See 'Three years she grew' (l. 18) in *'Lyrical Ballads' and Other Poems, 1797–1800*, ed. James Butler and Karen Green (Ithaca, NY: Cornell University Press, 1992). Hereafter indicated as *LB*; poems in this volume are cited by line numbers in the text.
4. See, for example, *The Excursion*, ed. Sally Bushell, James A. Butler, and Michael C. Jaye, with the assistance of David García (Ithaca, NY: Cornell University Press, 2007) 1.149–56. Hereafter indicated as *Excursion* and cited by book and line numbers in the text. Also see 'The Pedlar' (MS E, l. 128.) in William Wordsworth, *The Ruined Cottage and The Pedlar*, ed. James Butler (Ithaca, NY: Cornell University Press, 1979).

5. Sigmund Freud, 'Beyond the Pleasure Principle', in *The Standard Edition of the Complete Psychological Works*, trans. and ed. James Strachey, vol. 18 (London: The Hogarth Press, 1955), p. 38. Hereafter indicated as *BPP* and cited by page numbers in the text.

6. See 'A Long Way Round to Nirvana', in *Some Turns of Thought in Modern Philosophy: Five Essays* (Cambridge: Cambridge University Press, 1933), pp. 87–101. Freud himself (*BPP*, 55–6) mentions a 'Nirvana Principle' in this context.

7. Jones, quoting Bachelard, in *Gaston Bachelard, Subversive Humanist*, p. 91.

8. See Wallace Stevens, *Collected Poems* (London: Faber, 1984), p. 526.

9. I wish Bachelard had known passages from book one of *The Excursion* in which the Wanderer's imagination as a child is deeply affected by the impress of 'Great objects' from Nature that lay 'like substances' on his mind, 'and almost seemed / To haunt the bodily sense' (*Excursion*, 1.153–6). A material reverie is suggested that could also be a basis for the scientific imagination.

10. All biblical citations are from the King James Version.

11. A subtle description of one of these moments is found in 'Tintern Abbey': 'Once again / Do I behold these steep and lofty cliffs, / Which on a wild secluded scene impress / Thoughts of more deep seclusion' (ll. 4–7).

12. The semantic range of the word 'passion' is a complex one. Cf. 'Tintern Abbey''s 'The sounding cataract / Haunted me like a passion' (ll. 77–8). A 'passion' could mean an emotional flow of words. In Wordsworth it may also have a connotation opposing Descartes, or, more generally, mechanistic views that deny non-human natures a soul.

13. Wordsworth struggles to understand this intense developmental phase. We are not dealing, then, simply with projection, since he also mentions gratefully Nature's 'overflowing ... soul' (*1850 Prelude*, 2.398), not just his own emotional overflow. Indeed, he is mainly tempted to read into this phase Nature's socializing guidance. He admits, in any case, to an excess: that of an analytic habit of observation (nearest to 'creative agency') and leading to the discovery of affinities 'where no brotherhood exists / To passive minds', or, similarly, to an 'excess / Of the great social principle of life' (*1850 Prelude*, 2.386, 389–90). The excess is clearly what matters here even if the associationist terminology tends to conventionalize this phase as 'Love of Nature leading to love of Man' (the title of book eight). A problem for the reader is that what takes place bonds man and Nature, but not, necessarily, man and man.

14. One should include in this category borderline figures like the Old Man in 'Resolution and Independence' and 'Animal Tranquillity and Decay' who merges with the natural scene.

15. My discussion intersects at this point with Harold F. Searles, *The Nonhuman Environment: In Normal Development and in Schizophrenia* (New York: International Universities Press, 1960). Searles notes in his introductory pages a 'disregard of the significance of the nonhuman environment to psychology and psychiatry', and that 'the nonhuman environment, far from being of little or no account to human personality development, constitutes one of the most basically important ingredients of human psychological existence' (ibid., pp. 9–10). Searles also draws attention at one point to the work of D. W. Winnicott on the clinical issue of regression (Searles

himself tentatively suggests, in chapter nine, the therapeutic potential of a 'phylogenetic regression').

16. My formulation here of trauma as leading to the claiming of 'unclaimed experience' alludes to, and differentiates itself from, Cathy Caruth's concept.

17. Wordsworth values, sometimes uneasily, the 'involuntary sympathy / Of our internal being', stressing that 'thought' or 'meditation' cannot heighten such spontaneous motions, but also typing 'Fancy' as merely a propaedeutic faculty, expanding by its artificial, even forced analogies the sympathetic range of 'Imagination'. *The Thirteen-Book 'Prelude'*, ed. Mark L. Reed (Ithaca, NY: Cornell University Press, 1991), p. 228 (13.302–3, 305, 290–1). Hereafter cited as *1805 Prelude* by book and line numbers in the text. Wordsworth seems to wish to preserve the primacy of Imagination's agency against a more passive internal response to Nature's coercive agency.

18. See Philip Rieff, *Freud: The Mind of the Moralist* (Garden City, NY: Doubleday, 1961), p. 12.

19. Paul's well-known statement became a Christian proof-text justifying nature poetry. I still hear its echo in Paul Gauguin's comment about 'The Green Christ' (also known as 'The Breton Calvary'), that he wished to depict by this painting 'the power of nature with its cry'. See *45 Lettres à Vincent, Théo et Jo van Gogh*, ed. Douglas Cooper (Lausanne: La Bibliothèque des Arts, 1983), p. 165 (my translation).

20. Concerning poetry, Freud does remark cautiously in the last section of *BPP* that, on the human level, 'the hypothesis that all living substance is bound to die from internal causes' is 'strengthened in our thought by the writings of our poets', yet that such a belief may be 'only another of those illusions which we have created "to endure the burden of existence"' (*BPP*, 44–5; the translation of the quotation from Schiller's *The Bride of Messina* is mine). It is also quite possible that Freud would have viewed Wordsworth's sense for Nature's *anima* as a primitivistic trait reverting to a magical *Weltanschauung* that preceded the religious, which is itself surpassed by the scientific picture of the universe. See also his remarks on the notion of 'natural death' as foreign to 'primitive races', as well as his discussion of animism in chapter three of *Totem and Taboo* (1913). He also mentions biologists under whose hands 'the whole concept of death melts away' (*BPP*, 45). Towards the end of his treatise Freud admits to an 'artificial structure of hypothesis' (*BPP*, 60) due to having had to borrow from biology.

21. He may be fashioning a variant of Horace's famous boast that poems are more lasting than conspicuous material monuments.

22. See Edmund Spenser, *The Faerie Queene*, ed. A. C. Hamilton (New York: Longman, 1977), I.1.9, 1.6.

23. From the 'Intimations Ode', begun in 1802, playing on the dual meaning of 'through' (l. 188; my italics).

24. Percy Bysshe Shelley, *Poetry and Prose*, ed. Donald H. Reiman and Sharon B. Powers (New York: Norton, 1977), p. 406. This steadfast star is also, however, a lure that contributes to the suicidal drift Shelley expresses in the last stanza of his poem.

25. See below, however, pp. 16ff 206.

26. Wordsworth's prototype for the dead person, transformed into a *genius loci*, was most likely Milton's Lycidas, in the pastoral elegy of that title. Lycidas, a poet, dies by drowning, but survives as 'Genius of the [British] shore'

(l. 183). John Milton, *Poetical Works*, ed. Douglas Bush (Oxford: Oxford University Press, 1969), p. 147. For Wordsworth's most eloquent statement on 'the fore-feeling of immortality', see his first *'Essays upon Epitaphs'* published in Coleridge's *The Friend*, 22 February 1810. For a remarkably detailed examination of that fore-feeling, or the denial of death (Freud: 'In the unconscious every one of us is convinced of his own immortality') see Robert Jay Lifton, *The Broken Connection: On Death and the Continuity of Life* (New York: Simon and Schuster, 1979). For Freud's pronouncement just quoted see Sigmund Freud, 'Thoughts for the Times on War and Death', in *The Standard Edition*, vol. 14, p. 289.

27. Wordsworth's reticence when it comes to the serious use of myth in poetry is well known. Myth for him has to be 'founded in humanity'. Cf. the poet's remarks to Isabella Fenwick, on the 'Intimations of Immortality' Ode, in which he defends making use of Plato's myth of anamnesis by that criterion. See *'Poems, in Two Volumes', and Other Poems, 1800–1807*, ed. Jared Curtis (Ithaca, NY: Cornell University Press, 1983), p. 428.

28. *Home at Grasmere*, ed. Beth Darlington (Ithaca, NY: Cornell University Press, 1977), MS B, l. 1027. Also see MS D, l. 876.

29. Coleridge, in a tumult of thought about the death of his infant son Berkeley, and unable to grieve despite sadness and mental pain, because, he avers, he cannot conceive of any 'particle' of *'Life, Power, Being'* dying, quotes 'A slumber', speculating that it was an imaginary epitaph for Wordsworth's sister. *Collected Letters of Samuel Taylor Coleridge (1785–1800)*, ed. E. L. Griggs, vol. 1 (Oxford: Clarendon Press, 1956), pp. 478–50. (Wordsworth wrote, acknowledging Dorothy, 'She gave me eyes, she gave me ears'.) See 'The Sparrow's Nest' (l. 17) in William Wordsworth, *'Poems, in Two Volumes', and Other Poems 1800–1807*, ed. Jared Curtis (Ithaca, NY: Cornell University Press, 1983).

30. The phrase forms part of the title of chapter three of Freud's *Totem and Taboo*.

31. See Milton, *Poetical Works*, pp. 64–72.

32. It should not surprise – when we recall Freud – that the deathwardness of imagination in this proleptic epitaph occurs together with a 'development of consciousness'. Not only is there, via the second stanza, a recognition that the girl's deathlessness was illusory, but the poet's waking to this coincides ironically with the illusion's fulfillment. Nothing could touch Lucy now.

33. G. Wilson Knight, *The Starlit Dome: Studies in the Poetry of Vision* (London: Oxford University Press, 1971), p. 16.

34. For 'the unimaginable touch of Time' see 'Mutability' (l. 14), part of the *Ecclesiastical Sketches*, in William Wordsworth, *Sonnet Series and Itinerary Poems, 1820–1845*, ed. Geoffrey Jackson (Ithaca, NY: Cornell University Press, 2004). The phrase points there to dissolution, yet still to an image of eternity paradoxically insinuated by the endless, gradual wearing down of a material substance.

35. Dorothy Wordsworth, entry of 29 April 1802, in *The Grasmere Journals*, ed. Pamela Woof (Oxford: Clarendon Press, 1991), p. 92.

36. John Keats, *Complete Poems*, ed. Jack Stillinger (Cambridge, MA: Belknap Press, 1982), p. 281.

37. I developed that suggestion previously in the psycho-aesthetic context of 'A Touching Compulsion'. See *The Unremarkable Wordsworth* (Minneapolis: Minnesota University Press, 1987), p. 25. '-Metric' itself, compounded this way, connects with two issues. One foretells an important objectivist trend in modern poetry, which combines in a writer like John Crowe Ransom with agrarian sympathies close to those of Wordsworth. See *The World's Body* (New York: Scribner, 1938); also see suggestive comments in Douglas Mao, *Solid Objects: Modernism and the Test of Production* (Princeton, NJ: Princeton University Press, 1998), pp. 4–9. '-Metric' also brings attention to the role of metre and rhythm as affective poetic qualities. Wordsworth's comment in his Preface to *Lyrical Ballads* on the tempering and pleasuring function of metre are well known. Poetic metre and rhythm, from the perspective of my own essay, convey something of the active muteness, of the subarticulate undersong of non-human human being as well as of 'the ancient earth'.

38. I suspect that, in Wordsworth's case, Nature becomes geo-matric after the mother's 'phenomenal death' – becomes, that is, an absent presence, a permanent transitional object, a proxy holding and facilitating environment. Winnicott's aphorism in his posthumously published 'Fear of Break Down' that 'The underlying agony is unthinkable' is not far from Freud's 'The aim of all life is death'. A poetry that thinks, and is in turn thinkable by us, may be the closest we can come to imagining, even while defending against, an agony also defined by Winnicott as the haunting memory of a death not yet experienced. Winnicott writes as follows in 'Fear of Breakdown': 'When Keats was "half in love with easeful death" he was, according to the idea that I am putting forward here, longing for the ease that would come if he could "remember" having died; but to remember he must experience death now. ... What happened in the past was death as a phenomenon, but not as the sort of fact that we observe. Many men and women spend their lives wondering whether to find a solution by suicide, that is, sending the body to death which has already happened to the psyche.' D. W. Winnicott, 'Fear of Breakdown', *International Review of Psycho-Analysis*, 1 (1974), 106.

39. The source character of that integrative force – whether entropic like the death instinct or symbiotic and synthesizing like the countervailing 'life instincts' in *Beyond the Pleasure Principle* and Eros in *Civilization and its Discontents* – remains undetermined. One possible solution or reconciliation of these alternatives stresses the structural simultaneity of two types of integration, since 'both the archaic psyche's demand for "irrational nondifferentiation" and the synthetic function of the ego – the seat of rationality – have their source in the [pre-Oedipal] undifferentiated matrix'. My quotation comes from Joel Whitebook's 'Hans Loewald: A Radical Conservative', *International Journal of Psychoanalysis*, 85 (2004), 103.

40. See the poem as incorporated and extended in *1805 Prelude*, 5.389–422.

Index